W9-AFK-177

Volume II

Adolescent
Literature
as a

Complement
to the
CLASSICS

Volume II

Adolescent Literature as a Complement to the CLASSICS

Edited by

Joan F. Kaywell
University of South Florida

Indiana
Purdue
Library
Fort Wayne

PN
59
.A36
1993
v.2

Christopher-Gordon Publishers, Inc. — Norwood, MA

Credits...

Every effort has been made to contact copyright holders for permission to reprint borrowed material where necessary. We apologize for any oversights and would be happy to rectify them in future printings.

Chapter 4: Paraphrase from *Inside Out,* Second Edition, by Dan Kirby and Tom Liner with Ruth Vinz, Copyright (c) 1988 by Heinemann Education Publishers, used with permission.

Chapter 6: *"Thirty-Four Alternatives to Book Reports"* by Sharon L. Belshaw and Carolyn Warmington, in *Ideas for Teaching English in the Junior High and Middle School,* edited by Candy Carter and Zora M. Rashis, Copyright (c) 1980 by the National Council of Teachers of English. Reprinted with permission.

Chapter 9: Excerpts from *The Cay* by Theodore Taylor, Copyright (c) 1969 by Bantam Doubleday Dell, used with permission.

Chapter 12: Excerpts from *The Grey King* by Susan Cooper, Copyright (c) 1976 by Atheneum Publishers, used with permission.

Excerpts from *Anne of Green Gables* by L. M. Montgomery, are taken from the 1987 version published by Farrar, Straus & Giroux.

Excerpts from *Mossflower* by Brian Jacques, Copyright (c) 1988 by Avon Books used with permission.

"The Road Goes Ever On And On" from *The Fellowship of the Ring* by J.R.R. Tolkien. Copyright (c) 1954, 1965 by J.R.R. Tolkien. Copyright (c) renewed 1982 by Christopher R. Tolkien, Michael H.R. Tolkien, John F.R. Tolkien and Priscilla M.A.R. Tolkien. Reprinted by permission of Houghton Mifflin Co. All rights reserved.

Copyright (c) 1995 by Christopher-Gordon Publishers, Inc.

All rights reserved. Except for review purposes, no part of this material protected by this copyright notice may be reproduced or utilized in any form or by any means, electronic or mechanical, including photocopying, recording, or any information and retrieval system, without the express written permission of the publisher or copyright owner.

Christopher-Gordon Publishers, Inc.
480 Washington Street
Norwood, MA 02062

Printed in the United States of America

10 9 8 7 6 5 4 3 2 1   99 98 97 96 95

ISBN: 0-926842-43-9

INDIANA-
PURDUE
WITHDRAWN
LIBRARY
OCT 16 1995
FORT WAYNE

Adolescent
Literature
as a
Complement
to the
CLASSICS

DEDICATION and
ACKNOWLEDGMENTS

Dedication

To Susan S. Maida
and to all teachers
making a difference in this world

Thank God

Acknowledgments

My first thanks must go to my ever-faithful and talented graduate assistant, Heidi M. Quintana. Thanks for all of the library work, proofreading, and cheery notes.

Next, I'd like to thank my colleagues who agreed to write chapters, met their deadlines, and extended their friendship: Janet Allen, Lynne Alvine, Sissi Carroll, Pam Cole, Pat Daniel, Devon Duffy, Bonnie Ericson, Pat Kelly, Teri Lesesne, Charlie Reed, Bob Small, Lois Stover, and Connie Zitlow.

A VERY SPECIAL THANKS is extended to Sue Canavan, the Executive Vice President of Christopher-Gordon Publishers, whose patience and confidence launched this second book into becoming a reality. I am also grateful to the reviewers who made excellent suggestions along the way and to the teachers who used the first version of this text successfully.

And finally, I'd like to thank my family, friends, and various faculty and staff at the University of South Florida for supporting me and giving me the time and encouragement necessary to complete this task, especially Stephen M. Kaywell, Christopher S. Maida, Nancy Gonzalez, Carine Feyten, Jeff Golub, Howard Johnston, Kathy Oropallo, Dana Parrish, and Connie Brinson.

Adolescent
Literature
as a

Complement
to the
CLASSICS

TABLE OF CONTENTS

Adolescent
Literature
as a
Complement
to the
CLASSICS

PREFACE

Introduction

Adolescent Literature as a Complement to the Classics, Volume 2 was written because of the outstanding response received from teachers who have used the first volume of *Adolescent Literature as a Complement to the Classics* in their classrooms. Consistent with the first book, this text is based on two assumptions: (1) The classics comprise the canon of literature that is mostly taught in our schools; and (2) most teachers are familiar with adolescent literature, or young adult novels, but are unsure how to incorporate their use in classrooms. This book provides the necessary information so that teachers may confidently use young adult novels in conjunction with commonly-taught classics.

Why should teachers try to get students to read more when it is already difficult getting them to read the required material? I'll tell you. Part of the problem, as most teachers are fully aware, is that the classics are often too distant from our students' experiences or the reading level is too difficult. Students often question why they have to study something, read the Cliff's notes, or watch the movie version of the required classic. As a result, not only are students not reading the classics, but they are not reading much of anything!

By using young adult novels in conjunction with the classics, teachers can expose students to reading that becomes relevant and meaningful. Additionally, the reading levels of most young adult books are within a range of ease that most students can master. Reading, as with any type of human development, requires practice. The problem that occurs in our schools, however, is that we often place our students into reading practice that we require, a practice our students view as forced, meaningless, and too difficult. To make my point, let me draw an analogy to the developmental process of eating.

Just as a newborn baby has to be fed milk, a newborn reader needs to be read to. Babies begin with baby foods that are easily digested; something too solid will cause the baby to reject it. So, too, with reading. Young readers need to start with easy readers, ones that are easily consumed. Eventually, young children desire foods that have a little more substance—vegetables, eggs, and some palatable meats. Similarly, young readers might find delight in such books as Nancy Drew or Hardy Boys mysteries. Just as children regurgitate and learn to hate certain foods if forced too early to consume them, so will novice readers learn to hate certain books, or books in general, if forced to read books that are beyond their capabilities. As children reach adolescence, they will consume vast quantities of "hamburgers" in the form of adolescent literature — if we let them.

Like any concerned parent, we want our children to eat a proper diet, so we make them eat balanced meals in much the same way as we have our children read certain books. Ideally our children will learn to appreciate fine cuisine in the form of the classics. For some, they may find the experience too much for their stomachs to handle and will turn up their noses at lobster newburg and *Julius Caesar* for something a bit lighter. For others, unfortunately, they may never get exposed to that level, but they still can survive, unaware of what they are missing. Some of our students, however, will learn to enjoy and appreciate the delicacies of fine literature. It's all in the presentation, and adolescent literature can help make our teaching of the classics more appealing.

Now you are probably saying, "I am sold on exposing my students to adolescent literature, but why should I use *this* book?" First, some of the biggest names in the field of adolescent literature have contributed chapters: Janet Allen, the author of *It's Never Too Late: The Power of Literacy in the Secondary School* (Heinemann); Bonnie O. Ericson, reviewer of young adult books for *The ALAN Review* and editor of the "Resources and Reviews" column for *English Journal*; Joan F. Kaywell, author of *Adolescents At Risk: A Guide to Fiction and Nonfiction for Young Adults, Parents, and Professionals* (Greenwood Press); Patricia Kelly, former president of the Assembly on Literature for Adolescents (ALAN) and co-editor of *The ALAN Review*; Teri S. Lesesne, reviewer of young adult books for *The ALAN Review* and editor of the "Books for Adolescents" column in *The Journal of Reading*; Arthea J.S. "Charlie" Reed, the past editor of *The ALAN Review* and author of *Reaching Adolescents: The Young Adult Book and the School* (Merrill); Bob Small, the current co-editor of *The ALAN Review*; Lois T. Stover, co-editor of the 13th edition of *Books for You*, editor of the "Young Adult Literature" column for *English Journal,* and a member of the Board of Directors for ALAN; among others.

Second, all chapters stand alone, but an experienced teacher can easily adapt the strategies employed in one chapter to fit his or her particular situation. For example, a teacher may not be required to teach *The Odyssey* but may choose to incorporate the multi-text strategy in teaching whatever classic is required. Or, a teacher might be required to teach the aforementioned novel but could choose to approach its teaching under the theme of "the clash of cultures," incorporating the strategies suggested for teaching *Things Fall Apart*. In other words, several different approaches are suggested so that a teacher who likes a certain strategy could omit the suggested novels and insert the ones of choice. Because young adult novels are frequently out of print, there are enough suggestions and other resources listed to assist teachers and their students with their search for complementary novels. Single novels that are out of print are often found in used bookstores.

Third, this book is on the cutting edge, incorporating all of the latest research in reader response theory, student ownership, and collaborative learning. Each chapter is written so that each student, from the least to the most talented, can learn at his or her optimum level. Each student is a vital contributor to the class, and each student gets exposed to the classics in meaningful, relevant ways. The book is written for middle and high school English teachers; however, university professors who teach preservice teachers and graduate students may also find this text valuable.

Joan F. Kaywell
September, 1994

Adolescent
Literature
as a
Complement
to the
CLASSICS

ORGANIZATION

Introduction

The first three chapters focus on three classics—*The Odyssey, The Red Badge of Courage*, and *Narrative of the Life of Frederick Douglass: An American Slave, Written by Himself*—that deal with the themes of heroism, relationships, and war. The unit described in Chapter 1 begins with the whole class reading of *The Odyssey*, including a variety of introductory reading and response activities that engage all students. The students' reading experience is extended by reading young adult (YA) novels that deal with heroism and relationships. In Chapter 2, students share the reading of six YA novels in preparation for the reading of *The Red Badge of Courage*. The YA novels explore the human response to war and aid students in developing a deeper understanding of issues raised by Crane's work. Chapter 3, students read a nonfiction book prior to reading Douglass' narrative and participate in several concurrent reading activities. By combining Douglass' work with YA literature, most students can deeply experience and respond to this important and moving narrative.

Chapters 4, 5, and 6 are multicultural in design and feature *The Awakening* and *Things Fall Apart*. For teachers required to teach world literature, there is enough material included in these three chapters to last the entire school year. Over 100 YA novels representing several different countries are included.

Chapters 7, 8, and 9 focus on identity issues and friendships. The pre-reading of YA novels help students identify with the characters in *Julius Caesar*; whereas the post-reading of YA literature helps students relate to the conflicts inherent in *A Separate Peace*. Students all listen to *The Cay* prior to reading *The Miracle Worker*, and then participate in several activities that are designed to help students develop empathy for people with disabilities. An individual selection of a complementary YA novel completes the unit.

Chapters 10, 11, and 12 deal with science fiction and fantasy. In Chapter 10, students may choose to read from several YA books that deal with the theme of the duality of humanity found in Shelley's *Frankenstein*. These books are grouped into five categories: historical fiction, futurism—science fiction, fantasy fiction, modern realism, and humor. In Chapter 11, students predominantly compare and contrast one YA novel, *The*

Giver, with the classic, *Brave New World*. In that way, students are able to better understand the individual's responsibility to society. Several other related YA novels are included. Chapter 12 invites students to read several YA fantasy novels in order to help them appreciate Tennyson's "The Lady of Shalott."

CHAPTER 1

Heroes and Journeys in *The Odyssey* and Several Works of Young Adult Literature

BONNIE O. ERICSON

Introduction

Life and literature can sometimes overlap in remarkable ways. My 9th grade daughter had just finished reading *The Odyssey* in her English class when I was approached about writing a chapter connecting a classic with young adult (YA) literature. When I asked her—for the record—if she and her friends had liked this epic, she'd replied, "Yeah, it's like Indiana Jones, only in the old Greek days. But it wasn't easy." Her comments settled my choice.

Two months later, the day after I'd gathered all my materials and completed my initial readings of numerous works of YA fiction and rereadings of both Butler's prose (1988) and Fitzgerald's poetic (1963) translations of *The Odyssey*, the Northridge earthquake occurred. With all these materials trapped in my office for weeks, I had time to ponder the numerous connections between this memorable event and the classic classroom literary selection. Firefighters worked for hours to free a man caught below two stories of a collapsed parking structure, displaying the bravery of Odysseus as he descended to the House of Hades. The ground continued to shake, much as the harbor waters must have heaved as the Lastrygonians threw rocks at Odysseus's ships. Tabloid headlines warned those of us standing in grocery store lines that 17 demons had escaped to the earth's surface through a quake–caused fissure; similarly, Calypso advises Odysseus of the perils of the frightening six–headed monster, Scylla. The generosity of Alcinous and Menelaus to Odysseus and Telemachus was paralleled by discount stores' and individuals' donations to the newly homeless of everything from Big Macs to disposable diapers. And dealing with closed freeways and disaster relief and insurance agencies surely required the cunning of Odysseus as he tricked the Cyclops Polyphemus into calling out, "Noman is killing me by force!" (If you're unfamiliar with the allusions here, you're in for a treat when you read *The Odyssey* or reread it after many years.)

Seeing these connections gave me renewed appreciation of *The Odyssey*, and led to me realize, yet again, just how crucial it is that our students be able to connect the characters, events, and themes of their reading with the people, occurrences, and meanings of their own lives. Beyond inviting students to make these connections with their whole class reading through student–directed discussions and writing assignments, asking them to read and respond to thematically related YA works is a powerful technique for encouraging them to explore the links between literature and life.

The unit described in this chapter begins with the whole class reading of *The Odyssey*, including a variety of introductory, reading, and responsive activities. Group work in which students take responsibility for their reading and understanding particular aspects of *The Odyssey* is a key feature of this part of the unit. Next follows an explanation of the group workshop reading of thematically related YA novels, with shared response journals. While participating in the reading workshop, students also choose one of two personal writing assignments to complete to help connect the reading and their own experiences.

Whole Class Reading of *The Odyssey*

The Odyssey is a timeless adventure story frequently read by 9th graders as part of a heroes or mythology unit; or, it is sometimes read in the senior year in a world literature course. The themes of heroism, journeys of discovery, growing up, and family relationships make *The Odyssey* a work most students, 9th or 12th graders, could readily read and appreciate—*if only* the text were a bit shorter and easier to comprehend, *if only* there weren't so many complicated names and different characters, and *if only* the story were told in a straightforward manner instead of skipping around and changing places so often! Students do sometimes find themselves between a rock and a hard place (or, if you prefer, Scylla and Charybdis) in reading *The Odyssey*. They want to enjoy this work for its Indiana Jones–like excitement, but they may be hindered by the challenges of length, myriad proper names, and changes in setting.

Even with these challenges and even at the risk of an "incomplete" reading, it is important that students take ownership of their reading. I want them to think about, discuss, and ultimately enjoy and value the literature, rather than wait for and accept my interpretation of it. The following activities are provided as possible ways to help students maneuver smoothly past the challenges presented in *The Odyssey* while remaining largely in charge of their own course.

Introducing *The Odyssey*

Before beginning this classical work itself, students contemplate one of the unifying ideas of the unit: heroism. What does it mean to be a hero? (I use the term "hero" to refer to both male and female heroes.) Odysseus is certainly a brave hero, but he's also a character of many dimensions:

courageous, yes, but also vengeful, loving, sly, loyal, and sometimes foolish or greedy. Additionally, Penelope and Telemachus could be considered heroic in their own ways. Penelope raises her son and remains faithful to her absent husband for 20 years, while Telemachus as a young man displays courage in facing the suitors and embarking on a journey to locate his father. To prepare students to see the complexity of these characters, as well as the many facets of the heroes in the YA fiction they'll encounter later and of the heroes of their own lives, I use the following introductory activities.

Defining Hero

Play Mariah Carey's "Hero" (1993) and provide students with copies of the lyrics. (A related song concerning heroes could certainly replace this selection.) Discuss with the students what the song's "definition" of a hero seems to be. Also, share Joseph Campbell's comment that "A hero is someone who has given his or her life to something bigger than oneself" (1988, p. 143). Then have them freewrite about their own ideas concerning the topic "hero" or "heroism." What does it mean to be a hero? What are heroes like? Who are your heroes? Do you agree or disagree with Carey's and Campbell's views on heroism? Pairs share their written responses, and then a class discussion can lead to the development of a semantic map of this concept. Such a map might look similar to the one in Figure 1-1 developed by 9th graders.

Cubing Activity

Alternatively, students participate in a cubing activity (Neeld, 1986). Paper dice are constructed (See Figure 1-2) so that each group of four students in the class can have a die. Each face should have a different direction: define it, compare and contrast it, give examples of it, tell what color it is and explain why, tell what its symbols are and explain them, tell what actors (male and female) could portray it in a movie and explain why.

A student in each group rolls the die, and all group members freewrite on the topic "hero" according to the directions (define it, etc.) rolled. Students within each group then discuss and compare their responses. A second student in each group rolls the die again, so that different directions are given, and the groups again freewrite and discuss their responses. This process is repeated two more times, and then each group is directed to write three or four statements on a transparency that summarize their thoughts about heroes and heroism. These statements are then presented to the whole class, compared, and discussed.

Figure 1-1 Semantic Map

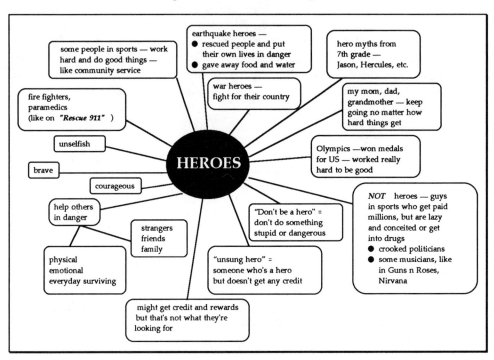

some people in sports — work hard and do good things — like community service

earthquake heroes —
● rescued people and put their own lives in danger
● gave away food and water

hero myths from 7th grade — Jason, Hercules, etc.

fire fighters, paramedics (like on *"Rescue 911"*)

war heroes — fight for their country

my mom, dad, grandmother — keep going no matter how hard things get

unselfish

HEROES

brave

Olympics —won medals for US — worked really hard to be good

courageous

help others in danger

strangers friends family

"Don't be a hero" = don't do something stupid or dangerous

NOT heroes — guys in sports who get paid millions, but are lazy and conceited or get into drugs
● crooked politicians
● some musicians, like in Guns n Roses, Nirvana

physical emotional everyday surviving

"unsung hero" = someone who's a hero but doesn't get any credit

might get credit and rewards but that's not what they're looking for

Figure 1-2 Pattern for Cubing

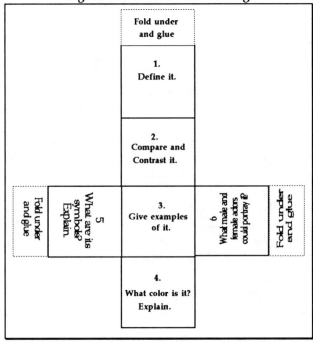

Fold under and glue

1.
Define it.

2.
Compare and Contrast it.

Fold under and glue

5
What are its symbols? Explain.

3.
Give examples of it.

6
What male and female actors could portray it?

Fold under and glue

4.
What color is it?
Explain.

Providing Background Information

In addition to an activity that has students explore their own ideas and beliefs about heroism, some background information is required before students begin their reading of *The Odyssey*. If they have not studied mythology recently, information about some of the Greek gods and goddesses should be provided or reviewed. In particular, students should be familiar with Zeus, Athene, Poseidon, and Hades; additional deities that may be presented or reviewed prior to reading include Apollo, Hephaestus, Hermes, Calypso, and Circe. Students may also be given a brief background on the Trojan War and perhaps on the Greek hero. This information is not intended to be an end in itself but will allow students to better understand and appreciate the story and characters.

Reading *The Odyssey*

In teaching *The Odyssey*, I divide the text into three major blocks: Books I–IV, Books V–XII, and Books XIII–XXIV. Books I–IV tell of the gods' decision to allow Odysseus to leave Calypso's island, Telemachus' attempts to rid his home of the suitors, and his subsequent voyage to Sparta to visit Helen and Menelaus. Books V–XII chronicle Odysseus' escape from Calypso, his adventures since the end of the Trojan War, and his arrival in the land of the Phaecians. Books XIII–XXIV detail Odysseus' and Telemachus' return to Ithaca, their reunions with family and friends, and their revenge on the suitors.

I use a variety of approaches with the reading. I read aloud Book I or play a tape recording of this chapter as students follow along. Other chapters are read aloud in a readers–theater fashion, that is, with students reading aloud the roles of different characters and a narrator, much as they would read a script. Students may also read aloud "round robin" style within established small groups; such a technique effectively involves numerous students at once. Some books are assigned for homework. How quickly you decide to progress through the book will depend mainly on your students' abilities but, in general, 9th graders can read and respond in about five weeks, and most 12th graders in about four weeks. When an abridged version from a literature anthology is read, the time will be reduced.

Responding to *The Odyssey* in Groups

The Odyssey reading and response groups of four students are established at the beginning of the unit. My best results have occurred when I form the groups based on a variety of abilities, personalities, and interests. These groups meet almost daily throughout the reading of *The Odyssey* for 5–15 minutes to address two main tasks. First, members of all groups should be certain that the other students in their group understand the characters and plot developments from the previous day's class reading or the homework reading. Some days the groups are asked to develop questions based on the previous reading assignment, and these are listed on the board so that several can be selected by the class for discussion.

Second, each group chooses a different topic from those listed below. On a daily basis each group discusses and makes notes on its topic as details and evidence emerge from the reading. While some of the group's questions for class discussion may address their insights or uncertainties about the topic, a more formal sharing of the findings takes place at the end of each of the three main blocks of *The Odyssey*. Students prepare a poster that encapsulates their discussions for their peers.

After the first block, each group shares its poster and their main ideas thus far. Some groups will have more to present at this time than others. Similarly, after completing the second section, the groups update their posters and information and share their findings with the rest of the class. Some groups' information will change markedly during the second section, but other groups' may develop less. A third report with a final version of the poster is made after completing the final block. The topics listed here have been effective for this ongoing group project.

Heroism Group

List all heroic characters and justify why they should be included on this list. How do they compare to today's heroes?

Odysseus Group

List character traits of Odysseus and note episodes and evidence to validate the selected traits. How is Odysseus like or unlike other protagonists in literature read by the class during the current school year?

Journeys Group

Chart the travels of Telemachus and Odysseus on a map of the Greek islands, including Ithaca, Pylos, Sparta, Ogygia, the land of the Phaecians, and so forth. Distances may be computed. What do Odysseus or Telemachus learn (if anything) on the various legs of their journeys?

Generosity Group

Cite examples of generosity throughout the work. Who is generous? To whom? What are their reasons or motives? What examples of present–day generosity compare to those in *The Odyssey*?

Deception Group

Cite examples of deception and duplicity. Who deceives another? Who is deceived? What are the reasons or motives? Are they justifiable? Why or why not?

Father–son Relationships Group

List and describe the father–son relationships (Odysseus–Laertes, Telemachus–Odysseus, Pisistratus–Nestor, Laodamas–Alcinous). Are these good relationships? Why or why not? How do these relationships compare to father–son relationships with which you are familiar?

Husband–wife Relationships Group

List and describe the marital relationships (Odysseus–Penelope, Menelaus–Helen, Alcinous–Arete). Are these good relationships? Why or why not? How do these relationships compare to the husband–wife relationships with which you are familiar?

Role of the Gods Group

List the occasions when the gods (Athene, Zeus, Poseidon, etc.) intervene or influence events in the story. What seems to be the function of the gods? Who or what are their modern-day counterparts?

Growing up Group

Trace the changes in Telemachus from the early chapters through his standing and fighting by his father's side. Is his "coming of age" similar to what most adolescents experience? Explain.

Role of Women Group

List and describe the traits and roles of some of the different women in *The Odyssey*, including Penelope, Helen, Euryclea, Nausicaa, Calypso, Circe, and Scylla. How do their traits and roles compare with those of today's women?

Revenge Group

List all acts of revenge in this work. Who gets revenge? Who is on the receiving end? What are the reasons for wanting revenge? Are these justifiable? Why or why not?

Language Group

Identify extended metaphors, similes, and especially powerful passages. Describe the effects of these passages, and use them to develop a description of Homer's style. How do the language and style compare with those of other literature read this year?

Responding to *The Odyssey* Individually

In addition to this group work throughout the reading of *The Odyssey*, it is important to encourage individual responses. To accomplish this, I ask individuals to complete *one* of the responsive activities for *each* of the three blocks of *The Odyssey*. These allow a variety of responses, from analytic to creative, and from drawing to dramatic reading. Displaying as many of these individual responses as possible in the classroom or even in a hallway display case will generate much interest!

Block One: Books I–IV

1. Read the Fitzgerald translation (I: 1–15; II: 1–14) and the corresponding portions of Butler's translation (Book I, first three paragraphs; Book II, first paragraph). In writing, compare and contrast these two translations. Which do you like better and why?

2. Write Telemachus' diary or journal entry for the day he discovers from Menelaus that his father is alive and the prisoner of Calypso.

3. You are Penelope's oldest and most trusted friend. Write her a letter in which you commiserate with her predicament and give her your best advice.

4. Write Penelope's "Dear Abby" for the day she discovers that Telemachus has left Ithaca on a quest to find his father.

Block Two: Books V–XII

1. Develop a storyboard of five to eight frames showing key scenes of Odysseus' adventures. A 5 × 8 index card may be used for each frame, which consists of a drawing of the scene and a corresponding quotation. Arrange these in sequential order for display.

2. Select several vivid and appealing quotations from these books. Work with these words, putting different quotations together,

rearranging them into poetic form, and cutting or adding words to form a "found poem." Give your poem an appropriate title.

3. In Book X, Odysseus and his crew are close enough to Ithaca to see the home fires burning. Assume you are a member of the crew. You've been gone from home for 10 years, and now you're almost home. What thoughts are going through your mind? What are your feelings? Write an interior monologue of these thoughts and feelings (Sauve, 1993).

4. Collect two magazine or newspaper stories that depict heroism and staple or glue them to a piece of paper. On another sheet of paper, (a) compare and contrast the heroic qualities of the people in the article with those of Odysseus, Penelope, or Telemachus; and b) compare and contrast the challenges faced by those in the article with those faced by the selected character.

Block Three: Books XIII–XXIV

1. Draw a picture of a key scene or develop a collage based on a key scene in this portion of *The Odyssey*. Include a paragraph explaining why you think this scene is important.

2. Suppose Odysseus appears as a guest on the "Oprah Winfrey Show." At one point, Oprah asks Odysseus which he loves more——the comfort of family and home or the adventures of a journey and war. Write Odysseus' response. He should discuss fully his answer and be persuasive to the audience.

3. Practice and tape record a dramatic reading of a key scene in these books. Along with the tape recording, provide a written account of why you chose this particular scene and what you attempted to convey in your recording.

4. You are Odysseus, and you've been back in Ithaca for several years. Menelaus comes to visit you, and asks what happened to the suitors and serving women. Write the dialogue that occurs between Odysseus and Menelaus, attempting to employ the language each would use.

This portion of the unit comes to a close after the groups have presented their final posters on their topics and after individuals have completed a final response activity. The remaining time is divided between student–directed reading and writing workshops.

Heroes and Journeys in YA Literature

Why take the time after weeks devoted to *The Odyssey* to read thematically related works of YA literature, especially when that time is so precious and there is pressure to move on to other core works? I would argue that the reading workshop portion of this unit is more than an enriching, although perhaps optional, component. It is integral! High school students benefit greatly from opportunities to read YA literature; these opportunities should not be limited to junior high or middle school pupils. Reading good YA literature tends to increase all secondary students' enjoyment of books, an essential experience for developing life–long readers. Such a result is well worth the time.

YA Literature for the Reading Workshop

Because *The Odyssey* is most often taught at grade nine or grade twelve, I have developed two separate lists of suggested YA works for group reading in this unit. Those recommended for grade nine are easily read by most 14–year–olds, have younger protagonists, and tend to be shorter and contain simpler plots. The recommendations for grade twelve tend to be a little more difficult to read, have older protagonists, and some are longer and have more complex plots. Certainly, you may wish to modify these lists, or even include some works from one list with the other, according to the talents, interests, and personalities of your students.

The recommended books fulfill a number of criteria. First, all have a heroic or potentially heroic character who undertakes some sort of journey. In most, a character develops or "grows up" over the course of the book, and a family relationship figures prominently. I have also attempted to provide a balance of male and female protagonists and to include protagonists from different cultural backgrounds. A final standard used in selecting these books is much less objective: In reading these books, I came to care about their central characters.

Ninth Grade Recommended Titles

Sounder by William Armstrong (116 pp.). Set in the South of the early 1900s, a boy finds an opportunity for education on one of his trips to learn where his father is. Like Odysseus' faithful Argus, Sounder knows when his master has returned, even after many years.

The True Confessions of Charlotte Doyle by Avi (232 pp.). Charlotte is 13 years old when she makes a voyage across the Atlantic in 1832. As the only passenger, she must decide whether her loyalty is to a mad captain or a mutinous crew.

Children of the River by Linda Crew (213 pp.). Sundara has survived an escape from the terrible war in Cambodia. But can she adjust to the memories and her new life in America with her aunt and uncle?

Checking on the Moon by Jenny Davis (208 pp.). Cab goes to spend the summer in Pennsylvania with her grandmother after her mother remarries and leaves for a European trip. As Cab works at her grandmother's restaurant, she comes to play a key role in addressing the community's problems with crime.

Monkey Island by Paula Fox (151 pp.). Alone in New York City after his mother abandons him, Clay is cared for by two remarkable homeless men. Clay is determined to find his mother, but what will happen if he does?

The Big Wander by Will Hobbs (181 pp.). Fourteen–year–old Clay and his older brother go to a remote area of Utah to search for their uncle in this story set in 1962. The brother returns home, but Clay stays and experiences a number of adventures before he locates his uncle. (Other Hobbs' titles are also good choices.)

For the Life of Laetitia by Merle Hodge (213 pp.). Lacey Johnson leaves her remote Caribbean village to live in the city with the father she hardly knows in order to further her education. Is the price too high?

The Brave by Robert Lipsyte (195 pp.). In this sequel to *The Contender*, Alfred Brooks is now a New York City police officer. He befriends Sonny Bear, an angry Native American boxer who leaves the reservation and his grandfather for the streets of New York City. Will he be able to meet the challenges of those mean city streets?

Somewhere in the Darkness by Walter Dean Myers (168 pp.). When Jimmy's father, Crab, returns from prison unexpectedly, the two travel to Chicago and Arkansas. Jimmy must decide whether to stay with his father, who's very ill and swears he's innocent of the murder charges, or return to live with his loving grandmother.

My Name Is Not Angelica by Scott O'Dell (130 pp.). Raisha, her friends, and family are kidnapped from their African homes to be sold as slaves in the West Indies. This is her story of the slave revolt of 1733 and its unexpected outcome.

Canyons by Gary Paulsen (184 pp.). This story of mystery and adventure is actually two connected stories. The first is of a young Apache who is murdered in the 1860's by white soldiers. The second is of present–day Brennan, who finds the skull of the Apache brave, Coyote Runs. What is it that Brennan must do with the skull? (Other works by Paulsen are also good choices.)

Missing May by Cynthia Rylant (89 pp.). Summer has lived with her aunt and uncle since she was young, but when Summer is 12 and her Aunt May dies, Summer and her Uncle Ob travel to Charleston to attempt to contact May through a psychic medium. Their trip is successful in unexpected ways.

12th Grade Recommended Titles

Midnight Hour Encores by Bruce Brooks (263 pp.). Sib Spooner is a gifted musician who has had anything but a typical childhood living with her father, Taxi. When Sib and Taxi drive across the country so that she can meet her mother, both are in for surprises and discoveries.

2001: A Space Odyssey by Arthur C. Clarke (236 pp.). Dave (the human) and Hal (the computer) venture through space on a mission initiated by a mysterious monolith left in the moon's crater by an alien intelligence. Where will the journey lead? (This novel was made into the classic movie.)

I Am the Cheese by Robert Cormier (233 pp.). Adam is bicycling along a highway in Massachusetts as this novel begins. Readers soon discover there's much more going on, although it's difficult to know what that is because Adam's journeys are both physical and psychological. Gradually the suspense builds and the pieces begin to fit together. If they have been prepared for the organizational difficulty, students will enjoy this classic Cormier work.

Lizard by Dennis Covington (198 pp.). Lizard has been living in a home for the mentally retarded because of a disfigurement, but being odd-looking doesn't mean he can't think. When a stranger claims to be his father, Lizard grabs the chance to leave the home and find some kind of life. His adventures on the road with Callahan are sometimes humorous and often memorable.

The Crazy Horse Electric Game by Chris Crutcher (215 pp.). After a water-skiing accident, former baseball hero Willie Weaver is left with slurred speech and a bad limp. He leaves his friends and family in Montana and goes to Oakland where he learns a great deal from an unlikely group of friends. Crutcher's typical blend of irreverence and poignancy works exceptionally well in this novel.

A Yellow Raft in Blue Water by Michael Dorris (372 pp.). This beautifully written novel is told in three sections by three voices: 15-year-old Rayona, her Native American mother Christine, and Christine's mother Ida. Their stories weave together giving insights into all three characters—heir secrets, their misunderstandings, and their love.

The Bean Trees by Barbara Kingsolver (232 pp.). Taylor Greer leaves her home in rural Kentucky, driving west to escape what she sees as an inevitable and dreary future. But could she have expected to live in Tucson in a sanctuary for refugees from Central America? Could she have foreseen adopting a young American Indian child? Kingsolver's readers will find themselves mixing laughter and tears.

A Wizard of Earthsea by Ursula K. Le Guin (183 pp.). Young Sparrowhawk has many magical powers, and so he leaves home to attend a school for magicians where he is renamed Ged. In a moment of reckless pride, he releases a terrible evil shadow and eventually must go on a quest to face his fear—the shadow. What makes this book so highly successful is Le Guin's marvelous and inimitable style.

Fallen Angels by Walter Dean Myers (309 pp.). Richie Perry is the book's narrator, and his story leads readers to feel they've experienced the Viet Nam War. Myers neither glorifies nor vilifies war, but he does let us into the hearts and minds of Richie and his friends as they struggle to survive and to come to terms with this war, their pasts, and their futures.

Shabanu: Daughter of the Wind by Suzanne Fisher Staples (240 pp.). Shabanu is a charming and strong–willed young woman, no small feat given the Pakistani culture which restricts many of her choices. However, since there are no sons in her family, she's been given unusual freedoms. What will she do when she learns she must marry a man who is much older and whom she does not love, or bring dishonor to her family?

The Road to Memphis by Mildred D. Taylor (290 pp.). Cassie Logan is 17 in this third volume of the Logan family saga set just before World War II. When her friend Moe breaks down after continued taunting and strikes a white man with a tire iron, Cassie and her brother help him escape to Memphis, an adventure in itself. Some students will find it challenging to read the dialect, but they'll be rewarded with a powerful story.

Homecoming by Cynthia Voigt (318 pp.). The four Tillerman children are left alone when their mother deserts them. Now it's up to 13–year–old Dicey to keep the children together. She is afraid, but she's also courageous and resourceful. Will she be able to find a new home for her siblings and herself with their grandmother?

The Reading Workshop

Prior planning is extremely helpful in multi–text class reading situations like this reading workshop. If possible, simply order copies of the books for your classroom library. Otherwise, ask the school's media specialist to order multiple copies of the YA works you'd like to use well in advance of the unit, call several local bookstores to inform them that students may be selecting particular books for a reading project, or check with your local public library to see if they have or can get copies of the books you wish to have students read.

Allow three of the five class periods per week for three weeks for the reading workshop. Explain to the students that they'll be in charge of most of these days. You may wish to modify the calendar to fit your students' needs, but the explanation that follows is based on a three–week period of time.

On the first day, I give a brief overview of the unit and introduce the book choices. I like to dramatically read a short selection from each book, show the cover, and very briefly summarize the story, without giving away the ending, of course. I think of this as being like a movie preview: The intention is to generate interest and present a general idea of who the characters are and what the story is about. Students write down their first, second, third, and fourth choices. By the following day, I organize the groups based on student choices.

On the second day, groups are announced and books are provided. Because I truly want to encourage minimal teacher guidance and greater student responsibility during the reading workshop time, I ask students to organize the designated class periods as they see fit. The time may be used for silent or group reading, discussion, or writing the response journal entries. On this day, each group establishes a schedule for reading the books and writing the response journal entries and turns this schedule in to me. If the book is 200 pages in length, for example, the students will want to decide how to read those pages over six class sessions (a final class session is described below). They write down how many pages or chapters of their book will be read by each day of the workshop.

All groups also decide how they will schedule the response journal entries, which go into thin, floppy three–ring binders. Each member of a group is expected to write a total of four entries: two initial entries and two responding to another's initial entry. With a group of four, this means there will be a total of 16 entries. Many groups organize their schedules so that initial entries are written by two group members at points about a quarter and half way through the book, with the other two group members writing their initial responses at points about three quarters of the way through the book, as well as at the end of the book. Those group members who do not write initial responses write their reactions to the initial responses at the various points in the novel. Each response entry is signed and dated. Other groups have decided on more elaborate schemes based on days of the week. At some point during the two weeks, the groups should also plan to design covers for their shared response logs, giving them titles and including the names of all writers. The schedule is up to the students, but it is turned in with the reading schedule just to be certain there is no confusion.

It may not be necessary to provide journal topics if your students are familiar with writing response logs; however, if you think your students would benefit from optional questions, you could provide the following:

1. Describe a relationship in your book. Explain your thoughts and feelings about this relationship.

2. At some point, one of the characters in your book probably could use some help in making an important decision. What is your best advice to him or her?

3. Choose a passage you especially like or find intriguing, important, or interesting. What are your thoughts about this passage? How do you think it relates to the rest of the book?

4. Are you pleased with your choice of books for the group reading? Should it be recommended for use in this unit next year? Why or why not?

5. Does a character in your book undergo any significant change? When did you first notice this change and what was its cause? Is this a change for the better?

On this second day, there may be some time for the groups to actually begin reading. If not, groups usually assign themselves reading for homework. During the other workshop days, I monitor each group's progress and provide time at the class's end for each group to quickly report to their classmates.

After students have finished reading, have held their final discussions, and have completed the journal entries, I use the final day of the three-week period to conclude the reading workshop. First, I ask the groups to skim their entire response logs and choose two entries—an initial entry and a reaction entry—which best capture the spirit of their book and their response to it. These become a bulletin board display for all students to read. Second, I "jigsaw" or reorganize the groups so that new groups of four are established. Different YA book readers are represented in each new group. These groups discuss the following questions:

1. Do any of the characters in your book possess heroic qualities? Identify these characters, tell something about them to the others in the group, and discuss how they're heroic.

2. Odysseus had the Lotus Eaters, Cyclopes, Poseidon, Scylla, and perhaps his own greed as obstacles to his returning home. What obstacles does a character in your book face, and how does he or she deal with them?

3. What journey or trip is made in your book? In your opinion, what is the effect of this trip? How would the story and a character change if the trip had not been made?

4. Which of these books would you recommend to a friend in another class for outside reading? Why? Which would you not recommend? Why not?

5. Which of the two books you've read, **The Odyssey** or the workshop book, seems to relate more to the issues and people in your own lives? Explain.

A recorder can make notes of answers to the questions, and each group can briefly share the highlights of its discussion with the class.

Figure 1-3 Continued

Writing Workshop Questionnaire

4. List two important comments made by one or two of your classmates as they responded to a draft. Did you agree or disagree with what was said? What revisions (if any) resulted from the comments?

     A. _____'s comment:
                  (Name)

       My response:

     B. _____'s comment:
                  (Name)

       My response:

5. What do you think are the strengths of your essay? Which are your favorite parts, and why?

6. What grade do you think your essay will earn, and why?

7. What did you learn as a result of writing this essay? Your response may be about the content of your essay or about your experience with writing it.

Conclusion

     This unit on heroes and journeys is one that connects a classroom classic with YA literature. Students are frequently involved in group activities, and responsibility for reading and responding lies, for the most part, with them. The first time I relinquished this amount of control I was very nervous. I worried that students wouldn't understand the book without my expert input. But I was also worried that students were relying too heavily on me for the "correct" answers and interpretations. So I undertook my own small odyssey. What I discovered was that we need to trust students with their reading in the same way that we have learned to trust them with their writing. Given the opportunity, they made good sense of the book and, furthermore, they appeared to enjoy their reading experience. This may not have led to complex analyses of the Homeric epic, but I do believe students found much food for thought. When some of the students are presented with Homer in a college class in a few years from now, I don't think they will groan loudly. And, finally, it is my hope that this positive experience with two different works will, along with other class experiences, be reinforced and encourage a life–long love of reading.

List of References

Armstrong, W. (1969). *Sounder*. New York: Harrow Books.

Avi. (1990). *The true confessions of Charlotte Doyle*. New York: Avon.

Brooks, B. (1986). *Midnight hour encores*. New York: Harper Keypoint.

Campbell, J. & Moyers, B. (1988). *The power of myth*. New York: Doubleday.

Carey, M. (1993). Hero. *Music box* (Columbia compact disc 53205), Carey (lyrics) and Carey and Afanasieff (music). Nashville: Sony Songs, Inc.

Clarke, A. (1968). *2001: A space odyssey*. New York: Penguin.

Cormier, R. (1977). *I am the cheese*. New York: Dell.

Covington, D. (1991). *Lizard*. New York: Delacorte Press.

Crew, L. (1990). *Children of the river*. New York: Delacorte Press.

Crutcher, C. (1987). *The crazy horse electric game*. New York: Greenwillow.

Davis, J. (1993). *Checking on the moon*. New York: Dell.

Dorris, M. (1987). *A yellow raft in blue water*. New York: Warner Books.

Fox, P. (1993). *Monkey island*. New York: Dell.

Glasser, J.E. (1994, February). Finding Ithaca: *The Odyssey* personalized. *English Journal*, **83** (2), 66–69.

Hobbs, W. (1992). *The big wander*. New York: Atheneum.

Hodge, M. (1993). *For the life of Laetitia*. New York: Farrar, Straus & Giroux.

Homer. (1963). *The Odyssey*. Translated by Robert Fitzgerald. New York: Anchor Books.

Homer. (1988). *The Odyssey*. Translated by Samuel Butler. New York: Amsco School Publications.

Kingsolver, B. (1988). *The bean trees*. New York: HarperCollins.

Le Guin, U.K. (1968). *A wizard of Earthsea*. New York: Bantam.

Lipsyte, R. (1991). *The brave*. New York: HarperCollins.

Myers, W.D. (1988). *Fallen angels*. New York: Scholastic.

Myers, W.D. (1992). *Somewhere in the darkness*. New York: Scholastic.

Neeld, E.C. (1986). *Writing*. Glenview, IL: Scott, Foresman.

O'Dell, S. (1989). *My name is not Angelica*. Boston: Houghton Mifflin.

Paulsen, G. (1990). *Canyons*. New York: Delacorte Press.

Rylant, C. (1992). *Missing May*. New York: Orchard Books.

Sauve, P. (1993). Class handout. Campbell Hall School, North Hollywood, CA.

Staples, S.F. (1989). *Shabanu: Daughter of the wind*. New York: Alfred A. Knopf.

Taylor, M.D. (1990). *The road to Memphis*. New York: Puffin.

Voigt, C. (1981). *Homecoming*. New York: Fawcett Juniper.

CHAPTER 2

Bridging *The Red Badge of Courage* with Six Related Young Adult Novels

PAM B. COLE

Introduction

Three years ago, as a high school English teacher, I recommended *The Red Badge of Courage* by Stephen Crane to one of my 11th grade students. Knowing Tim was one of my better readers, I was confident he would both understand and enjoy a story about a soldier's reactions to warfare. Two days later, however, he dropped the book, unfinished, on my desk. "That's no good," he said. "There's no story to it."

Though research in reader-response theory has affirmed our belief that we must recognize and honor readers' rights to interact with texts and to create individual meaning, we remain aware that some literature, most notably the "classics," is difficult for young readers because they cannot easily relate the literary experience to their own lives (Phillips, 1989). The gap between the text and students' life experiences is simply too great. Tim, like many other high school students, grappled with the complexities of Crane's masterpiece. Although Tim's an able reader, he was unprepared to deal with the complexity of psychological realism, impressionism, and naturalistic philosophy evident in the classic; thus, he was unable to connect with important issues raised by the work: the psychological complexities of fear and courage on the battlefield, the brutality and horror of war, and the nature of the individual and his relation with society. Tim looked only for the story and could not find it. Had I insisted that Tim read the novel, forcing my own explications of the text on him, his reading would have been meaningless.

Pairing this American classic, so often taught in secondary classrooms, with similar, but less sophisticated, young adult (YA) novels that explore the human response to war can aid students in developing a deeper understanding of issues raised by Crane's work. Moreover, when the gap between students' prior experiences and *The Red Badge of Courage* is eased by comparable YA literature, students may also begin understanding a bit more about Crane's technique: his use of psychological realism, impressionism, and naturalistic philosophy.

Through the use of literary circles, this unit will illustrate how six YA novels can prepare students for reading *The Red Badge of Courage*. The unit, designed for a six-week period, is divided into three primary parts: pre-reading, concurrent, and post-reading activities. Though numerous books deal with the effects of war, the following books are similar to *The Red Badge of Courage* in that they deal primarily with the protagonist's inner struggles to understand the conflicting emotions caused by war: *Fallen Angels* by Walter Dean Myers, *The Fighting Ground* by Avi, *Gentle Annie: The True Story of a Civil War Nurse* by Mary Francis Shura, *I Had Seen Castles* by Cynthia Rylant, *My Brother Sam Is Dead* and *The Winter Hero* by James and Christopher Collier. Other possible novels are listed in "Other YA Literature Worth Considering" and complete bibliographic information can be found at the end of this chapter.

Novel Summaries

The Classic

The Red Badge of Courage by Stephen Crane (192 pp.)

Having dreamed of fierce and bloody battles all of his life in which he saw himself in numerous heroic struggles, young Henry Fleming burns to enlist as a private in the Civil War. His mother's resistance, however, discourages him. But reading of marches, sieges, and conflicts in newspapers and listening to gossip in the village fuel his desire. Shivering with ecstasy, Henry enlists in a Northern company that forms near his home and sets off filled with pride and grand illusions of his heroic prowess. His grand illusions are shattered, however, when he finds himself on the battlefield. Amid the cold realities of war, Henry begins questioning his own courage and fears he may run when confronted with battle. Henry experiences the brutality, horrors, and exaltation of war and moves through periods of doubt, fear, anxiety, and bravery. As he does so, he becomes a symbolic representation of human nature in the face of war.

Six Young Adult Novels

Fallen Angels by Walter Dean Myers (309 pp.)

Believing that he is just an observer in life and lacking the finances to pursue his dream of attending college, 17-year-old Richie Perry enlists in the army, confident of his immortality and having no thoughts of seeing actual combat. Nonetheless, Perry finds himself assigned to combat duty in Viet Nam as a result of a paperwork foul-up. Once in Nam, his days are filled with frequent patrols into Vietcong territory in which he and his comrades are to sight and report on any Vietcong movement. Their assignments are considered "light stuff" until they begin encountering frequent, intense conflicts with the Vietcong. Perry and his comrades express doubt, fear, anxiety, and courage and begin questioning what they are doing in Nam. Their single dream becomes that they will get out of Nam alive.

Myers has written a superb example of psychological realism. Through the eyes of Richie Perry, Myers recreates the mental theater of war. The reader shares Perry's doubts, fears, and apprehensions as he deals with the stark realities of war. Like Crane's Henry Fleming, Perry comes to understand the senselessness and ruthlessness of war.

In addition, the novel is an excellent choice for discussing the meaning of naturalistic philosophy. The central characters are people who are caught up by forces of nature and society that are beyond their understanding or command. Readers can question how much control Perry and his comrades have over their own fate, that is, who is in control—the individual, society, or nature. Furthermore, the patrol scenes in which Perry and his comrades encounter the enemy lend a naturalistic quality to the work. Sites and events are very detailed, grim, and illustrate the animalistic nature of human beings; moreover, the weather is an imposing force that works perpetually against the soldiers.

The novel can also be used to introduce students to the concept of impressionism. Chapters are frequently disjointed or episodic. The story unfolds, not through a series of events, but through a series of psychological stages that occur within the mind of the protagonist. Additionally, sites and events are frequently filtered through Richie Perry's impressions. In describing the Vietcong, for example, Perry remarks, "The darkness seemed to eat their bodies. Black" (p. 288).

The story not only provides a riveting account of the Viet Nam War, but also is an excellent choice for introducing students to the concepts of psychological realism, naturalistic philosophy, and impressionism. It is, however, written for more able readers and contains mature language.

The Fighting Ground by Avi (152 pp.)

April 1778. The American Revolution. Thirteen-year-old Jonathan, dreaming romantic thoughts of the glory and valor of war, runs to the local tavern to learn the reason for the tolling bell. Upon arrival, he learns that a small number of untrained farmers have gathered to fight against professional Hessian soldiers. Against his father's wishes, Jonathan borrows a musket from the tavern keeper and joins the ranks. However, Jonathan's romantic thoughts of battle are soon shattered when he is taken prisoner by the Hessians. He learns that war is not glory and valor, but pain, senseless brutality, and death.

By providing a minute-by-minute account of one youth's experiences during the Revolution, Avi reveals how the protagonist struggles to understand the intense and conflicting emotions brought on by war. The novel is an excellent choice for introducing students to the idea of psychological realism.

Gentle Annie: The True Story of a Civil War Nurse by Mary Francis Shura (184 pp.)

During the Civil War, the Union recruited several hundred women, known as Daughters of the Regiment, whose primary role was to serve as laundresses—washing clothes, darning stockings, and mending torn seams. Among these female recruits was young Anna Blair Etheridge. Not only did Anna perform laundry services for the army, she also served as a nurse on the front line of almost every major battle fought by the Army of the Potomac. Praised by soldiers and journalists in letters, journals, and newspapers, Anna became widely known for her courage, duty, modesty, and gentle nature.

Female contributions to war efforts have long been silenced in history. Drawing from factual records, Shura recreates a seldom-told story of a woman's war experiences. In doing so, she paints numerous detailed and grim battle scenes. These scenes can be used to introduce students to the concept of naturalistic philosophy. As a result of her war experiences, the protagonist struggles with the psychological complexities of war. The novel, therefore, can also be used to introduce students to the idea of psychological realism.

I Had Seen Castles by Cynthia Rylant (97 pp.)

It is 1941, and the Japanese bomb Pearl Harbor. Seventeen-year-old John Dante is outraged at the bombing and thinks only of getting even. While eagerly awaiting his 18th birthday so he can enlist, John falls in love with Ginny, a lovely pacifist. Despite her objections to the war, John enlists shortly after his birthday and loses her forever. Fifty years later, John reflects on his youth—haunted by his war experiences and by Ginny's memory. Rylant has created a heartfelt story of lost innocence that can be used to introduce students to psychological realism.

My Brother Sam Is Dead by James and Christopher Collier (216 pp.)

The American Revolution is being fought, and the Meeker family loyalty is divided. Young Tim Meeker finds himself torn between allegiance to his father, an English supporter, and allegiance to his older brother Sam, a "rebel" partisan. Tim does not engage in actual combat, but his hometown becomes a scene of intense conflict. He is forced to take on adult responsibilities while observing death and brutality on both sides. When his brother is executed by American loyalists and his own father dies as a prisoner on a British ship, Tim begins seeing war as a meaningless way of resolving differences.

The novel is a sharp revelation of the human aspects of war and can serve to introduce the concept of psychological realism. Sam's imprisonment can also serve as a springboard for a discussion on naturalistic philosophy.

The Winter Hero by James and Christopher Collier (152 pp.)

Young Justin is an orphan living with his sister and her husband, Peter, a hero of the Revolutionary War. Justin idolizes his brother-in-law and wishes to do something "glorious and brave" so that Peter will be proud of him. But the war is over, and Justin does not foresee any opportunities. When the local farmers protest against unfair taxation levied against them by the Boston government, Justin finds his chance. Anxious to be a hero, he spies for the local farmers and eventually takes up military arms with the farmers in Shay's Rebellion. Justin's glorified visions of war vanish, however, when he sees death, experiences hunger and cold, and realizes that his brother-in-law may be executed for his role in the rebellion. The novel is particularly effective as a vehicle for discussing the psychological complexities of war.

Pre-reading Activities

All readers bring prior knowledge and experiences to their reading; none are a tabula rasa. Thus, pre-reading activities provide a means by which students can begin connecting their frames of reference to the task at hand. They are a means by which students begin reflecting on a given subject and begin wrapping their prior knowledge around the text, thus shaping and altering it (Milner & Milner, 1993; p. 87). Any of the following activities will encourage students to begin making connections with what they already know and what they are about to encounter in their reading of both the YA novels and *The Red Badge of Courage*.

Children's Literature

I have used children's literature in the secondary classroom as read-alouds and have found its use stimulating and thought provoking. Ten children's books that carry the war theme follow. As a pre-reading activity, choose one and read it aloud to the class. Give students approximately 10 minutes to freewrite after the reading, and then allow them to discuss their responses. Since the stories are quick reads, you may wish to share more than one with the class.

The Dove's Letter by Keith Baker

While in flight, a dove spots a beautiful letter lying abandoned on the ground below. Sensing that the letter carries an important message for its receiver, the dove begins a search for the letter's owner. A woodsman, a farmer, a baker, a weaver, and finally a soldier find different messages in the letter. The story is one in which the reader may reflect on a soldier's homecoming. Is home the same? Will it ever be?

The Wall by Eve Bunting

This story, written from a small boy's point of view, is a very moving account of a father and son's visit to the Viet Nam Veterans' Memorial in Washington, D.C. The two search for the name of the boy's grandfather who was killed in conflict.

Sadako and the Thousand Paper Cranes by Eleanor Coerr

Based on a true event during World War II, this story is a heart-wrenching account of a young girl who is poisoned by radiation gases during the dropping of the bomb on Hiroshima.

Drummer Hoff by Barbara Emberley

This is a story that illustrates military hierarchy. Each army person is involved in carrying out orders to fire a large cannon. The lowest in command, Drummer Hoff, actually fires the cannon while the general imparts the command.

The Lotus Seed by Sherry Garland

This story is a moving account of a Vietnamese family's life during a civil war. When the emperor is dethroned, a young Vietnamese girl takes a lotus seed from his garden as a remembrance. She keeps the seed a secret from her family and carries it with her to America when she and her family are forced to flee Viet Nam. Years later, her grandson finds the precious seed and plants it in his garden. The seed symbolizes life, hope, and cultural heritage.

The Butter Battle Book by T.S. Geisel (Dr. Seuss)

This book offers an excellent discussion on the absurdity of war. In this story, the Yooks and Zooks go to war over a ridiculous disagreement concerning which side of the bread should be buttered.

The Story of Ferdinand by Munro Leaf

The Banderilleros, the Picardores, the Matador, and the spectators all expect Ferdinand to fight; however, when Ferdinand reaches the middle of the ring, he is attracted by fragrant flowers in a beautiful woman's hair.

Rather than charging the Matador, Ferdinand sits down quietly to smell the flowers. The story is a good discussion of individual versus societal expectations.

Potatoes, Potatoes by A. Lobel

This story is about two boys and their mother who live in a house surrounded by a wall that protects them from their warring neighbors. They live a content life until the two boys see armies marching outside the wall. Attracted by the glory of war, the boys join opposing sides and end up fighting one another on their mother's land. This is an excellent springboard for a discussion on humanity's capacity for self-destruction.

Faithful Elephants: A True Story of Animals, People, and War by Yukio Tsuchiya

The Japanese government orders the death of all zoo animals during World War II for fear that the animals will run wild if the zoo is hit during bombing raids. The story is a reminder that humans are not the only victims of war; all of nature pays a price.

Waiting for the Evening Star by Rosemary Wells

Wells captures a family's life before World War I. The younger brother, Berty, envisions no place better than the family farm in Vermont. His older brother, however, dreams of travel and seeing the world. This is a story of coming-of-age and brotherly love and is an excellent springboard for a discussion on the effects of war on the home front.

Short Stories

Short stories also make thought-provoking pre-reading activities. Tim O'Brien's short story "Ambush," about a haunting memory of death in Viet Nam, is brief and makes a stimulating read-aloud. Short stories such as Ernest Hemingway's "In Another Country," Ambrose Bierce's "A Horseman in the Sky," Pearl Buck's "The Old Demon," Liam O'Flaherty's "The Sniper," and John Hersey's "Survival" are a bit longer but work just as well. If longer stories are chosen, I suggest having small groups participate in a collaborative reading, with each student reading a section agreed upon by the group. As one student reads, the other students underline words, phrases, and passages they find meaningful. After the story is complete, students then freewrite about the aspects of the story that were meaningful for them and then discuss their responses within their group. You may wish to have small groups share their stories and their responses with the larger group after the small group discussions.

Choral Reading

Choral reading, the oral interpretation of poetry by two or more voices, is yet another viable pre-reading activity. Divide students into groups of four or five and provide them with several poems from which they can choose. Poetry carrying war themes is plentiful, of course, and easily found in any number of anthologies. Consider poetry by Siegfried Sassoon, Ivor Gurney, Walt Whitman, and Wilfred Owen; war is a recurring theme in much of their writing. Explain to students that choral reading may take many different forms. For example, one student may read a particular line or stanza; then a second student may read a line or stanza; then a third; and so on until the poem is finished. One student may also read particular lines and then ask the group to join in on refrains. Other methods will work, and students should not hesitate to be creative. Allow them time to make a choice, design a plan for reading, and rehearse the choral reading. After rehearsal, small groups present their choral reading to the larger group. Time should be allowed for large group reaction and interaction with the reading. Freewriting may also follow choral reading.

Art Activities

Wartime newspapers and magazines are literally filled with satirical war cartoons. Working in either small groups, pairs, or as individuals, students locate some of these cartoons in the library and bring them to the class for a large group discussion of the serious issues they raise. This activity may be followed by sharing with the class James Thurber's "The Last Flower," an illustrated fable about the senseless, destructive nature of war. Paintings carrying war themes or war photography may be used in a similar fashion.

Predictions

This activity is stimulating and takes little preparation. You may choose to read the opening sentence or paragraph of each YA novel to the class, and ask students to make predictions about what they think will occur in the story. Or you may ask students to speculate about the meaning of the title or the nature of the book cover. Either approach will require reflection on the students' part and will provide a means by which students begin tapping their prior experiences.

Selecting YA Novels

After pre-reading activities, introduce students to the YA books by giving brief booktalks on each novel. Next, have students form literary circles (groups of four preferably, and not more than five students) around a novel of their choosing. If one novel appears more popular than others, you may ask students to make a first and second choice, or you may allow two or more circles to form around the same novel. Set deadlines for the novels to be finished. Two weeks per novel should be sufficient.

Journal Keeping

Students need to record their thoughts and feelings in logs or journals as they work through a piece of reading. Such "recordings" aid students in thinking through their reading. They act as springboards for small or large group discussions and help students develop projects later on in the unit.

Since the purpose of pairing the YA novel with *The Red Badge of Courage* is to enable readers to better understand the classic and draw comparisons and contrasts between the classic and the YA novel, a three-column journal works well. Ask students to design a three-column journal, using legal-sized paper turned crossways, that they will bring with them to all group discussions. During the reading of the YA novel, have students note in the first column important words, passages, or ideas they encounter in their reading. Below the notation(s), ask them to note their personal response(s). The second column is used in the same manner with *The Red Badge of Courage*. The third column is used as the bridge between the two works: In this column, students note similarities or differences they find between the two works as they read.

Presenting Literary Conventions

Understanding how literary conventions are used in YA novels will aid students in gaining a better understanding of their use in *The Red Badge of Courage*. Therefore, as students become immersed in their YA novels, periodically draw their attention to literary conventions. Listed below are examples of how imagery, metaphor, and point of view might be addressed. Once you have introduced each convention to students, ask them to look for examples in their YA novels as they read. Then later, when they read *The Red Badge of Courage*, ask them to do the same. You may want to ask them to set aside a section in their journal for this assignment. It is important, however, not to force your explications of the novel on the students; doing so will discourage them from exploring their own thoughts concerning the text.

Imagery

Imagery is a powerful and complex element in *The Red Badge of Courage*. Understanding how words and phrases can appeal to the reader's senses and imagination can aid students in developing a deeper understanding of Crane's masterpiece. Since the word *red* carries significant symbolic meaning in *The Red Badge of Courage* and is a recurring image in the other YA novels, an activity in which students are asked to think about sensory reactions to the word can help them to develop a deeper understanding of this writing technique. One idea is to have students create poems from words they associate with the color *red* (Phillips, 1989).

Write, for example, the word *red* on the chalkboard. Ask students to brainstorm on paper all the nouns and descriptive words that the word *red* evokes in their minds. Have students form groups and create short poems from the words they have listed. What feelings do the poems evoke? Do they evoke feelings of excitement? Danger? Fear? Follow by asking students to watch for words in their reading that appeal to their senses and to consider various questions: What emotion(s) do these words elicit? Or what mood(s) do they create? Have them repeat the activity with the words *black* or *darkness* (e.g. *My Brother Sam Is Dead*, p. 106; *Fallen Angels*, p. 288).

Metaphor

Metaphor is another recurring element in *The Red Badge of Courage* and can be more easily understood if students begin thinking about the meanings of metaphors as they read their YA novels. Demonstrate the form and content of a metaphor. You might, for example, project on an overhead the metaphor *Love is a rose*, and explain that a metaphor is an abstract relationship between two unrelated items. You may then choose any number of short poems that demonstrate metaphor—Eve Merriam's "Metaphor" and Sylvia Plath's "Metaphors" are excellent choices—and have students discuss the relationships being compared. Also, students will readily identify metaphor in the children's story *Two Bad Ants* by Chris Van Allsburg, a metaphorically rich story about two ants who stray from their ant kingdom and experience a number of dangerous perils before being reunited with the ant army. You may wish to read this story out loud and then ask students to discuss its metaphoric language. Follow by asking students to watch for metaphors in their novels and to consider this question: How do these metaphors define characters, explain themes, or describe settings?

Point of View

The perspective from which a story is told greatly influences what and how the reader is able to see. Using limited third-person point of view, Crane describes the thoughts and actions of the protagonist and filters the events of the story through Henry Fleming's "impressions." To Henry, for example, the regiment emerges as "grunting bundles of blue."

To help students better understand point of view, select any one of the children's books listed earlier in this chapter, share the book with the class, and ask them to consider the story in light of alternative points of view. You might, for instance, share Bunting's *The Wall* and ask students how the story would be different if an adult had narrated the story instead of the child. Ask students to consider diverse points of view while they are reading their novels and discuss them in their literary circles: How might, for example, John's experiences be different in *I Had Seen Castles* had Ginny narrated the story rather than John? What if Peter narrated *The Winter Hero* rather than Justin? What if a Viet Nam news reporter narrated Perry's experiences in Nam in *Fallen Angels*? and so forth. At this point, you may want to have students choose a short, but powerful, scene and rewrite it from a different point of view.

Literary Circle Discussions

Allow students at least two days to get immersed in their reading, and then begin allowing them to meet three times a week to share their responses to the novels. During these meetings, student journals should serve as springboards for discussing their reading. Ask students to share their responses to important words, lines, or passages that they reacted to in their journals. To encourage group participation, occasionally alter this format. You may, for example, ask students to bring admit slips—slips of paper containing questions or topics of discussion about their reading—for admission to group meetings. Or, when literary groups convene, have students take turns giving story summaries—reports on what is happening thus far in their reading. A more challenging group activity is to have students perform think-alouds.

Before their groups convene, have students choose passages that depict levels of growth and psychological changes that occur in the characters. When they meet in their groups, have students read their chosen passages to the group and then speculate about the changes that are taking place within the characters. These activities, while encouraging group participation, will allow students to explore their own questions and reactions to the text.

Although discussion of the novels should primarily focus on issues that students themselves raise from their reading, you may occasionally want to draw their attention to a particular issue or question. When groups meet, for instance, you may ask them to consider such questions as the following: Are the protagonists heroes? Why or why not? What is heroism? Is courage displayed? How? By whom? What is courage?

These are only five ideas to encourage group discussion; certainly there are many others. Through these and other similar activities, students will become involved in an interpretive community, a "gathering of students in which each student's personal responses are elaborated, informed and enlarged by interaction with others" (Milner & Milner, 1993; p. 100). Students will encounter a variety of responses and interpretations of the texts which will broaden individual perspectives and lay to rest the idea that any one reading is the definitive reading of the text (Milner & Milner, 1993; p. 100).

Concurrent Activities

Responding to literature through group discussions can be very meaningful, enjoyable, and rewarding. Because there are multiple ways of knowing, understanding, and expressing what we know and what we feel (Gardner, 1983), a deeper appreciation of the texts can be fostered if students are encouraged to use other intelligences—other talents, skills, abilities, and interests while they are reading the novels. Listed below are only a few activities—intended as examples—that will encourage both you and your students to begin thinking about ways of exercising alternative ways of knowing. Possibilities naturally are endless.

Drama Activities

Students may wish to feign the identity of the characters and dramatize a number of "what if" situations. For example, from *I Had Seen Castles*, what would happen if John met Ginny after more than fifty years? From *My Brother Sam Is Dead*, what would happen if Sam and his father met prior to Sam's execution? From *The Fighting Ground*, what would happen if Jonathan's father followed him to the tavern? and so forth.

Some groups may be interested in reader's theater. Groups may choose a particularly moving scene and develop and practice a performance for the rest of the class. Good readers, however, may wish to choose a scene to rehearse and read aloud individually to the class. Still other groups may feel comfortable choosing a particularly moving scene and dramatizing it for the class.

Students may also enjoy such activities as on-the-scene reporting of a battle. One student takes on the role of a soldier while another becomes the field reporter. The pair develops a script and then performs it before the rest of the class.

Some students may find panel debates appealing. Students choose sides to debate the issue of war in the novel. Which side, if either, is justified in its military actions? Students may wish to research the causes of any war involved in this unit—the Revolutionary War, the Civil War, Shay's Rebellion, World War II, or the Viet Nam War—as preparation for this panel debate.

Art Activities

Students may design a book cover for one of the books, or they may choose a scene that is vivid in detail and recreate it either through sketches, paintings, dioramas, mosaics, murals, or collages. Other possibilities are to sketch, paint, or mold from clay favorite characters. Here, students with artistic flair will develop their own ideas.

Writing Activities

Literary circles may wish to create their own newspaper that relates the events that they read about in their novel. For example, some students reading Avi's *The Fighting Ground* may write about Jonathan's disappearance when he is taken prisoner by the Hessians, while others in the group may write about the brutal murder of the young boy's parents.

Students may, however, wish to create a more historically accurate account of any of the wars covered in the unit by researching the battles or events described and creating a scrapbook of war clippings.

Another possibility is to have students choose an emotionally intense scene and rewrite it from an alternative point of view. For example, after having read the scene in *The Red Badge of Courage* in which Henry flees from battle, students may have an onlooker relate Henry's actions. Those students reading *My Brother Sam Is Dead* may wish to narrate Sam's thoughts prior to his court martial.

Some students may wish to become the character. Feigning the character's identity, students may write a letter home detailing war experiences, keep a diary expressing thoughts, feelings, decisions, and experiences during the war or, looking ahead to old age, students may reminisce about their war experiences. (Since the novel *I Had Seen Castles* is a story in which an elderly man recounts his war experiences, group(s) that have read this novel may wish to share favorite passages with others who are particularly interested in this writing assignment.)

Math Activities

Students may create a timeline that illustrates the major events in their novels. Or, those who enjoy working with math coordinates may graph an x and y axis. On the x axis they list 10 major occurrences in the story; on the y axis they rate the significance of the events from one to ten. Other students may wish to plot a military strategy map indicating where armies are located, where battles have occurred, and where the next likely encounters will be.

Music Activities

Students interested in music may wish to compile a collection of songs that were popular during the setting of their novels and either present or teach one such song to their class. Some students may enjoy setting a poem with a war theme to music or performing a dramatic reading of a scene using music as supporting background. Still others may enjoy writing a ballad about one of the protagonists in the novels or writing their own song with a war theme.

Post-Reading Activities

After students have had the opportunity to explore both *The Red Badge of Courage* and a YA novel of their choosing, post-reading activities should concentrate on commonalties running through the novels. Students should first be encouraged to discuss in their literary circles similarities and differences in their novels. Several ideas for discussion activities follow.

Discussion Activities

Have students compare and contrast any of the following:

- The settings of each novel and the effect they have on the novel.

- The structure of their novels. Do chapters flow smoothly from one event to another or are chapters episodic in nature?

- Symbolism in their novels.

- A scene from each novel they read that is particularly rich in color, sight, and/or sound imagery.

- The points of view used by the authors of their novels.

- Character development in their novels.

- Figurative language in their novels.

- The goals, dreams, or motives behind the actions of each protagonist.

- The changes that take place within the protagonists.

- Naturalistic philosophy within the novels.

Culminating Activities

After students, in group discussions, have had an opportunity to explore similarities and differences among their novels, they should be encouraged to choose or develop a culminating activity for their work. A few suggestions for activities that bridge the novels follow, but students should be encouraged to develop their own activities—either individually, in pairs, or in small groups—based on their own personal interactions with the texts. Allow adequate time for students to complete their projects. Time will vary, of course, depending on your schedule and the nature of the projects chosen. Have students present their projects to the class as their culminating activity for the unit.

Speech/Drama Activities

Meet the Protagonist

Students interested in drama may wish to stage a meeting between the protagonists from their two novels. Characters may meet as either friend or foe on the battlefield, as guests on a talk show, or as prisoners of war; or, they may meet several years after the war and reminisce about their war experiences. Possibilities for this project are endless. Whatever encounter is chosen, students should speculate on what words the characters might exchange, create a dialogue, and perform the text for the rest of the class.

Panel Discussion

Some students may wish to organize a panel to discuss the similarities and differences among characters. Or students may wish to take on the role of characters and participate in a panel discussion in which they talk about their experiences in the war. Any of these activities, or others that are similar, will encourage students to reflect on the inner struggles of the characters.

Open Forum

One literary circle may wish to facilitate an open forum. Students in the literary circle involve other students in a group discussion of similarities and differences that span all the novels. For example, a literary circle that has read *Gentle Annie: The True Story of a Civil War Nurse* might raise the issue of character development: The protagonist of *The Red Badge of Courage* is a rather one-dimensional character, but the protagonist in their YA novel is much more developed. The literary circle may ask other students to respond to the idea of character development in their YA novels.

Writing Activities

Comparison/Contrast Paper

Students may opt for a traditional comparison/contrast paper based on any of the discussion activities listed earlier or on another idea of their own choosing.

Skit

Some students may enjoy writing an original skit that has characters from both of their novels. Students who write the skit may wish to perform the skit, or they may wish to direct the skit and ask other students who are more interested in drama to audition for parts.

Letters

Students may feign a relationship of sorts between two characters from both novels. For example, Annie from *Gentle Annie: A True Story of a Civil War Nurse* encounters Henry Fleming from *The Red Badge of Courage* on the battlefield and dresses his "wound." They exchange addresses and promise to write. What would they talk about in their letters? Would Henry reveal the truth about his wound? His fear of dying? Would Annie talk about her former marriage? Her reasons for joining the Union cause?

Reader's Support Kit

Some students, working alone or in small groups, may wish to develop for future readers of *The Red Badge of Courage* a reader's support kit—a collection of support materials that prepare students to encounter a novel, that aid them during their reading, and that foster reflection afterward (Small & Kenney, 1978). Reflecting on activities that would strengthen and deepen responses to the novel, students put together a collection of written activities, pictures, puzzles, questionnaires, and appropriate objects for students to examine. Such kits can then be placed in either the classroom or school library for other students to use. As a spin-off of this project, some students may be interested in developing a "bridging kit," a reader's support kit that contains activities that link the two novels they read. Either activity would deepen students' own understanding of their reading.

Other YA Literature Worth Considering

Jayhawker by Patricia Beatty (214 pp.).
Toliver's Secret by Esther Wood Brady (166 pp).
I'm Deborah Sampson: A Soldier in the War of the Revolution by Patricia Clapp (176 pp.).
The Tamarack Tree by Patricia Clapp (256 pp.).
The Bloody Country by James and Christopher Collier (183 pp.).
War Comes to Willy Freeman by James and Christopher Collier (178 pp.).
The Forgotten Heroes: The Story of the Buffalo Soldiers by Clinton Cox (174 pp.).
Undying Glory: The Story of the Massachusetts 54th Regiment by Clinton Cox (167 pp.).
April Morning by Howard Fast (202 pp.).
Johnny Tremain by Esther Forbes (269 pp.).
Early Thunder by Jean Fritz (255 pp.).
Which Way Freedom? by Joyce Hansen (120 pp.).
Across Five Aprils by Irene Hunt (190 pp.).
Rifles for Watie by Harold Keith (332 pp.).

Touchmark by Mildred Lawrence (184 pp.).
Carlota by Scott O'Dell (141 pp.).
Sarah Bishop by Scott O'Dell (184 pp.).
Sing Down the Moon by Scott O'Dell (146 pp.).
The Slopes of War by N.A. Perez (202 pp.).
Shades of Gray by Carolyn Reeder (152 pp.).
Behind Rebel Lines: The Incredible Story of Emma Edmonds, Civil War Spy by Seymour Reit (114 pp.).
A Ride into Morning: The Story of Tempe Wick by Ann Rinaldi (289 pp.).
Time Enough for Drums by Ann Rinaldi (249 pp.).
Children of the Fire by Harriette Robinet (134 pp.).
The Killer Angels by Michael Shaara (355 pp.).

Conclusion

The Red Badge of Courage has much to offer adolescents. But it is a complex novel that requires teachers to seek ways that will make it more accessible to young readers. Pairing this classic with similar YA novels can aid students in reading, understanding, and making connections with their lives and that of the protagonist, Henry Fleming. The six novels used in this unit pair well with *The Red Badge of Courage*, for like Crane's classic, each deals with the individual's inner struggles to understand war. However, the field of YA literature is far from being stagnant: There are currently many more novels that could be successfully paired with the work, and there will certainly be many more written in the future.

List of References

Avi. (1984). *The fighting ground*. Philadelphia: J.B. Lippincott Company.
Baker, K. (1993). *The dove's letter*. New York: Harcourt, Brace, & Jovanovich.
Beatty, P. (1991). *Jayhawker*. New York: William Morrow.
Bierce, A. (1992). A horseman in the sky. In B. Bernstein (Ed.), *Language and literature*. Evanston, IL: McDougal Littell, 304–309.
Brady, E.W. (1976). *Toliver's secret*. New York: Bullseye.
Buck, P. (1992). The old demon. In R. Craig Goheen (Ed.), *Language and literature*. Evanston, IL: McDougal Littell, 35–43.
Bunting, E. (1990). *The wall*. New York: Clarion.
Clapp, P. (1986). *The tamarack tree*. New York: Penguin USA.
Clapp, P. (1977). *I'm Deborah Sampson: A soldier in the war of the revolution*. New York: Lothrop, Lee, & Shepard.
Coerr, E. (1977). *Sadako and the thousand paper cranes*. New York: Yearling.
Collier, J.L. & Collier, C. (1987). *War comes to Willy Freeman*. New York: Dell.
Collier, J. & Collier, C. (1985). *The bloody country*. New York: Scholastic.
Collier, J. & Collier, C. (1978). *The winter hero*. New York: Four Winds Press.

Collier, J., & Collier, C. (1974). *My brother Sam is dead*. New York: Scholastic.

Cox, C. (1993). *The forgotten heroes: The story of the buffalo soldiers*. New York: Scholastic.

Cox, C. (1991). *Undying glory: The story of the Massachusetts 54th Regiment*. New York: Scholastic.

Crane, S. (1981). *The red badge of courage*. Mahwah, NJ: Watermill Press.

Emberley, B. (adaptor). (1967). *Drummer Hoff*. Englewood Cliffs, NJ: Prentice-Hall.

Fast, H. (1961). *April morning*. New York: Crown.

Forbes, E. (1971). *Johnny Tremain*. New York: Dell.

Fritz, J. (1967). *Early thunder*. New York: Coward, McCann, & Geoghegan.

Gardner, H. (1983). *Frames of mind: The theory of multiple intelligences*. New York: Basic Books.

Garland, S. (1993). *The lotus seed*. New York: Harcourt, Brace, & Jovanovich.

Geisel, T.S. (Dr. Seuss). (1984). *The butter battle book*. New York: Random House.

Hansen, J. (1992). *Which way freedom?* New York: Avon.

Hemingway, E. (1989). In another country. In Scribner's literature series: *American literature*. Mission Hills, CA: Glencoe, 490–495.

Hersey, J. (1992). Survival. In B. Bernstein (Ed.), *Language and literature*. Evanston, IL: McDougal Littell, 795–805.

Hunt, I. (1964). *Across five Aprils*. New York: Pacer.

Keith, H. (1957). *Rifles for Watie*. New York: Troll.

Lawrence, M. (1975). *Touchmark*. New York: Harcourt, Brace, & Jovanovich.

Leaf, M. (1984). *The story of Ferdinand*. New York: Scholastic.

Lobel, A. (1967). *Potatoes, potatoes*. New York: Harper & Row.

Meridiam, E. (1992). Metaphor. In J. Beatty (Ed.), *Literature and language*. Evanston, IL: McDougal Littell, 576.

Milner, J.O. & Milner, L.F.M. (1993). *Bridging English*. New York: Merrill.

Myers, W.D. (1988). *Fallen angels*. New York: Scholastic.

O'Brien, T. (1992). Ambush. In B. Bernstein (Ed.), *Language and literature*. Evanston, IL: McDougal Littell, 331–332.

O'Dell, S. (1980). *Sarah Bishop*. Boston: Houghton Mifflin.

O'Dell, S. (1977). *Carlota*. Boston: Houghton Mifflin.

O'Dell, S. (1970). *Sing down the moon*. New York: Dell.

O'Flaherty, L. (1992). The sniper. In Richard Craig Goheen (Ed.), *Language and literature*. Evanston, IL: McDougal Littell, 649–651.

Perez, N.A. (1990). *The slopes of war*. Boston: Houghton Mifflin.

Phillips, L. (1989, March). First impressions: Introducing Monet to Megadeth. *English Journal*, 78 (3), 31–33.

Plath, S. (1960). Metaphor. In X.J. Kennedy (3rd Ed.), (1983). *Literature: An introduction to fiction, poetry, and drama*. Boston: Little, Brown & Company, 1461.

Reeder, C. (1989). *Shades of gray*. New York: Avon.

Reit, S. (1988). *Behind rebel lines: The incredible story of Emma Edmonds, Civil War spy*. New York: Gulliver Books.

Rinaldi, A. (1991). *A ride into morning: The story of Tempe Wick*. New York: Gulliver Books.

Rinaldi, A. (1986). *Time enough for drums*. Mahwah, NJ: Troll.

Robinet, H. (1991). *Children of the fire*. New York: Macmillan.

Rylant, C, (1993). *I had seen castles*. New York: Harcourt, Brace, & Jovanovich.

Shaara, M. (1974). *The killer angels*. New York: Ballantine.

Shura, M.F. (1991). *Gentle Annie: The true story of a Civil War nurse.* New York: Scholastic.

Small, R., & Kenney, D.J. (1978). The slide-tape review and the reader support kit. In Gene Stanford (Ed.), *Activating the passive student*. Urbana, IL: NCTE, 7–11.

Sutcliff, R. (1980). *Frontier wolf*. New York: E.P. Dutton.

Thurber, J. (1939). *The last flower, a parable in pictures*. New York: Harper & Brothers.

Tsuchiya, Y. (1988). *Faithful elephants: A true story of animals, people, and war*. Translated by Tomoko Tsuchiya Dykes. New York: Harcourt, Brace, & Jovanovich.

Van Allsburg, C. (1988). *Two bad ants*. New York: Houghton Mifflin.

Wells, R. (1993). *Waiting for the evening star*. Bergenfield, NJ: Penguin USA.

CHAPTER 3

Using Young Adult Literature to Encourage Student Response to the *Narrative of the Life of Fredrick Douglass: An American Slave, Written by Himself*

ARTHEA J. S. REED

Introduction

Frederick Douglass' slave narrative is readily accessible to high school students. It is short (slightly more than 120 pages), easy to read and understand, and filled with warmth and wisdom. In addition, it presents a vivid picture of a horrifying period of American history that far too few students understand. Students may read about the institution of slavery in history textbooks, some of which attempt to show the cruel inhumanity of many slave owners, but no textbook allows students to see and feel the fear, pain, and hate quite like literature can. Douglass' autobiography portrays his fear when he was separated from his mother as a small child and allows us to experience, with him, the pain inflicted by undeserved whippings and weakness caused by too little food and too much physical exertion. Douglass helps us to understand the hatred of slaves for their masters as well as the sickness of hate, in general, that allowed human beings to keep other human beings as chattel.

Frederick Douglass not only provides students with an understanding of the horrors of slavery but also helps students understand how they can overcome personal adversity. Although a slave, Douglass' mind was never enslaved. He, who was denied any formal education and deprived of books and paper, writes eloquently about the importance of knowledge. He tells readers that the only way a person can be enslaved is by remaining ignorant, that learning is "the pathway from slavery to freedom" (p. 49). It is ironic that someone who was denied the right to learn can best teach the importance of education often taken for granted by today's students.

Although the *Narrative of the Life of Frederick Douglass* is appropriate reading for many grade levels and subjects and can be read and understood as early as middle school, the values examined in the book may be too mature for most middle school students and many average high school students. Likewise, many immature, egocentric readers are unable to relate to books in which they cannot picture themselves. By combining Douglass' work with young adult (YA) literature, most students can deeply experience and respond to this important and moving narrative. In addition to having younger students read such historical novels as *Jump Ship to Freedom* by James L. and Christopher Collier, *The Slave Dancer* by Paula Fox, and *Freedom Road* by Howard Fast as an accompaniment to Douglass' narrative, I read parts of the narrative aloud so that a community of students can experience the emotion of his words and the strength of his character.

By late high school most students are able to read and understand the narrative independently. One of the wonderful elements of the work is that its content is mature, making it appropriate for the most able students, while its easy reading level makes it accessible to older students who have difficulty reading. However, even with older students, combining this book with YA and adult novels that deal with slavery help bring the horror of the institution to life and help adolescents understand the importance of Douglass' accomplishments which, by today's standards, may seem minimal.

In the pages that follow, prereading, during reading, and after reading strategies, including oral and written responses to questions and quotations, are discussed. Small and large group activities are included that allow students to understand the plight of slaves and the horror of this period in our history. In addition, two bibliographies (see "Selected Nonfiction for Student Choice and Group Reading" and "Selected Fiction Related to the Unit") suggest how this narrative can be incorporated with YA and adult books in units on several related topics: the Civil War, African Americans from Slavery to the 20th Century, and Slavery and Freedom. These bibliographies are designed to help teachers build units in which Douglass' narrative is one book in an inclusive unit that includes YA novels, adult novels, modern classics, other nonfiction slave narratives, and other works of nonfiction. Throughout, there are many possibilities for extending the learning beyond Douglass' narrative to other literature, research, and interdisciplinary studies.

Selected Nonfiction for Student Choice and Group Reading

Slave Ships from Africa

Black Odyssey: The Case of the Slave Ship Amistad by Mary Cable (183 pp.).

Great Slave Narrative by Arna Bontemps (331 pp.).

The Slave's Narrative by Charles T. Davis & Henry Louis Gates, Jr. (Eds.) (384 pp.).

The Classic Slave Narratives by Henry Louis Gates, Jr. (Ed.). (518 pp.).

Five Slave Narratives: A Compendium by William Loren Katz (Ed.).

To Be a Slave by Julius Lester (160 pp.).

The Black Americans: A History in Their Own Words 1619–1983 by Milton Meltzer (306 pp.).

American Slavery as It Is: Testimony of a Thousand Witnesses by Theodore Weld (224 pp.).

Recent Critical Studies of Frederick Douglass

Critical Essays on Frederick Douglass by William L. Andrews.

Frederick Douglass: Critical Perspectives Past and Present by Henry L. Gates, Jr. & K. A. Appiah (Eds.).

Slave & Citizen: The Life of Frederick Douglass by Nathan I. Huggins.

Frederick Douglass by William S. McFreeley.

Frederick Douglass: New Literary and Historical Essays by Eric J. Sundquist.

Underground Railroad

The Underground Railroad: First Person Narratives of Escapes to Freedom in the North by Charles L. Blockson (320 pp.).

Harriet Tubman: Conductor on the Underground Railroad by Ann Petry (175 pp.).

Black Abolitionists by Benjamin Quarles (310 pp.).

The Underground Railway from Slavery to Freedom by Wilbur H. Siebert (478 pp.).

The Underground Railroad by William Still (780 pp.).

Fugitive Slaves

Anthony Burns: The Defeat and Triumph of a Fugitive Slave by Virginia Hamilton (193 pp.).

"Escape from Slavery: Five Journeys to Freedom" by Doreen Rappaport.

The Civil War (For more titles refer to P. Cole's chapter in this text).

Lincoln: A Photobiography by Russell Freedman (150 pp.).

The Boys' War: Civil War Letters to Their Loved Ones from the Blue and Gray by Jim Murphy.

Behind Blue and Gray: The Soldier's Life in the Civil War by Delia Ray.

All for the Union: The Civil War Diary and Letters of Elisha Hunt Rhodes by Robert Hunt Rhodes (248 pp.).

End of Slavery and Beginning of Reconstruction

Dry Victories by June Jordan (80 pp.).

The Black Americans: A History in Their Own Words 1619–1983 by Milton Meltzer (306 pp.).

First Taste of Freedom

This Strange New Feeling by Julius Lester (164 pp.).

African Americans

Young and Black in America by Rae Pace Alexander & Julius Lester (Eds.).

I Know Why the Caged Bird Sings by Maya Angelou.

Black Ice by Lorene Carey.

Growing Up Black by Jay David (Ed.).

Paul Robeson: The Life and Times of a Free Black Man by Virginia Hamilton.

Black Dance in America: A History Through Its People by James Haskins.

Black Music in America: A History Through Its People by James Haskins.

One More River to Cross by James Haskins.

The Story of Stevie Wonder by James Haskins.

Witchcraft, Mysticism and Magic in the Black World by James Haskins.

A Pictorial History of Black Americans by Langston Hughes, Milton Meltzer, & Eric Lincoln.

Black People Who Made the Old West by William Katz.

Now Is Your Time! The African-American Struggle for Freedom by Walter Dean Myers.

Selma, Lord, Selma: Girlhood Memories of the Civil Rights Days by Sheyann Webb & Rachel West Nelson.

Prereading Activities

Prior to reading the *Narrative of the Life of Frederick Douglass: An American Slave, Written by Himself,* have students select nonfiction books related to the narrative. Introduce the books to the students by doing a short booktalk or by orally reading from each book. When the students choose and settle on the book they will read, group them by common books. Students write personal reactions to their reading in reader response journals that they are required to keep throughout the unit. Possible early journal prompts include the following:

1. What is the topic and who are the historical figures (if any) mentioned in the first few chapters of your nonfiction book?

2. What is the viewpoint of the author? Is the author critical or sympathetic?

3. Does the book appear to be accurate from your knowledge of history?

4. Are you enjoying the book? Why? Why not?

After students share these early reader response journal entries and have had time to discuss their books, have a spokesperson from each group briefly share their progress. Further reader response suggestions attempt to get the students into the mind of the book's protagonist or the author of the book. Students can select among the following for future discussions:

1. If you were _____, what would you do?

2. Why do you think the author selected the particular title of the book?

3. Could _____ have selected a different course of action? How would this have changed the narrative?

4. What do you believe will be the outcome or consequence of the protagonist?

5. What do you know about the history of the period in which this book takes place? How do think the events of this time affect or will affect the outcome of the book?

These assignments, group discussions, and whole class sharings continue throughout a week's reading of these books. By bringing so many different perspectives, the class has both breadth and depth that cannot usually be obtained by studying just one perspective. Because the nonfiction books require different reading skill levels, all students may participate. Also during this week of independent reading, it is helpful to introduce Frederick Douglass' narrative with some of the following whole class activities:

1. Develop a timeline related to the history in the books that they are reading that places the Douglass narrative in a historical framework.

2. Discuss what was occurring in the United States between the birth of Douglass and the publication of his narrative (1818–1845).

3. Define the terms *nonfiction, autobiography,* and *narrative.*

4. Discuss the concept of "primary source," and read aloud excerpts from one or more of these secondary sources about slaves: Virginia Hamilton's ***Anthony Burns: The Defeat and Triumph of a Fugitive Slave***, Arna Bontemp's ***Great Slave Narratives***, Julius Lester's ***To Be a Slave***, or Dorothy Sterling's ***Black Foremothers***.

5. Provide a chronology of the narrative, which only digresses in some chapters. (See Figure 3-1 for a "Timeline of the Life of Frederick Douglass").

6. Introduce and define the following words: slavery, abolition, abolitionist, and chattel.

7. Ask students to write about a time they were not allowed to do something and describe how it made them feel. Then have students write about and discuss what life would be like as a slave.

8. Discuss the meaning of the word *irony* and provide some examples.

9. Discuss the concept, "there can be no freedom without education," and have students write about and discuss how they would be different if they could not read or write.

10. Read the first chapter aloud to the class and discuss it.

During Reading: Questions and Quotations for Discussion

The primary strategies employed during the reading of *Narrative of the Life of Frederick Douglass: An American Slave, Written by Himself* are oral and written response strategies that allow the students to move from basic reactions to deep understanding and analysis. Questions are designed to help students comprehend the narrative and move beyond comprehension to analysis and evaluation. (See Figure 3-2 for "Levels of Student Response".) The questions and quotations from the narrative can be used as discussion starters for small groups or as writing prompts to help students deal with the concepts in a more personal way. A combination of written and small group oral discussion allows more students to be involved in the process.

The reading response log technique is appropriate for all grade levels. In it, students respond to the various quotations in writing. I try to encourage the students to respond in a variety of increasingly complex ways. This allows them to develop thinking and writing skills at the analytical and evaluative levels. I find it helpful to distribute one question and quotation per chapter per group. In this way, students focus and elaborate on one response deeply and are exposed to all responses made by their peers.

Figure 3-1
Timeline of the Life of Frederick Douglass

Note: All dates are approximate since slaves were kept ignorant of the concept of time or dates.

1818	Frederick Bailey (Douglass) born in Tuckahoe, near Hillsborough, Maryland. Mother — Harriet Bailey, a slave; father — a white man, perhaps the master. Separated from mother in infancy.
1824	Harriet Bailey dies; seen only by son four or five times when she'd travel 12 miles by foot at night.
1817–1825	Lived on the "Great House Farm" plantation of Colonel Edward Lloyd; master was Captain Anthony, Colonel Lloyd's clerk.
1825	Moved to Baltimore, Maryland, home of Mr. Hugh Auld, brother of Colonel Lloyd's son-in-law, Captain Thomas Auld.
1825	Mrs. Sophia Auld, new mistress, begins to teach Frederick to read; Mr. Auld finds out and forbids it, calling it "unlawful" and "unsafe."
1825–1832	Lived with Aulds; continues to learn to read and write, often bribing the poor white children to help him.
1828	Returns to Colonel Lloyd's plantation after death of Captain Anthony and his youngest son Richard so that property, including horses and slaves, can be divided between two surviving children, Mrs. Lucretia and Master Andrew; falls to the portion of Mrs. Lucretia and is returned to Baltimore.
1829	Reads "The Columbian Orator," giving words to his feelings about slavery; learns the meaning of the word "abolition"; meets two kind Irishmen who advise him to run away to the North; "from that time on I resolved to run away" (p. 57).

Note: The following dates are more accurate since Frederick has learned to read and understands dates.

March 1832	Mrs. Lucretia and Master Andrew have both died; Master Thomas Auld, Lucretia's husband, remarries and has a misunderstanding with Master Hugh. As punishment of Hugh, Frederick goes to live with Master Thomas in St. Michael's, Maryland. Master Thomas is not as good a master; he feeds his slaves very little.
Jan. 1, 1833	Sent to live with Mr. Covey who has a reputation "for breaking young slaves" (p. 70); Frederick is frequently whipped.
Aug. 1833	Frederick becomes ill in the fields; Mr. Covey, whips him. Frederick runs away from Mr. Covey and files a complaint with Master Auld which is rejected. When Frederick returns to Mr. Covey's he vows to fight which he does; Mr. Covey's treatment toward him begins to change; Frederick vows that he never will be whipped again. "This battle with Mr Covey . . . rekindled the few expiring embers of freedom, and revived within me my own manhood" (p. 82).
Jan. 1, 1834	Moved to home of Mr. William Freeland, three miles from St. Michael's. Mr. Freeland was "an educated southern gentleman" and much kinder to the slaves. Frederick begins a Sabbath school for slaves; if they were caught they would be whipped, but they wanted to learn to read and write.

Figure 3-1 Continued
Timeline of the Life of Frederick Douglass

Jan. 1835	Mr. Freeland again hires Frederick from his master. Frederick and several other slaves plot an escape but are discovered and sent to jail. For a reason unknown to Frederick, Master Thomas Auld decides to send him back to Baltimore to Hugh Auld.
1835	Sent to learn the trade of caulking at a shipyard; severely injured in fight with white carpenters; Mr. Hugh Auld takes Frederick to work in shipyard where he is foreman; Frederick learns quickly and is soon earning wages that he must turn over to Master Hugh Auld.
Spring 1838	Frederick applies to Master Thomas to allow him to hire his time; Thomas refuses. Later, Hugh agrees, making a deal that guarantees him more money. Frederick agrees to the plan since it is the only way he can earn money to escape. When Frederick goes out of the city on work without permission, Master Hugh tells him to "bring my tools and clothing home forthwith" (p. 109). This makes Frederick more committed to find a way to escape.
Sept. 3, 1838	Frederick escapes to New York; he does not reveal the means in his narrative, stating that it could embarrass some and keep others from escaping; he is helped by Mr. David Ruggles who houses Frederick in his boarding house and helps him get Anna Murray, a free black woman, to New York.
Sept. 15, 1838	Anna Murray and Frederick Johnson (name changed from Frederick Bailey) marry; this is particularly important since slaves were not permitted to marry; they leave for New Bedford. In New Bedford the couple is helped by Mr. and Mrs. Nathan Johnson. Frederick asks the Johnsons to help him pick a new name; Mr. Johnson who is reading "Lady of the Lake" selects Douglass.
Aug. 11, 1841	At the anti-slavery convention at Nantucket, Mr. William C. Coffin urges Frederick Douglass to speak. Douglass writes, "It was a severe cross, and I took it up reluctantly. The truth was, I felt myself a slave, and the idea of speaking to white people weighed me down" (p. 119).

Chapter 1

Sets the scene; Frederick tells us about his early life and begins to explain life on the plantation.

Questions and Quotations

1. "By far the larger part of the slaves know as little of their ages as horses know of theirs, and it is the wish of most masters to keep their slaves thus ignorant" (p. 21). Why would slaveholders want to keep a slave ignorant about such a simple thing as the date of his or her birth? [The intentional ignorance of slaves plays an important role in Frederick's understanding of the system.]

2. "It was the blood-stained gate, the entrance to hell of slavery, through which I was about to pass" (p. 25). Why is a slaveholder who has fathered a slave likely to be tougher on that child?

3. "He was a cruel man, hardened by a long life of slaveholding" (p. 24). Why does Frederick tell the story of Lloyd's Ned? [This is an important point that Frederick will continue to make throughout the narrative.]

Chapter 2

Describes the plantation system of Colonel Lloyd; discusses the daily existence of slaves on the plantation.

Questions and Quotations

1. "The same traits of character might be seen in Colonel Lloyd's slaves, as are seen in the slaves of the political parties" (p. 30). Was there a pecking order among slaves? Explain.

2. Why would a slave whose life on a plantation was very bad fear being sold to a slave-trader? Explain.

3. "Crying for joy, and singing for joy, were alike uncommon to me while in the jaws of slavery" (p. 32). Why does Frederick suggest that slaves sing out of sorrow rather than out of joy, and why is it difficult to find copies of slave songs?

Chapter 3

Relates several anecdotes that tell readers more about plantation life and the thinking of slaves.

Questions and Quotations

1. What is ironic about Colonel Lloyd's treatment of his horses compared to the treatment of his slaves?
2. The following is a slave maxim: "A still tongue makes a wise head" (p. 36). What is a maxim and what does this one mean?

3. Discuss the prejudice that existed among slaves from different plantations, and examine the irony of this prejudice.

Figure 3-2
Levels of Student Response

A. Engaging

      The articulation of the reader's emotional reaction or level of involvement, from "This is BOR—ING," to "I couldn't put it down," is called engaging. The first is called lack of engagement; the second engagement. However, the reader's articulation of her or his level of engagement with the text may be the first step in responding to it. For example, tell students, "Write about how the chapter makes you feel."

B. Describing

      By selecting some important aspect of the text and restating or reproducing the information, students describe what they know. For example, tell students, "Select any quotation from this chapter, and write about what you think it means."

C. Conceiving

      Students make statements about meaning or infer important aspects of the text. For example, tell students, "Write about this quote, and discuss not only what it means to you, but what it means in relationship to Frederick's life as a slave."

D. Explaining

      The reader explains why the characters do what they do, and examines their motivations. For example, ask students to explain why learning to read was so important to Frederick. Ask them, "What did he believe the ability to read would give him?"

E. Connecting

      The reader connects her or his own experiences with the text. Whenever a reader responds to text, connecting is a recurrent movement between the text and one's experiences, knowledge, and attitudes. The reader may first recall a similar experience, thent elaborate on that experience, next apply the experience to the text, later use the text to reflect on her or his own experience and, finally, interpret the text and the experience. For example, ask the students to write about a time when they felt like they were trapped. At first, they might write or discuss how this experience would have been different if they saw little hope of escaping. Next, they might write or discuss what they would try to do to escape. Finally, they might put themselves in Frederick's place: What would they do to attempt to become free?

F. Interpreting

      The reader uses all of the reactions above to interpret an overall theme or meaning of the text. For example, ask these types of questions: "Why did Frederick write this narrative? What was the danger in writing it? When did Frederick conceive that freedom was a possibility?"

G. Judging

      The reader makes judgments about the text concerning the truth of the text, the importance of the text, the quality of the text, and so forth. For example, ask students questions such as these: "Why is this narrative still read today? Are there any lessons in it for you? Any lessons for the country?"

Chapter 4

Tells readers more about overseers and relates incidents of slave murders.

Questions and Quotations

1. Why is Mr. Austin Gore a "first-rate overseer," and what is the irony of this description of him?

2. Discuss this maxim laid down by slaveholders: "It is better that a dozen slaves suffer under the lash, than that the overseer should be convicted, in the presence of the slaves, of having been at fault" (p. 38).

3. "To be accused was to be convicted, and to be convicted was to be punished" (pp. 38–39). "He dealt sparingly with his words, and bountifully with his whip, never using the former where the latter would answer as well" (p. 39). Discuss the system of justice on the plantation. [Another important point that continues throughout the narrative.]

4. What other examples does Frederick give of his statement "that killing a slave, or any colored person, ... is not treated as a crime, either by the courts or the community" (p. 41)?

Chapter 5

Examines Frederick's life as a slave child and discusses his leaving the plantation.

Questions and Quotations

1. What was life like for Frederick on the plantation, and why was he so happy to be leaving? Compare this with chapter 2's, question 2.

2. What does Frederick mean when he says, "I may be deemed superstitious, and even egotistical, in regarding this event as a special interposition of divine Providence in my favor" (p. 47)?

Chapter 6

Discusses learning to read and explains its importance.

Questions and Quotations

1. "If you teach that nigger (speaking of myself) how to read, there would be no keeping him. It would forever unfit him to be a slave. He would at once become unmanageable, and of no value to his master" (p. 49). Why is learning to read so important to practicing freedom?

2. "I now understood what had been to me a most perplexing difficulty—to wit, the white man's power to enslave the black man. It was a grand achievement, and I prized it highly. From that moment, I understood the pathway from slavery to freedom" (p. 49). Why does the inability to read keep men enslaved? Respond first as Frederick, then as Mr. Auld, and then as yourself.

3. "In learning to read, I owe almost as much to the bitter opposition of my master, as to the kindly aid of my mistress. I acknowledge the benefit of both" (p. 50). Why does Frederick call Mr. Auld's forbidding his learning how to read "invaluable instruction"?

4. Discuss the irony of what Mr. Auld taught Frederick when he forbids Mrs. Auld to teach him to read. In education we refer to the school's "hidden curriculum," that which is not intentionally taught but is learned by the students. What are some of the "hidden curricula" in the school you attend? How does Mr. Auld's lesson to Frederick relate to the concept of the "hidden curriculum?"

5. "A city slave is almost a freeman, compared with a slave on the plantation" (p. 50). Why is the life of a city slave so much better than the life of a plantation slave?

Chapter 7

Relates what Mrs. Auld learned from keeping slaves; how Frederick came to hate slavery and how he learned to write.

Questions and Quotations

1. "Slavery soon proved its ability to divest her [Mrs. Auld] of these heavenly qualities. Under its influence, the tender heart became stone, and the lamblike disposition gave way to one of tiger-like fierceness" (pp. 52–53). How did Mrs. Auld change and why did she change?

2. "The first step had been taken.   Mistress, in teaching me the
    alphabet, had given me the *inch*, and no precaution could prevent
    me from taking the *ell*" (p. 53).   What plan did Frederick adopt to
    learn how to read now that Mrs. Auld was no longer teaching
    him, and what was ironic about his plan?

3. What irony does Frederick find in this statement: "It is almost an
    unpardonable offense to teach slaves to read in this Christian
    country" (p. 54)?

4. "I would at times feel that learning to read had been a curse
    rather than a blessing.   It had given me a view of my wretched
    condition, without the remedy.   It opened my eyes to the horrible
    pit, but to no ladder upon which to get out" (p. 55).   Is Frederick
    correct that learning is a curse rather than a blessing?   Is learning
    ever a curse?   Readdress this issue after you finish reading the
    book.

5. Discuss how you learned how to read and write.   Discuss how
    your experiences differed from the methods encountered by
    Frederick.

Chapter 8

Discussion of slaves as property; plight of old slaves; return to
Baltimore.

Questions and Quotations

1. "At this moment [valuation of the property], I saw more clearly
    than ever the brutalizing effects of slavery upon both slave and
    slaveholder" (p. 60).   How was the value of the master's property
    determined; specifically, how are slaves valued when compared
    to livestock?   [The ironic comparison of slaves to livestock is a
    continuous theme of the narrative.]

2. "The hearth is desolate.   The children, the unconscious children,
    who once sang and danced in her presence, are gone.   She
    gropes her way, in the darkness of age, for a drink of water.
    Instead of the voices of her children, she hears by day the moans
    of the dove, and by night the screams of the hideous owl.   All is
    gloom.   The grave is at the door" (p. 62).   What happened to
    Frederick's grandmother after the deaths of Lucretia and Andrew,
    and how does this anecdote help explain the value of slaves?

3. Why does Frederick put John Greenleaf Whittier's poem (p. 62) in his narrative immediately following the anecdote about his grandmother?

Chapter 9

Moves to St. Michael's, Maryland, with Master Thomas Auld; the irony of the Christian slaveholder is discussed.

Questions and Quotations

1. "After his conversion, [Master Thomas Auld] found religious sanction and support for his slaveholding cruelty" (p. 67). What, according to Frederick, happens to Master Thomas Auld after his conversion to Christianity? Why? [This is an important point that Frederick continues to make throughout the rest of the narrative.]

2. Why does Frederick find irony in the fact that the slaves' Sabbath school is discontinued?

3. "Master Thomas was one of the many pious slaveholders who hold slaves for the very charitable purpose of taking care of them … . He resolved to put me out, as he said, to be broken" (p. 69). How does Master Thomas propose to "break" Frederick, and why is the use of the verb "to break" ironic?

4. Why was Mr. Covey's reputation for "breaking" slaves of great value to him, and why does Frederick suggest that his "pious soul" adds to Mr. Covey's "reputation as a 'nigger-breaker'" (p. 70)?

Chapter 10

How a man is made a slave; a slave made a man.

Questions and Quotations

1. "I do verily believe that he sometimes deceived himself into the solemn belief, that he was a sincere worshipper of the most high God; and this, too, at a time when he may be said to have been guilty of compelling his woman slave to commit the sin of adultery" (p. 74). Why does Mr. Covey buy a slave to use as a *breeder*? Why does he hire Mr. Samuel Harrison, a married man? What irony does Frederick find in this?

2. "Mr. Covey succeeded in breaking me. I was broken in body, soul, and spirit. My natural elasticity was crushed, my intellect languished, the disposition to read departed, the cheerful spark that lingered about my eye died; the dark night of slavery closed in upon me; and behold a man transformed into a brute!" (p. 75). How does Mr. Covey succeed in breaking Frederick?

3. Read aloud and discuss Frederick's discussion of sailing vessels, beginning with the last line on page 75 and continuing through the end of the first paragraph on page 77. Why does Frederick find the sailing vessels so abhorrent to watch? What do they symbolize for him? At the same time he finds hope in them. What is his hope? What are the sailing vessels a metaphor of?

4. "You have seen how a man was made a slave; you shall see how a slave was made a man". (p. 77). How does Frederick succeed in again becoming a man?

5. How does Frederick win the fight with Mr. Covey, and why is this battle "the turning-point in my career as a slave" (p. 82)? He resolves "that, however long I might remain a slave in form, the day had passed forever when I could be a slave in fact" (p. 83). Discuss how this is possible.

6. Beginning with the final paragraph on page 83 and continuing to the end of the first paragraph on page 86, Frederick provides his readers with an anecdote about the purpose of the Christmas holiday for slaveholders. Read this section orally. Discuss why slaves are given the Christmas holiday. "The mode here adopted [is] to disgust the slave with freedom, by allowing him to see only the abuse of it" (p. 85). How are the holidays used to "disgust the slave with freedom"?

7. "I assert most unhesitatingly, that the religion of the south is a mere covering for the most horrid crimes,—a justifier of the most appalling barbarity,—a sanctifier of the most hateful frauds,—and a dark shelter under which the darkest, foulest, grossest, and most infernal deeds of slaveholders find the strongest protection" (p. 86). Why does Frederick include the anecdotes about the two religious slaveholders, Mr. Hopkins and Mr. Weeden? What point is he attempting to make?

8. Frederick makes the point that many slaves would "rather bear those ills we had, than fly to others, that we knew not of" (p. 93). How does this help explain why so few slaves escaped?

9. "All at once, the white carpenters knocked off, and said they would not work with free colored workmen. Their reason for this, as alleged, was, that if free colored carpenters were encouraged, they would soon take the trade into their own hands and poor white men would be thrown out of employment" (p. 100). Why might "poor white men be thrown out of employment"?

10. Frederick says, "I have observed this in my experience of slavery,—that whenever my condition was improved, instead of its increasing my contentment, it only increased my desire to be free, and set me thinking of plans to gain my freedom. I have found that, to make a contented slave, it is necessary to make a thoughtless one" (p. 103). Why do improved conditions make Frederick less content?

Chapter 11

Escape from slavery; becoming a free man; involvement in the anti-slavery movement.

Questions and Quotations

1. "I have never approved of the very public manner in which some of our western friends have conducted what they call the *underground railroad*, but which I think, by their open declarations, has been made most emphatically the *upperground railroad*" (p. 106). Why does Frederick not approve of the *underground railroad*?

2. "He [Master Hugh] received all the benefits of slaveholding without its evils; while I endured all the evils of a slave, and suffered all the care and anxiety of a freeman. I found it a hard bargain" (p. 108). What does Master Hugh do to attempt to encourage Frederick to continue to earn money, and what effect does his encouragement have? Why does Frederick agree to it?

3. "I had very strangely supposed, while in slavery, that few of the comforts, and scarcely any of the luxuries, of life were enjoyed at the north, compared with what were enjoyed by slaveholders of the south... I had somehow imbibed the opinion that, in the absence of slaves, there could be no wealth, and very little refinement" (p. 115). What conditions did Frederick find for "colored people" in the North, and why was he surprised?

4. "It [speaking publicly against slavery] was a severe cross, and I took it up reluctantly. The truth was, I felt myself a slave, and the idea of speaking to white people weighed me down. I spoke but a few moments, when I felt a degree of freedom and said what I desired with considerable ease" (p. 119). Why is it that some people can overcome great obstacles and fears while others cannot? Can you think of some modern examples of people who have "spoken out" about something?

Appendix

Defense of his speaking out against the Christianity of slave holders. (*Note*: Teachers of younger or less mature student might prefer to eliminate the appendix from their reading assignments.)

Questions and Quotations

1. "Between Christianity of this land, and the Christianity of Christ, I recognized the widest possible difference... . To be the friend of the one, is of necessity to be the enemy of the other" (p. 120). Why does Douglass contend that the church looks the other way on the treatment of slaves?

2. Read orally the hymn/poem on page 122. What point is Douglass making by inserting this poem?

3. "They love the heathen on the other side of the globe. They can pray for him, pay money to have the *Bible* put into his hand, and missionaries to instruct him; while they despise and totally neglect the heathen at their own doors" (p. 123). Douglass points to many ironies in how slaveholding Christians practice their religion. Discuss these ironies.

4. Read aloud and discuss the parody Douglass "copies" on pp. 124–125. What is his intent in using it in his narrative? Why is the word "union" used throughout it? In this parody is he only criticizing the Christians of the South or is he also criticizing the Christians of the North? Explain.

5. Why do you think Douglass added the appendix?

During Reading: Activities to Accompany Group Discussion

The activities are designed for small group active participation with the narrative. I prefer to have groups choose which activities they will be responsible for throughout the reading of the narrative. Many of them have the potential to move the students beyond the narrative into other literature; others allow for research opportunities. Have students choose one assignment from each group: In-Class Activities and Out-of-Class Activities.

In-Class Activities

1. Chart the relationship of slaveholder to overseer to slave on chart paper. Discuss life on the plantation for each of these people.

2. Draw a diagram of the holdings (including plantations and slaves) of Colonel Lloyd. Write a diary and then make a chart of a day in the life of a slave. Draw pictures of slave children in summer and in winter.

3. Conduct a role play of Master Auld, Mistress Auld, and Frederick discussing Frederick's learning how to read.

4. Trace the ownership of Frederick from the beginning of the narrative through Chapter 8. Explain why he is owned by so many different people. On a map plot the route that Frederick followed to get to Baltimore.

5. Frederick points out many ironies in this narrative. Identify as many as you can and relate two of them to modern examples.

6. Write a poem, song, essay, play, or short story that dramatizes your feelings about one or more parts of the narrative.

7. Review the names of all Douglass' masters, and discuss whether you believe they were their real names or not. Explain how it was possible for Frederick to have more than one master, and discuss who actually owned Frederick.

8. Place this narrative in the context of other historical events in your additional nonfiction reading. Make a timeline and present it to the class.

9. Throughout the narrative Douglass makes several important points over and over; these might be considered the themes of the work. Review the narrative to find quotations related to these points.

   A. Justice for slaves (and all men of color) is different from justice for whites.

B. No one can be enslaved if she or he has the ability to read, write, and think.

C. The way to enslave someone is to keep them from all learning.

D. Slaves were treated no better than, and sometimes worse than, livestock.

E. By encouraging depravity, men come to learn to hate freedom.

F. The Christianity of the slaveholders is hypocritical and used to justify their actions.

G. White men fear that men of color will steal their jobs if they are educated and learn how to perform the job.

10. What was the intended purpose and who was the audience for Douglass' narrative? Read the preface and the letter that is included before the narrative. What point is each of these men making? Why are these included with the narrative? Does the inclusion of these tell us something about how African Americans were regarded in the North? Notice the frontispiece prior to Chapter 1: "Entered, according to Act of Congress, in the year 1845, By Frederick Douglass, In the Clerk's Office of the District Court of Massachusetts." What does this mean? What is its significance?

Out-of-Class Activities

1. Go to the library and find some songs sung by slaves. Discuss the meaning of these songs, and examine if they were likely to be sung because of sorrow, as suggested by Frederick.

2. Why was education essential for white children in New England and illegal for slave children in the South? Use several different sources to document your response.

3. Frederick's contention that men use religion to justify cruelty is not new. Look for examples of this throughout history.

4. Frederick talks about the superstition of slaves when Sandy Jenkins gives him the root to place in his right pocket. Go to the library and see what other slave superstitions you can find. What were the reasons for these superstitions? Who besides slaves have superstitions? What are some superstitions you, your family, or your friends hold? Where do they come from?

5. Research slaves and marriage. Did slaves marry? How were couples treated in slavery?

6. Frederick becomes an apprentice caulker. Research the apprentice system of education in the Middle Atlantic states. Was it common for slaves or free African Americans to be apprentices?

7. Several times in Chapter 10, Frederick refers to free colored men and women. Research the free African Americans of the South. Why were some free even though most were slaves?

8. Again in Chapter 10, we hear about the legal system and slaves. Research cases in which slaves were tried. What occurred?

9. Chapter 11 deals with the names of slaves. Notice that Frederick Douglass changed his name three times. Discuss why he changed his name. See if you can find out any information about the names of slaves. You might also explore some of the other men named in Chapter 11. See what other information you can find about Wendell Phillips and William Lloyd Garrison. Can you find information about any of them? Report your findings to the class.

10. Research information about the underground railroad. What did it do? Where and for how long was it in existence? Is Frederick fair in his criticism of it?

11. Research documented slave escapes. How did many slaves escape? Where did they escape to? From this, can you guess how Frederick might have escaped from Maryland to New York?

12. Douglass tells us of his attitudes about the North. Research attitudes about the North held by various Southerners: slaveholders, slaves, free blacks, politicians, others. What made them believe these things about the North? How might these beliefs have contributed to the outbreak of Civil War?

13. Douglass makes the point that many of the ex-slaves in New Bedford lived better than average slaveholders in Maryland. Research the lives of ex-slaves in the North. Was his perception correct? Did they live comfortable lives?

14. Research slavery in the South. Which were the slave states? What was the philosophic/economic rationale for slavery? How many slaves were in each state at the time Frederick was a slave? What did the slaves do in each state? How did their treatment differ? From which states did most slaves escape? How did slavery end? When? Report your findings to the class.

15. Research the history of slavery. In what other cultures has it existed? What happened to those cultures? How did it get started in the American colonies? When? By whom? Where does it exist today? Present your findings to the class.

16. Research the life of Frederick Douglass. What were his accomplishments after escaping from slavery? Present your findings to the class.

Extending the Unit: After Reading Activities

The after reading activities allow the students to reflect on Douglass' narrative, place it in historical context, and compare it with other works of literature. Again, the emphasis is on students' response to the work rather than on gaining specific information from it. Have students choose from among the following possibilities:

1. Do a readers' theater production of *Escape to Freedom: A Play about Young Frederick Douglass* by Ossie Davis (89 pp.).

2. Go to the library and find other poems by John Greenleaf Whittier. What other poems did he write about slavery? Why does Frederick call him the slave poet?

3. Read "Lady of the Lake." Why does Mr. Johnson, who had just finished reading it, choose the name Douglass for Frederick?

4. Read one or more other slave narratives (listed in the bibliography "Selected Nonfiction for Student Choice and Group Reading"). Compare them to Douglass'. Were their lives as slaves similar? Do they make some of the same points about slavery? Report your comparisons to the class.

5. Harriet Tubman also came from the Eastern Shore of Maryland, specifically Cambridge, just a few miles from St. Michael's. Go to the library and research her role in the underground railroad or read *Harriet Tubman: Conductor on the Underground Railroad* by Ann Petry.

6. Read the fictional account of the underground railway, *Runaway to Freedom: A Story of the Underground Railroad* by Barbara Smucker and compare it to a nonfiction account such as *The Underground Railroad: First Person Narratives of Escapes to Freedom in the North* by Charles L. Blockson.

7. In 1993, Toni Morrison won the Nobel Prize for Literature. Her novel *Beloved* about three generations of African American women is considered one of the great literary works dealing with the theme of slavery. Read Morrison's fictional account, write about and discuss how the lives of these women were affected by slavery.

8. Go to the library and do research on the U.S. justice system and people of color. Read Lee's *To Kill a Mockingbird* or Gaines's *The Autobiography of Miss Jane Pittman,* and discuss whether and how the U.S. justice system has changed in its treatment of people of color. Present your findings to the class.

9. Read sections of Mark Twain's *The Adventures of Huckleberry Finn* to find what the superstitions of the slave Jim were. Discuss why slaves were superstitious. Why would slaves attribute their deaths to trickery?

10. Read one of the suggested works of fiction related to the unit. Compare the effectiveness of the fiction with that of the nonfictional account.

Selected Fiction Related to the Unit

Slave Ships from Africa
The Slave Dancer by Paula Fox (152 pp.).
Middle Passage by Charles Johnson (209 pp.).

Slave Narratives
A Girl Called Boy by Belinda Hurmence (168 pp.).
Tancy by Belinda Hurmence (203 pp.).

Underground Railroad
The Autobiography of Miss Jane Pittman by Ernest J. Gaines (254 pp.).
The Mystery of Drear House by Virginia Hamilton (217 pp.).
The House of Dies Drear by Virginia Hamilton (279 pp.).
Runaway to Freedom: A Story of the Underground Railroad by Barbara Smucker (154 pp.).
Uncle Tom's Cabin by Harriet Beecher Stowe (496 pp.).

Fugitive Slaves
Black Thunder by Arna Bontemps (224 pp.).
A Girl Called Boy by Belinda Hurmence (168 pp.).

Runaway to Freedom: A Story of the Underground Railroad by Barbara Smucker (154 pp.).
Uncle Tom's Cabin by Harriet Beecher Stowe (496 pp.).

The Civil War (For more titles refer to P. Cole's chapter in this text.)
Eben Tyne, Powdermonkey by Patricia Beatty & Phillip Robbins (227 pp.).
Which Way Freedom? by Joyce Hansen (120 pp.).
Across Five Aprils by Irene Hunt (190 pp.).
Rifles for Watie by Harold Keith (332 pp.).
Gentle Annie: The True Story of a Civil War Nurse by Mary Frances Shura (184 pp.).

End of Slavery and Beginning of Reconstruction
A Gathering of Days: A New England Girl's Journal by Joan Blos (160 pp.).
Tancy by Belinda Hurmence (203 pp.).

First Taste of Freedom
Jump Ship to Freedom by James L. & Christopher Collier (198 pp.).
War Comes to Willy Freeman by James L. & Christopher Collier (178 pp.).
Who is Carrie? by James L. & Christopher Collier (158 pp.).
Freedom Road by Howard Fast (263 pp.).
Beloved by Toni Morrison (275 pp.).
Wolf by the Ears by Ann Rinaldi (252 pp.).
Amos Fortune, Free Man by E. Yates (181 pp.).

African Americans
And I Heard a Bird Sing by Rosa Guy (176 pp.).
The Disappearance by Rosa Guy (159 pp.).
Edith Jackson by Rosa Guy (179 pp.).
The Friends by Rosa Guy (185 pp.).
My Love, My Love or the Peasant Girl by Rosa Guy (119 pp.).
Ruby by Rosa Guy (224 pp.).
A Raisin in the Sun by Lorraine Hansberry (151 pp.).
A White Romance by Virginia Hamilton (191 pp.).
Junius Over Far by Virginia Hamilton (277 pp.).
A Little Love by Virginia Hamilton (207 pp.).
The Magical Adventures of Pretty Pearl by Virginia Hamilton (311 pp.).
Sweet Whispers, Brother Rush by Virginia Hamilton (215 pp.).
Justice and Her Brothers by Virginia Hamilton (282 pp.).
Arilla Sun Down by Virginia Hamilton (269 pp.).
The Planet of Junior Brown by Virginia Hamilton (217 pp.).

Zeely by Virginia Hamilton (122 pp.).

M.C. Higgins, the Great by Virginia Hamilton (278 pp.).

I Be Somebody by Hadley Irwin (170 pp.).

To Kill a Mockingbird by Harper Lee (238 pp.)

Somewhere in the Darkness by Walter Dean Myers (168 pp.).

Mop, Moondance, and the Nagasaki Knights by Walter Dean Myers (150 pp.).

The Mouse Rap by Walter Dean Myers (186 pp.).

Scorpions by Walter Dean Myers (216 pp.).

Me, Mop and the Moondance Kid by Walter Dean Myers (154 pp.).

Fallen Angels by Walter Dean Myers (309 pp.).

Crystal by Walter Dean Myers (198 pp.).

Motown and Didi: A Love Story by Walter Dean Myers (174 pp.).

Hoops by Walter Dean Myers (183 pp.).

The Young Landlords by Walter Dean Myers (197 pp.).

It Ain't All for Nothin' by Walter Dean Myers (217 pp.).

Fast Sam, Cool Clyde, and Stuff by Walter Dean Myers (190 pp.).

Mojo and the Russians by Walter Dean Myers (151 pp.).

Words by Heart by Ouida Sebestyen (135 pp.).

The Road to Memphis by Mildred Taylor (304 pp.).

Let the Circle be Unbroken by Mildred Taylor (394 pp.).

Roll of Thunder, Hear My Cry by Mildred Taylor (276 pp.).

Song of the Trees by Mildred Taylor (52 pp.).

The Color Purple by Alice Walker (290 pp.).

Conclusion

I have taught Frederick Douglass' slave narrative successfully to students from 7th grade to graduate school in three different subject areas. This, in itself, makes Douglass' narrative a remarkable work. It is unusual to find a primary source that brings the history and human tragedy of slavery to life for so many readers. In addition, the narrative speaks to values all of us hope to inculcate in our students: an understanding of the privilege of freedom and the responsibility inherent in it. I have read aloud to hundreds of students the section of the narrative in which Douglass explains how he learned to read and write and how without education he would have always been enslaved. Far too many of our students believe that education is their right, and that we are responsible for giving it to them. It is critical that they understand that historically and globally schooling was a privilege given only to a few. Today's students need Douglass' message that knowledge comes through individual effort and is required to preserve freedom. I have combined Douglass' narrative with many other fiction and nonfiction works to deal with important themes and historical concepts that are merely dry facts when taught only through textbooks. Using this inclusive approach, I have taught the values of knowledge, responsibility, and freedom and helped students discover how exciting learning can be.

List of References

Alexander, R.P. & Lester, J. (Eds.). (1970). *Young and black in America*. Westminster, MD: Random House.

Andrews, W.L. (1991). *Critical essays on Frederick Douglass*. New York: Macmillan.

Angelou, M. (1971). *I know why the caged bird sings*. New York: Bantam.

Beatty, P. & Robbins, P. (1990). *Eben Tyne, Powdermonkey*. New York: William Morrow.

Blockson, C.L. (1987). *The Underground Railroad: First person narratives of escapes to freedom in the North*. New York: Prentice Hall.

Blos, J. (1990). *A gathering of days: A New England girl's journal*. New York: Macmillan.

Bontemps, A. (1992). *Black thunder*. Boston: Beacon Press.

Bontemps, A. (1969). *Great slave narratives*. Boston: Beacon Press.

Cable, M. (1971). *Black odyssey: The case of the slave ship Amistad*. New York: Viking.

Carey, L. (1991). *Black ice*. New York: Alfred A. Knopf.

Collier, J.L. & Collier, C. (1987). *Jump ship to freedom*. New York: Dell.

Collier, J.L. & Collier, C. (1987). *War comes to Willy Freeman*. New York: Dell.

Collier, J.L. & Collier, C. (1987). *Who is Carrie?* New York: Dell.

David, J. (Ed.). (1969). *Growing up black*. New York: Pocket Books.

Davis, C.T. & Gates, H.L., Jr. (Eds.). (1991). *The slave's narrative*. Cary, NC: Oxford University Press.

Davis, O. (1990). *Escape to freedom: A play about young Frederick Douglass*. New York: Puffin.

Dionisio, M. (1991, January). Responding to literary elements through mini-lessons and dialogue journals. *English Journal, 80* (1), 40–44.

Fast, H. (1974). *Freedom road*. New York: Bantam.

Fox, P. (1991) *The slave dancer*. New York: Dell.

Freedman, R. (1987). *Lincoln: A photobiography*. New York: Clarion.

Gaines, E.J. (1987). *The autobiography of Miss Jane Pittman*. New York: Doubleday.

Gates, H.L., Jr. (Ed.). (1987). *The classic slave narratives*. New York: The New American Library.

Gates, H.L., Jr. & Appiah, K.A. (Eds.). (1994). *Frederick Douglass: Critical perspectives past and present*. New York: Amistad Press.

Guy, R. (1992). *Edith Jackson*. New York: Dell.

Guy, R. (1990). *And I heard a bird sing*. New York: Puffin.

Guy, R. (1990). *My love, my love or the peasant girl*. New York: Henry Holt & Company.

Guy, R. (1989). *Ruby*. New York: Puffin.

Guy, R. (1985). *The disappearance*. New York: Puffin.

Guy, R. (1983). *The friends*. New York: Bantam.

Hamilton, V. (1993). *Anthony Burns: The defeat and triumph of a fugitive slave.* New York: Alfred A. Knopf.

Hamilton, V. (1993). *M.C. Higgins, the great.* New York: Aladdin.

Hamilton, V. (1989). *Justice and her brothers.* San Diego: Harcourt, Brace, & Jovanovich.

Hamilton, V. (1987). *The mystery of Drear house.* New York: Greenwillow.

Hamilton, V. (1987). *A white romance.* New York: Philomel.

Hamilton, V. (1986). *The magical adventures of pretty Pearl.* New York: Harper & Row.

Hamilton, V. (1986). *The planet of Junior Brown.* New York: Collier.

Hamilton, V. (1986). *Zeely.* New York: Aladdin.

Hamilton, V. (1985). *Junius over far.* New York: HarperCollins.

Hamilton, V. (1985). *A little love.* New York: Berkeley Books.

Hamilton, V. (1984). *The house of Dies Drear.* New York: Collier.

Hamilton, V. (1983). *Sweet whispers, brother Rush.* New York: Avon.

Hamilton, V. (1979). *Arilla sun down.* New York: Dell.

Hamilton, V. (1979). *Paul Robeson: The life and times of a free black man.* New York: Dell.

Hansberry, L. (1988). *A raisin in the sun.* New York: Signet Classic/NAL.

Hansen. J. (1992). *Which way freedom?* New York: Avon.

Haskins, J. (1992). *One more river to cross.* New York: Scholastic.

Haskins, J. (1990). *Black dance in America: A history through its people.* Scranton, PA: Thomas Y. Crowell.

Haskins, J. (1987). *Black music in America: A history through its people.* Scranton, PA: Thomas Y. Crowell.

Haskins, J. (1979). *The story of Stevie Wonder.* New York: Dell.

Haskins, J. (1976). *Witchcraft, mysticism and magic in the black world.* New York: Dell.

Huggins, N.I. (1987). *Slave & citizen: The life of Frederick Douglass.* New York: HarperCollins.

Hughes, L., Meltzer, M., & Lincoln, E. (1973). *A pictorial history of black Americans.* Westminster, MD: Crown.

Hunt, I. (1986). *Across five Aprils.* New York: Berkeley Books.

Hurmenče, B. (1984). *Tancy.* New York: Clarion.

Hurmence, B. (1982). *A girl called boy.* New York: Clarion.

Irwin, Hadley. (1984). *I be somebody.* New York: Athenaeum.

Johnson, C. (1991). *Middle passage.* New York: Plume.

Jordan, J. (1972). *Dry victories.* New York: Holt, Rinehart & Winston.

Kane, S. (1991, February). Turning teenagers into reader response researchers. *Journal of Reading,* 34 (5), 400–401.

Karolides, N.J. (1992). The transactional theory of literature. In N.J. Karolides (Ed.), *Reader response in the classroom: Evoking and interpreting meaning in literature.* White Plains, NY: Longman, 21–32.

Katz, W. (1977). *Black people who made the old West.* Scranton, PA: HarperCollins.

Katz, W.L. (Ed.). (1968). *Five slave narratives: A compendium.* Arno Press and *The New York Times.*

Keith, H. (1957). *Rifles for Watie.* New York: Troll.

Lee, H. (1988). *To kill a mockingbird.* New York: Warner Books.

Lester, J. (1986). *To be a slave.* New York: Scholastic.

Lester, J. (1985). *This strange new feeling.* New York: Scholastic.

McFreeley, W.S. (1992). *Frederick Douglass.* New York: Simon & Schuster.

Meltzer, M. (1987). *The Black Americans: A history in their own words 1619–1983.* New York: Harper Trophy.

Morrison, T. (1992). *Beloved.* New York: Alfred A. Knopf.

Murphy, J. (1990). *The boys' war: Civil War letters to their loved ones from the blue and gray.* New York: Clarion.

Myers, W.D. (1992). *Somewhere in the darkness.* New York: Scholastic.

Myers, W.D. (1992). *Mop, Moondance, and the Nagasaki knights.* New York: Delacorte Press.

Myers, W.D. (1991). *Now is your time! The African-American struggle for freedom.* Scranton, PA: HarperCollins.

Myers, W.D. (1992). *The mouse rap.* New York: Harper Trophy.

Myers, W.D. (1990). *Scorpions.* New York: Harper.

Myers, W.D. (1989). *The young landlords.* New York: Puffin.

Myers, W.D. (1988). *Fallen angels.* New York: Scholastic.

Myers, W.D. (1988). *Fast Sam, cool Clyde, and stuff.* New York: Puffin.

Myers, W.D. (1988). *Me, Mop and the moondance kid.* New York: Delacorte Press.

Myers, W.D. (1987). *Crystal.* New York: Viking.

Myers, W.D. (1987). *Motown and Didi: A love story.* New York: Dell.

Myers, W.D. (1983). *Hoops.* New York: Dell.

Myers, W.D. (1978). *It ain't all for nothin'.* New York: Viking.

Myers, W.D. (1977). *Mojo and the Russians.* New York: Viking.

Petry, A. (1991). *Harriet Tubman: Conductor on the Underground Railroad.* North Bellmore, NY: Marshall Cavendish Corporation.

Probst, R.E. (1984). *Adolescent literature: Response and analysis.* New York: Merrill.

Quarles, B. (1991). *Black abolitionists.* New York: Da Capo Press.

Rappaport, D. (1988). Escape from slavery: Five journeys to freedom. In Dorothy Sterling (Ed.). *Black foremothers.* New York: Feminist Press.

Ray, D. (1991). *Behind blue and gray: The soldier's life in the Civil War.* New York: Lodestar Books.

Reed, A.J.S. (1994). *Reaching adolescents: The young adult book and the school.* New York: Merrill.

Reed, A.J.S. (1993). *A teacher's guide to the signet edition of Narrative of Frederick Douglass: An American slave, written by himself.* New York: Penguin.

Rhodes, R.H. (1992). *All for the Union: The Civil War diary and letters of Elisha Hunt Rhodes.* New York: Vintage Books.

Rinaldi, A. (1991). *Wolf by the ears.* New York: Scholastic.

Robertson, S.L. (1990, January). Text rendering: Beginning literary response. *English Journal,* 79 (1), 80–84.

Rosenblatt, L.M. (1983). *Literature as exploration.* (4th ed.). New York: Modern Language Association.

Rosenblatt, L.M. (1978). *The reader, the text, the poem: The transactional theory of the literary work.* Carbondale, IL: Southern Illinois University Press.

Rosenblatt, L.M. (1991). The lost reader of democracy. In *The triumph of literature: The fate of literacy: English in the secondary school curriculum.* New York: Teachers College Press, 114–144.

Rosenblatt, L.M. (1989). Writing and reading: The transactional theory. In J.M. Mason (Ed.), *Reading and writing connections.* Needham Heights, MA: Allyn Bacon, 153–176.

Sebestyen, O. (1983). *Words by heart.* New York: Bantam.

Shura, M.F. (1991). *Gentle Annie: The true story of a Civil War nurse.* New York: Scholastic.

Siebert, W.H. (1968). *The Underground Railway from slavery to freedom.* Arno Press and the *New York Times.*

Small, R.C. (1979, October). The YA novel in the composition program: Part II. *English Journal,* **68** (7), 75–77.

Small, R.C. (1977, October). *The junior novel and the art of literature. English Journal,* **66** (7), 55–59.

Smucker, B. (1977). *Runaway to freedom: A story of the Underground Railroad.* New York: Harper & Row.

Still, W. (1968). *The Underground Railroad.* Arno Press and the *New York Times.*

Stowe, H.B. (1852). *Uncle Tom's cabin.* New York: Signet Classic/NAL.

Sundquist, E.J. (Ed.). (1990). *Frederick Douglass: New literary and historical essays.* Cambridge, NY: Cambridge University Press.

Taylor, M. (1992). *The road to Memphis.* New York: Penguin.

Taylor, M. (1991). *Let the circle be unbroken.* New York: Puffin.

Taylor, M. (1991). *Roll of thunder, hear my cry.* New York: Puffin.

Taylor, M. (1978). *Song of the trees.* New York: Bantam.

Twain, M. (1981). *The adventures of Huckleberry Finn.* New York: Bantam.

Walker, A. (1992). *The color purple.* New York: Harcourt, Brace, & Jovanovich.

Webb, S. & Nelson, R.W. (1980). *Selma, Lord, Selma: Girlhood memories of the Civil Rights days.* New York: William Morrow.

Weld, T. (1968). *American slavery as it is: Testimony of a thousand witnesses.* Arno Press and the *New York Times.*

Yates, E. (1989). *Amos Fortune, free man.* New York: Puffin.

Zaharias, J. (1984, fall). Promoting response agility through literature for young adults. *The ALAN Review,* **12** (1), 36–41.

CHAPTER 4

The Awakening and
Young Adult Literature:
Seeking Self-Identity in Many Ways
and in Many Cultures

PAMELA SISSI CARROLL

...she had apprehended instinctively the dual life—that outward pressure which conforms, the inward life which questions—Kate Chopin, The Awakening, p. 14

Introduction

When Kate Chopin's *The Awakening* was published in 1899, the author, a widowed young mother of six children, was almost instantly condemned by and ostracized from the society in which she had been raised. How could a novel have had such an immediate and powerful impact? It occurred because the turn-of-the-century novel violated conventions for pleasantly palatable literature written by and about respectable women. The work is a study of protagonist Edna Pontellier's internal struggle to balance the paradoxical demands of the mother-woman, an image that others imposed upon her, and the self-woman, an image she felt compelled to explore. Chopin's protagonist rebukes society when she chooses to ignore the traditional mother-woman roles: receiving the town's matriarchs during weekly social calls, knitting winter sweaters for her sons while sitting on the beach during summer vacation, responding delicately and with little emotion to powerful piano performances, and sacrificing her own art in order to oversee her cook and servants. Kate Chopin herself was condemned by society merely because of her association with the fictitious character whom she created, Edna Pontellier.

Edna Pontellier's quest for her own identity, daring for its time, is fueled by the heat of a summer at the Louisiana coast and by the conflicts among which she lives. The men in her life are contrasts: On one hand is the condescending attitude of her good husband, Leonce; on the other, the adoring attention of her would-be lover, Robert. Similarly, the women in Edna's world are contrasts: There is her friend, the affable, porcelain mother-woman, Madame Ratignolle; there is also her artistic mentor, the contentious, scratchy pianist, Mademoiselle Reisz. Edna wants to be taken seriously as an individual by each of these people—as a wife, mother, lover, friend, and artist. What she ultimately realizes, though, is that her longing to be recognized as an individual pulls her away from a comfortable home and family and into self-imposed isolation that neither husband, lover, friend, nor mentor fully understands.

At issue in *The Awakening* are personal identity and the paradoxes that interfere with one's attempts to establish and maintain an identity. This theme is a sophisticated version of the question that is of central concern to adolescents: "Who am I?"

Why Should *The Awakening* Be Taught?

The Awakening offers high artistic quality, historic and cultural significance, thematic appeal for adolescents, and a wide range of literary elements which can be illuminated through instruction. *The Awakening* is a beautifully crafted short novel (125 pages), thus making it appropriate for in-class reading. It introduces student readers to many aspects of the culture and language of French Creoles of turn-of-the-century New Orleans. Readers are immediately met with the challenge of passages that have French terms intertwined with English. For example, the first sentence of the novel includes a parrot's demand, "Allez vous-en! Allez vous-en! Sapristi!" (with a footnote, "Get out! Get Out! Damnation!" provided).

Chopin delicately mixes a third-person omniscient point of view with glimpses into the protagonist's psyche in passages like the following:

> Mrs. Pontellier was not a woman given to confidences... . Even as a child she had lived her own small life inside herself. At a very early period she had apprehended instinctively the dual life—that outward existence which conforms, the inward life which questions. (p. 14)

The novel is appealing because it is a work about and by a woman who was not afraid to rattle her contemporaries out of complacent acceptance of the social order. The historic setting, cultural contexts, and uncomfortable theme that gave rise to strong objections upon the original publication of *The Awakening* interest adolescents. These elements also provide rich focal points for instruction that can enhance a class's experience with the novel.

While its literary quality is indisputable, the strongest recommendation for including *The Awakening* in a high school syllabus lies in its theme of self-identity. Adolescent readers of both genders recognize the kinds of struggles with which Edna deals. They experience their own conflicting contraries and paradoxical demands that require them to make decisions about which they are frequently unsure and often unhappy.

Why *The Awakening* Should Be Paired with Young Adult Literature

Although Chopin's novel is brief, her style—particularly the late 19th-century use of rich language, the smattering of French phrases, and the sometimes difficult syntax—will challenge many high school readers. Reading and studying selected young adult (YA) literature will prepare students for the predominant theme of *The Awakening*: seeking self-identity. With confidence in their understanding of the theme, students can turn their attention to the more difficult literary elements of the short yet complex novel.

Goals of this Thematic Unit

Some possible goals that may be achieved are as follows: (1) To help students address THE question of adolescence—"Who am I?"—in an environment that encourages interaction and collaboration; (2) to introduce teachers and students to literature outside of the mainstream—pieces by writers from diverse cultures and circumstances—which can be used in treating the omnipresent and virtually universal issue of adolescents' quest for their own identities; (3) to suggest strategies by which reading, writing, speaking, listening, and critical thinking can be integrated during the study of a novel, strategies that can be adapted for use during this and other units of study.

Materials Needed for this Thematic Unit

Because all students will read Kate Chopin's *The Awakening*, a class set of the novel will be necessary. Signet Classics (New York) publishes a text called *The Awakening and Selected Stories of Kate Chopin* that is sold for about $3.00 a copy. This book is valuable because, if readers get really hooked on Chopin, they can further explore her work by sampling the short stories included in the collection.

The teacher will need to assemble four "preparatory reading packets," each of which will include one selection (or more, according to the teacher's judgment) from the short story, novel, and autobiography categories listed below (See "Short Stories for Young Adults: Culturally Diverse Perspectives"). Labels of "low" and "average" refer to my estimations of the readability of the literary works in terms of the reading achievement levels of high school readers. The labels are intended as suggestions only and are not meant to restrict the potential readership of any piece of literature.

Divide the class into four large groups. Although the resulting groups will be larger than is typical for "small group" assignments, the increased discussion that will occur by virtue of larger "small groups" will serve to enhance the students' exploration of self-identity. Each group will receive a copy of the teacher-made preparatory reading packet that is individualized for each group.

Short Stories for Young Adults: Culturally Diverse Perspective

"The Story of My Life" by Anna Bender. A Chippewa Indian girl goes away to boarding school. Seven years later, when she returns home, she finds herself lost between two worlds. (low/average)

"A Summer Tragedy" by Arna Wendell Bontemps. Jeff and Jennie Patton, old black sharecroppers, believe that the changes in society and their failing health will soon render them useless to others. In a story that withholds their shocking destination until they arrive, Jim and Jennie carefully fulfill their promise to each other—to end their lives by driving their car into a river. (average)

Athletic Shorts: Six Short Stories by Chris Crutcher. Each story of this superior collection focuses on adolescents who are struggling to identify themselves.   Angus Bethune is the class nerd, and his parents are remarried—each to partners of their same gender. Johnny Rivers has the chance to wrestle his domineering father, but even when Johnny wins the match, he and his father lose. Lionel must recover from the tragic death of his family, a death caused by one of his classmates. Telephone Man, a racist, learns that his assumptions about people need revision. Louie Banks faces the pain of losing a new friend to AIDS and losing old friends to their own ignorance. These are characters with whom many teens have concerns and experiences in common; hence, each of the stories is appropriate in a thematic unit dealing with self-identity. (average)

"Everybody Knows Tobie" by Daniel Garza. Thirteen-year-old Joey, a Chicano living in north Texas, questions where he belongs in society—a society in which he is discriminated against as a Chicano migrant worker's child. His brother, Tobie, is known in the town because he has its best newspaper route. When Joey takes over Tobie's paper route and performs it with grace, the young Chicano finds that he, too, can be accepted by the Gringo businessmen; he feels that he has established his place in the community. The reader is left to question Joey's easy acceptance of the Gringos' apparent respect. (low)

"In the American Society" by Gish Jen. A Chinese-American couple are raising their children to dream the American dream. Even though the family–owned and –operated pancake house does good business and the dream seems attainable, the Chinese immigrant parents still have trouble assimilating. They embarrass their children when they misunderstand the unwritten rules for eating at a dinner party and when the father wears a jacket with an exposed price tag. In this story, not only the adolescents but the entire family must wrestle with their own and others' stereotypes and misunderstandings in order to define what it means to be Chinese-American. (low/average)

"Paths upon Water" by Tahira Naqvi. Sakina is a traditional Pakistani woman who, during a visit to the United States, is forced to see the world through the eyes of her son, Raza, a graduate of an American college and a resident of the United States. When Raza takes his mother to the beach, she is shocked by bikinis, sunbathing, and couples' open affection. She questions where—if anyplace—she fits into this scene and into her son's new life; she surprises herself with the non-traditional answer. (average)

"Where Are You Going, Where Have You Been?" by Joyce Carol Oates. Connie is the prototypical teen: She is not a bad girl, but she fights with her mother and prefers hanging out at the mall to spending time at home. She faces the decision of doing what her parents would choose or of taking a risky ride with a rough young man when he arrives at her house. (low/average)

"I Stand Here Ironing" by Tillie Olsen. A mother reflects on raising her daughter, Emily, a child who spent almost a year in a convalescent home because she remained weak and skeleton-thin after the measles. Emily suffers from asthma and loneliness and is quiet, dark, and vulnerable. She is disturbed that she does not look like other girls who are plump, blond, and smiling. The story may have more to do with the mother's questions about Emily's identity than it does about Emily's own quest for answers. (average)

"Tears of Autumn" by Yoshiko Uchida. Twenty-one-year-old Hana Omiya agrees to move from Japan to Oakland, California, to meet and marry the son of her uncle's friend. She questions her life-changing decision as she travels on the cold ship which is "transporting her soul to a strange new life." (low/average)

Autobiographical Pieces: Culturally Diverse Perspective (Mixed Genres)

Teacher selections from *I Know Why the Caged Bird Sings* by Maya Angelou (246 pp.). This popular autobiographical account of the writer's childhood in the segregated South forces readers to confront the ugly face of racism and note how strength can overcome it. Angelou's triumph is that she is not swallowed by negative circumstances, partly because of her grandmother's love and partly because she constantly questions where she belongs in society as a bright black child in the South. (average)

Teacher selections from *A Girl from Yamhill* by Beverly Cleary (279 pp.). As the child of a farmer who had to relocate to a city job during the Depression, Cleary never felt that she was accepted by her mother or was ever able to please her. Teen readers will easily identify with Cleary's struggles to establish her unique personality and yet find ways to become more connected to her family, too. (low/average)

"How It Feels to be Colored Me" by Zora Neale Hurston (2 pp.). In this engaging essay, Hurston presents her memories of "the very day [she] became colored" at 13 years of age. She claims not to be that way because she "do[es] not belong to that sobbing school of Negrohood who hold that nature somehow has given them a lowdown dirty deal and whose feelings are all hurt about it." This is an unusual treatment of a girl's growth toward self-identity. (average)

Speaking Out: Teenagers Take on Race, Sex, and Identity by Suaun Kuklin (Ed.) (165 pp.). Kuklin, the editor of this collection of student-written essays, spent a year among the students at a multicultural public high school in New York City. The book's entries resonate with the frustrations and celebrations that teens experience in their worlds. Students will recognize others like themselves and their friends in the writings and photographs in this useful collection. (low/average)

Essay excerpts from *Gift from the Sea* by Anne Morrow Lindbergh (127 pp.). Lindbergh's essay expresses her inner conflict over the simple life she believes she is meant to live and the life that she is living as a wife and mother of five children. In her poignant essay, Lindbergh begins with a hermit crab as a simile for herself, then expands her focus to life in 20th-century America and its "premise of ever-widening circles of contact and communication." This lovely piece encourages readers to ask themselves questions about their own and their society's expectations and realities. (average)

Teacher selections from *Kaffir Boy: The True Story of a Black Youth's Coming of Age in Apartheid South Africa* by Mark Mathabane (354 pp.). Mathabane shows readers the cruel realities he experienced while growing up black in Alexandra, near Johannesburg, South Africa. His story is engaging, troubling, and important. (average)

Somehow Tenderness Survives: Stories of Southern Africa by Hazel Rochman (Ed.) (171 pp.). This is a powerful collection of stories, some of which are autobiographical. Among the most profound are Geina Mhlope's "The Toilet" and Peter Abrahams' "Crackling Day." These stories are not for students who refuse to recognize that the world is not always beautiful and just. (average)

Teacher selections from *Hunger of Memory: The Education of Richard Rodriguez* by Richard Rodriguez (195 pp.). Rodriguez, a Mexican-American, speaks to teens who are ashamed of their cultural heritage, their skin color, and their social status in this honest and compelling autobiography. (average)

Teacher selections from *But I'll Be Back Again* by Cynthia Rylant (54 pp.). Rylant grew up in Appalachia embarrassed about the poverty in which she was raised. In her autobiography, she describes the circumstances and dreams of her childhood and adolescence, which produced in her the urge to write. (low)

"The Jacket" by Gary Soto (3 pp.). Soto describes the humiliation he felt as a 6th grader because he had to wear an ugly and too large jacket. He was convinced that the jacket was responsible for every problem he faced, including ridicule from teachers and bad grades on tests. Finally, he comes to regard the jacket as an "ugly brother who breathed over [his] shoulder" as he grows up. He eventually learns to accept the jacket and his own relationship to it and to his world. (low)

"The Konk" by Piri Thomas (12 pp.). Fourteen-year-old Piri, a Puerto Rican boy living in New York in the early 1900s, is ashamed of his curly hair. A trip to the barber turns disastrous, yet helps him learn to accept his hair and himself. (low)

"In Search of Our Mothers' Gardens" by Alice Walker (7 pp.). Walker evokes the image of her mother's colorful garden as a metaphor for the creativity and determination of the black woman in America. Walker explains that the realization that her mother, like other unknown black American women of her mother's generation, was a gifted artist in her own right who helped her connect to her heritage, and thus helped her define her own identity.

Novels for Young Adults: Culturally Diverse Expressions

Notes for Another Life by Sue Ellen Bridgers (250 pp.). Thirteen-year-old Wren Jackson and her older brother, Kevin, are living with their grandparents. Their mother, Karen, is cutting her ties with her family in order to establish herself as a career woman, and their father is wasting away in a mental hospital, a victim of depression. In contrast to Karen, the mother of Wren's boyfriend and Wren's own grandmother are examples of mother-women, Southerners who live for their families; yet Wren is torn. She has the potential to become a concert pianist but feels that she must decide whether a life like her self-centered mother's—or one like her selfless grandmother's—will be right for her. (low/average)

The Moves Make the Man by Bruce Brooks (280 pp.). The Jayfox is a terrific basketball player, and his talent helps him be accepted when he is the first black student in a North Carolina high school. The Jayfox begins to learn about the kind of integrity that transcends winning basketball games when he and a white athlete, Bix, become friends. With humor, careful attention to the game of basketball, and sensitivity to the adolescents' problems, Brooks's novel captures the interest of reluctant readers. (low/average)

Children of the River by Linda Crew (213 pp.). Seventeen-year-old Sundara is a high school student in Oregon, but she is also a refugee from the Khmer Rouge in war-ravaged Cambodia. Although Sundara wants to belong to the popular groups in her high school, her life with relatives is a mirror of life in Cambodia, with traditions that American high school students do not understand. Sundara is torn between her desire to be an average American, the despair of not knowing whether her parents are alive or dead, and her loyalty to the customs of her native culture. (average)

A Yellow Raft in Blue Water by Michael Dorris (372 pp.). Fifteen-year-old Rayona is half Indian and half black. She cannot seem to be ordinary; instead, she is often abandoned and always vulnerable. Despite a bleak life on a Montana reservation, Rayona has a strong spirit and an unquenchable desire to find her mother and to discover her own personal identity. Both Rayona's mother and grandmother share their perspectives on events as well. (average/high)

The Talking Earth by Jean Craighead George (151 pp.). Billie Wind is a Seminole who is disciplined for her lack of allegiance to the tribal beliefs by being sent to live alone in the Everglades. While there, she develops an understanding of herself and a respect for the heritage that she had previously not known. (low)

Bearstone by Will Hobbs (154 pp.). Cloyd is a troubled young teen. The son of a Navajo whom he has never known, Cloyd tries to run away from the Ute group home. When his attempt fails, he is sent to live with Walter, a gentle yet strict old white man who is a farmer and hunter. While living with Walter, Cloyd finds a turquoise bear hidden in a cave. The bear becomes the boy's symbol for his strength and identity. When hunters who come to stay at Walter's farm kill a bear, Cloyd retaliates by destroying Walter's prize peach trees. The two must work together to mend their torn relationship and to recognize that each has a place where he belongs. (low)

Annie John by Jamaica Kincaid (148 pp.). Annie grows up happily in the Caribbean on Antigua. As a teen, her relationship with her mother shifts from a trusting and positive one to a tormented and painful one. Annie struggles with herself as she tries to decide who she is and what her values are. (average)

There's a Girl in My Hammerlock by Jerry Spinelli (199 pp.). Eighth-grader Maisie Brown is an athlete, but instead of cheerleading, she sets her aim on being a wrestler. Her friends think she is crazy, and the guys show her no respect. Regardless, Maisie begins to believe in herself and stands up for her decisions. This novel treats a young adolescent's self-identity questions with a humorous, light touch. (low)

Dicey's Song by Cynthia Voigt (211 pp.). Thirteen-year-old Dicey is the strength of her family. Abandoned by their mother, she and her younger siblings have recently moved in with a grandmother they have never really known. The grandmother is a misunderstood, eccentric outcast, and Dicey and her siblings are soon similarly labeled. Dicey demonstrates mature strength of character as she helps her family adjust to their new arrangement, but she is also a child who needs love and direction as she begins to seek her own identity. (low)

The Runner by Cynthia Voigt (181 pp.). Seventeen-year-old Bullet isolates himself from racial prejudice by taking long lonely runs. He is forced to examine his fiercely-protected independence and his prejudice when he develops a relationship with a black runner, but he never relinquishes his right to define himself as a self-alienated outsider. (low/average)

Strategies

Students will read short stories, autobiographical essays and excerpts, and YA novels by and about people who represent a wide range of cultural backgrounds. Each piece asks the question, "Who am I?" in some way. Students should work collaboratively throughout the unit of study. Small groups will read and complete activities from one of four preparatory reading packets. After the small groups read the preparatory packet materials, all groups will read *The Awakening*, which is the heart of the unit.

There are at least two reasons why collaborative learning is the preferred method for both the preparatory packets assignments and for the reading of *The Awakening*. First, adolescents define themselves in terms of how others view them, but they often have misconceptions about what those perceptions are. Psychologist David Elkind (1967) explains that adolescence is a time of egocentrism, yet adolescents are, for the first time in their lives, able to "take account of other people's thought" (p. 386). Elkind further explains:

> One consequence of adolescent egocentrism is that, in actual or impending social situations, the young person anticipates the reactions of other people to himself. These anticipations, however, are based on the premise that others are as admiring or as critical of him as he is of himself. In a sense, then, the adolescent is continually constructing, or reacting to, *an imaginary audience*. It is an audience because the adolescent believes that he will be the focus of attention; and it is imaginary because, in actual social situations, this is not usually the case. (p. 387)

It is important for teachers to help adolescents explore their self-perceptions and their understandings of how others see them. The literature of this unit, when read and studied in collaborative groups, provides vehicles through which teachers can provide low-risk opportunities for such explorations.

Second, collaboration promotes critical thinking. When we collaborate we must crystallize and defend—or adjust—our own stances, opinions, and assumptions. Group work, then, will promote an exchange of ideas that requires careful examination of one's own ideas and will therefore reinforce the theme of this unit of study—the quest for self-identity.

Organization

I suggest that the teacher place students in heterogeneous groups so that each group is comprised of a combination of strong and weaker students. Because of the high interest level of the unit and with help provided by peers, even readers who are below the class average are likely to have a positive experience with the readings and activities related to, and including, *The Awakening*. Group work will occur in three separate phases.

Phase One

All students will select and complete one "Self-Identity" activity from each of three categories: visual, written, and oral/spoken. Group members will share their visual and written products with other members of their group and will collaborate to plan, develop, and present their choice of oral or dramatic segments to the entire class.

Phase Two

Groups will select one of the preparatory reading packets that the teacher provides (See "Materials Needed for this Thematic Unit" above). In each packet are literary selections, appropriate for young adult readers, that address the self-identity theme from each of the following genres: short stories, autobiographical essays and excerpts, and novels. The group work with these preparatory reading packets (that is, the supplemental texts in which themes that are important in *The Awakening* are introduced to readers) should be assigned and completed prior to whole-class reading of *The Awakening*. During and following each group's reading of these prepared materials, students will repeat a selection of the Self-Identity activities that they completed in Phase One. This time, however, they will respond as if they are speaking for characters from the literature instead of for themselves. This strategy will allow students to bring their personal perceptions to bear upon the literary texts. The intersection of the personal and the newly encountered information is where comprehension and growth occur.

Phase Three

Individuals will read *The Awakening* and complete a final activity, one in which the readers' personal experiences, experiences with the supplemental texts, and the actual event of reading *The Awakening* will be synthesized. Groups will meet for peer revision and editing of their drafts of the final product of the thematic unit.

Activities

During Phase One, each activity will be used independent of the literature by the students as individuals who are dealing with their own personal self-identity questions. Similarly, each activity will then be used in relation to the literature by students as a vehicle for responding to the texts during Phase Two.

The teacher may wish to have groups complete all or part of the activities described below before the actual reading of the literature begins. This approach encourages students to engage in thoughtful reflection on their own identities before they apply thoughts to others' searches for self-identity. I suggest that students select one or more Self-Identity activities from each category—visual, written, spoken/oral—and complete the same activity in both Phase One and Phase Two. Group cohesiveness may be strengthened if every member of the small group completes the same Self-Identity activities. Group members might be encouraged to read and think about the possibilities, then come to a consensus about which ones all members will complete. The nature of the Self-Identity activities ensures that each activity will be equally compatible in conjunction with any of the pieces of literature. The teacher and students decide which activities are most appropriate for Phase One and Phase Two activities.

Visuals

Visual activities give students from all social, cultural, and linguistic groups an equal opportunity to succeed in a class assignment. Since the purpose of these activities during Phase One is to encourage self-reflection and to move toward self-definition, care should be taken by teachers and students to respect the right of any student to keep his or her creations private if sharing them might cause embarrassment to the student.

Identity Bags

The teacher distributes a small paper bag to each student. Using markers, crayons, pencils, pens, magazine cutouts, and so forth, students create a bag with two dimensions. On the outside of the bag, students glue and write words and pictures that reflect the way they think others see them. On the inside of the bag, students place pictures and words (written on slips of paper or cut from magazines and other print materials) that represent ways they see themselves. In their small groups, students may put all bags in a pile and try to decide, based on the outside and the inside, whose is whose. Students then discuss the differences between others' images of them and their self-images. Students may also opt for simple sharing of their bags during group time and may choose to keep what is inside the bags to themselves if they feel uncomfortable revealing it to classmates. This activity works equally well, of course, with shoe boxes or other containers that can be decorated.

T-shirts and Bumper Stickers

The teacher provides each student with either a construction paper T-shirt (as large as possible for visual effect) or a strip of construction paper that is approximately the size of a bumper sticker. Students design slogans and visual symbols that represent themselves, original sayings that they might actually be proud to wear on their T-shirts or display as bumper stickers on their lockers, notebooks, cars, and so forth. Group members may wish to try to guess who designed the T-shirts or stickers and could then work as teams to guess who designed the products of classmates in other groups. The products may be displayed in the classroom. A "clothesline" on which all of the T-shirts are hung is an attention-getting classroom display.

Graph of the Ups and Downs of a Day, Month, Season, or Year

The teacher provides a model of this activity based on one of her or his own days, months, seasons, or school years. Students then complete their own graphs to share with their group members and then, if desired, display in the classroom. To make the graph, first list on a piece of paper all of the important events of a specified time (day, month, etc.) of choice. Next, on a large piece of paper or a poster, draw a simple grid with an x and y axis. Then use the list created in step one to generate a graph of the events of that time. Positive events will occupy points high on the y axis of the graph, while negative ones will occupy low points. The chronological order of the list should be reflected across the x axis, and each point that is plotted on the graph should be numbered in correspondence with the original list of events. The original list can be glued or taped to the back of the graph so that the graph itself is left free of the clutter of words. Groups should be allowed time to share their graphs with group members. Discussions of the differences in group members' life experiences may prove useful in helping to establish a comfortable work environment.

Life Map

Kirby, Liner, and Vinz (1988, pp. 33, 54–55) describe an excellent self-identity exercise called the life map. Whereas the graph may focus on a restricted time period, the life map allows students the opportunity to create a visual autobiography, one in which brief phrases illuminate drawings or cutouts. Students create a road map that features events from their lives; these events serve as landmarks along the way. The maps might be taped to the wall, side-by-side, in order to represent the one road that all students in a particular class have traveled collectively. This activity lends itself well to computer graphics, and it is recommended that the teacher participate by creating his or her own map to serve as a model.

Written

Group discussions of written compositions are encouraged as a means of helping each writer clarify thoughts. Additionally, group members are given insights into the writer's thinking.

Autobio/Biopoem

John and Kay Bushman (1993, pp. 72–73) provide a formula for getting students to write poetry about themselves. For this activity students are asked to compose poems about themselves during Phase One and about a character during Phase Two. The formula follows:

Line 1: first name
Line 2: 4 traits that describe you (or a character)
Line 3: relative of _____
Line 4: lover of _____, _____, and _____
Line 5: who feels _____, _____, and _____
Line 6: who needs _____, _____, and _____
Line 7: who fears _____, _____, and _____
Line 8: who gives _____, _____, and _____
Line 9: who would like to see _____, _____, and _____
Line 10: resident of _____
Line 11: last name

The poems may be collected and published as a class autobiography, or students may wish to write a stanza for each member of their family, for each of their close friends, and so forth. They may also wish to add lines to the formula as they feel lines are needed.

This is a Poem About [or for]... .

Rico's (1983, pp. 44–49) strategy for the creation of this personal kind of poem is simple. The writer merely clusters or lists things that come to mind about a person. During Phase One, the writer puts himself or herself at the center of the cluster or at the top of the list. During Phase Two, a character that is met through the preparatory reading packets is the focus. The cluster or list might include the person's likes, dislikes, activities, good qualities, problem spots, and the like. This cluster or list then becomes the source of information from which the writer draws to write a poem that begins with the clause, "This is a poem about [or for]... ." This strategy has proven successful with students of all ages, children through adults. Its simplicity belies its heuristic power.

Special Settings

Students select and write a description of a place that is special to them for some reason. To "test" the quality of the descriptive prose, members of the group could be asked to read the description and draw the place with accuracy. The teacher may pre-select passages from the preparatory reading packets or from *The Awakening* that are particularly effective descriptions of place and present those to the group as models. Students should evaluate the style of the writer and look for how the writer achieves the desired effect. Students are often surprised that, despite what they have learned during lessons on the descriptive essay, adjectives are not always the most promising way to give attention to details.

Mad, Soft, Fast Talking

Students will enjoy completing and sharing Kirby, Liner, and Vinz's (1988, pp. 142–143) activity with their group members. This activity gives them an opportunity to reveal three sides of themselves not typically revealed in students' standard classroom personalities. Using a timer, students complete each part of the assignment in three minutes. The teacher gives the following directions orally or has them written for students to follow:

1. In "Fast Talking," writers try to convince someone of something that is important to them. Examples of topics include trying to talk your teacher into a higher grade or a postponed deadline, trying to talk your coach into canceling holiday practices, and trying to talk a police officer out of writing you a well-deserved speeding ticket. At three minutes, time is called.

2. In "Soft Talking," writers try to comfort someone or something. Topic possibilities include comforting a child who has lost her doll while in the grocery store, consoling a friend whose pet has run away, or cheering up a pitcher after his last pitch led to a grand slam and a loss for his team. Again, when three minutes have elapsed, time is called.

3. During "Mad Talking," writers express anger, disbelief, or frustration over a troubling matter. The venting of emotional steam is important here. Topic examples include telling the one who left you dateless on the night of the big dance just how you feel, telling your parents how unreasonable the last punishment you received was, telling a referee that the game-determining call was wrong, and so forth.

After all three parts have been completed in the aforementioned order, the group members should reread their writing and make evaluations about their own "voices" as writers. Groups then discuss what these distinctly different voices say about them as writers and as people.

Spoken or Oral

Around the Dinner Table

This is a simple role-play activity in which group members imagine that they are seated around a dinner table or an equivalent setting if the membership issue revolves around a school or social group. One student is designated as the one with the problem who is trying to figure out where he or she "fits" in the family or within another group such as school, social, church, and the like. Students gathered around the table play the role of family members (or others) who both help and hinder the focal student's attempts to define his or her place. The issues that emerge are often those that are currently important to the members of the small group. Students hear their own fears, frustrations, and arguments, along with the counterarguments from a more objective position than they usually take. Thus, students may learn important lessons about their own assumptions and stances on certain problems.

One student might serve as recorder, keeping notes on the major points made by each participant in the role-play in order to facilitate discussion after the session has concluded. Audio- or videotapes of the sessions may also be helpful for the purpose of debriefing the sessions; but if participants decrease their participation in response to the audio- or videotapes, the technological aides are best left turned off.

Our Own Oprah Show

This activity works best when the whole class assists the host group that has chosen to do the activity. Students in a small group identify one problem that teens often face; members may use their own problems if they wish. One student in the host group is selected to be "Oprah," a popular star of television talk shows. Another student is designated as the one with the problem and is seated in a chair at the front center of the classroom. Other members of the group sit around the "problem student," and each role-plays someone who is involved in or affected by the particular problem.

"Oprah" stimulates conversation among audience members, or other students in the class, about the problem. The objective is for the cast and audience to strive for a consensus of opinion. After the "show" is over, students could be led into a discussion about which issues emerged, which were relevant and significant, which solutions are sound, and so forth. During Phase Two, the problems that are the focus for the "show" should be those of the characters encountered in one or more pieces of literature. If students decide that a character from one story has a problem that is similar to the problem of a character in another piece of literature, both characters, along with those with whom they are involved, should appear on the "stage" with "Oprah."

Songs

Students are asked to participate in this small group activity that requires simultaneous participation by group members. Students select songs that seem to speak for or about them in some way. The songs may describe moods or sides of their personalities that are rarely on display while they are in school. Students write or type the lyrics and distribute copies to their groups. Each student then plays his or her song for the group and asks members to identify at least two phrases that stand out for them for some reason and to underline those phrases on the lyrics' page. As the "expert" on the song, the student conducting the group activity will list the underlined phrases on a poster, chalkboard, transparency, computer, or the like. What emerges is a kind of poem that is generated from members' personal connections and responses to the song. The temporary group leader should read the new poem aloud and lead the group in a discussion of the new creation.

Literature Think-Alouds

Richard Beach (1993, p. 58) describes a promising activity that integrates the reading and writing of literature in a way that connects a personal response to literature with close attention to the text. First, students write a journal entry as a means of responding to a piece of literature they have read. Then, students get in pairs to read words, phrases, sentences, or longer portions directly from the literary text. The partner asks the reader to talk about why the particular passage is important enough to be singled out, then encourages the reader to continue responding to other questions. A discussion of the literature and the reader's response to it is stimulated, and soon both partners become engaged in talk about the text and their responses to it. Usually the portion that is selected for reading aloud is identified in the journal entry as an important passage; the journal entry prepares the first reader with a focus.

Synthesizing and Culminating Activity

There is no getting around the fact that the troubling ending of ***The Awakening*** demands attention. In the final scene, Edna walks into the sea, telling herself two things: (1) that she wants only to be with her lover, Robert, but that even her desire for him will eventually "melt out of her existence, leaving her alone" (p. 123); and (2) that she loves her husband and children but they "need not have thought that they could possess her, body and soul" (p. 124). Given these internal conflicts of the self-woman and the mother-woman and the larger social conditions that make it virtually impossible for a female like Edna, given her time and place, to define herself in any way except torn between conflicting demands, she chooses to end her life. Many students read this passage as Edna's most selfish and hateful act; others defend Edna, claiming that she had exhausted all possible options available to her in that time and place. The points of view that fuel these differences of opinion will quickly ignite discussions in most high school classrooms.

What can be done to deal productively with the energy that certain issues will produce? A group discussion, debate, or writing assignment on Edna's choice would, by necessity, develop into a consideration of ethical, moral, religious, and social issues related to suicide. A better direction, it seems to me, is to conduct a pre-writing discussion on the broader topic of "personal choice."

Throughout the unit, students have dealt with questions about their own identities—about how others see them and how they perceive themselves. Now, at the close of the unit, students are ready to reflect on what they have learned about themselves. They are ready, too, to look at the society in which they live and see its promises and blemishes. Instead of walking into the ocean because there are no options, they can look to their futures and see many possibilities. A discussion might be directed with questions such as the following:

> What are the choices that you have as a young person—male or female—in this place and time in history?

> Where do you see yourselves in the next year, the next decade?

> What differences will you make because of who you are?

Discussing these questions will help prepare students to write final essays about themselves. The essays will draw on the self-discoveries students have made while reading about people from a variety of cultures and with diverse sets of expectations and impediments. They will also draw on the ideas that emerged while students completed visual, written, and oral Self-Identity activities in Phase One and Phase Two.

Far more sophisticated than the "This Is What I Want to Do with My Life" essay of a child who has not thought realistically about who she or he is, this essay will encourage students to synthesize what they have learned and to use that information to make projections into their own futures. Writers might be encouraged to incorporate in their essays this key passage from *The Awakening*: "... she was becoming herself and daily casting aside that fictitious self which we assume like a garment with which to appear before the world" (p. 62). Students explain who their own "fictitious self" has been and which garments need "casting aside."

Students gather the visual and written products from Phase One and Phase Two and select their favorite works, along with the final essay, for peer review in their small groups. After peer reviews and resultant revisions have been completed, each student will have a small collection of works that focus on himself or herself. These works can be bound, placed in a portfolio, or otherwise displayed with the student's permission. Each class will also have a collection of works about classmates—a family scrapbook—to be treasured by those who now know that they belong.

The ideas presented for this thematic unit are, by necessity, merely a starting place. Teachers and students are encouraged to add poetry, songs, stories, nonfiction, drama, news articles, and other writings to the unit plan, according to the individual and collective interests and academic needs of each class. The teacher of literature who helps adolescents find answers to self-identity questions is like a successful piano teacher—he or she helps students gain the confidence they need in order to play from their hearts, and then, on recital night, hides behind the curtain to listen to the performances and celebrate the applause.

List of References

Angelou, M. (1971). *I know why the caged bird sings.* New York: Bantam.

Beach, R. (1993). *A teacher's introduction to reader response theories.* Urbana, IL: National Council of Teachers of English.

Bender, A. (1992). The story of my life. In A. Herschfelder (Ed.), *Rising voices: Writings of young Native Americans.* New York: Charles Scribner's Sons.

Bontemps, A. (1993). A summer tragedy. In D. Worley & J. Perry (Eds.), *African American literature: An anthology of nonfiction, fiction, poetry, and drama.* New York: National Textbook Company.

Bridgers, S.E. (1981). *Notes for another life.* New York: Alfred A. Knopf.

Brooks, B. (1984). *The moves make the man.* New York: Harper & Row.

Bushman, J.H. & Bushman, K.P. (1993). *Using young adult literature in the English classroom.* New York: Merrill/Macmillan.

Chopin, K. (1976, originally published in 1899). *The awakening.* In B. Solomon (Ed.), *The awakening and selected stories of Kate Chopin.* New York: Signet/NAL.

Cleary, B. (1989). *A girl from Yamhill.* New York: Dell.

Crew, L. (1989). *Children of the river.* New York: Delacorte Press.

Crutcher, C. (1991). *Athletic shorts: Six short stories.* New York: Greenwillow.

Dorris, M. (1987). *A yellow raft in blue water.* New York: Warner Books.

Elkind, D. (1967). Egocentrism in adolescence. In J. Gardner (Ed.), *Readings in developmental psychology.* 2nd. ed. Boston: Little, Brown & Company, 383–390.

Garza, D. (1990). Everybody knows Tobie. In C. Tatum (Ed.), *Mexican American literature.* Orlando: Harcourt, Brace, & Jovanovich.

George, J. (1983). *The talking earth.* New York: Harper Trophy.

Hobbs, W. (1989). *Bearstone.* New York: Avon Camelot.

Hurston, Z.N. (1994). How it feels to be colored me. In A. Applebee, A. Bermudez, J. Langer, & J. Marshall (Sr. Consultants), *Literature and language: American literature.* Evanston, IL: McDougal Littell, 786–788.

Jen, G. (1994). In the American society. In Laurie King (Ed.), *Hear my voice: A multicultural anthology of literature from the United States.* Menlo Park, CA: Addison-Wesley, 174–187.

Kincaid, J. (1985). *Annie John.* New York: Farrar, Straus, & Giroux.

Kirby. D., Liner, T., & Vinz, R. (1988). *Inside out: Developmental strategies for teaching writing.* 2nd ed. Portsmouth, NH: Heinemann.

Kuklin, S. (1993). *Speaking out: Teenagers take on race, sex, and identity.* New York: Putnam.

Lindbergh, A. (1975). *Gift from the sea.* New York: Pantheon.

Mathabane, M. (1986). *Kaffir boy: The true story of a black youth's coming of age in apartheid South Africa.* New York: NAL/Dutton.

Naqvi, T. (1994). Paths upon water. In L. King (Ed.), *Hear my voice: A multicultural anthology of literature from the United States.* Menlo Park, CA: Addison-Wesley, 12–23.

Oates, J. (1993). Where are you going, where have you been? In H. Rochman & D. McCampbell (Eds.), *Who do you think you are? Stories of friends and enemies.* Boston: Little, Brown/Joy Street, 14–35.

Olsen, T. (1994). I stand here ironing. In A. Applebee, A. Bermudez, J. Langer, & J. Marshall (Sr. Consultants), *Literature and language: American literature.* Evanston, IL: McDougal Littell, 756–762.

Rico, G. (1983). *Writing the natural way.* Los Angeles, CA: J.P. Tarcher.

Rochman, H. (1993). *Against borders: Promoting books for a multicultural world.* Chicago, IL: American Library Association Booklist.

Rochman, H. (Ed.). (1988). *Somehow tenderness survives: Stories of Southern Africa.* New York: HarperCollins.

Rodriquez, R. (1983). *Hunger of memory: The education of Richard Rodriquez.* New York: Bantam.

Rylant, C. (1989). *But I'll be back again.* New York: Orchard.

Soto, G. (1990). The jacket. In C. Tatum (Ed.), *Mexican American literature.* Orlando: Harcourt, Brace, & Jovanovich, 392–395.

Spinelli, J. (1991). *There's a girl in my hammerlock.* New York: Simon & Schuster.

Thomas, P. (1978). The konk. In Piri Thomas, *Stories from El Barrio.* New York: Alfred A. Knopf.

Uchida, Y. (1994). Tears of autumn. In A. Applebee, A. Bermudez, J. Langer, & J. Marshall (Sr. Consultants), *Literature and language: American literature.* Orlando: McDougal Littell, 647–652.

Voigt, C. (1982). *Dicey's song.* New York: Fawcett Juniper.

Voigt, C. (1985). *The runner.* New York: Athenaeum.

Walker, A. (1994). In search of our mothers' gardens. In L. King (Ed.), *Hear my voice: A multicultural anthology of literature from the United States.* Menlo Park, CA: Addison-Wesley, 127–134.

CHAPTER 5

Using Young Adult Literature as a Companion to World Literature: A Model Thematic Unit on the "Clash of Cultures" Centered on *Things Fall Apart*

LOIS T. STOVER AND CONNIE S. ZITLOW

Introduction

English curricula are being revised to include literature reflective of the cultural diversity of our shrinking world and more indicative of the contributions diverse cultures have made to humanity. Thematic units that allow students to explore the various ways different people respond to a topic will be a useful organizational structure during this transitional period. For instance, the Scott Foresman *Classics in World Literature* (1991) text includes selections from around the globe such as *Tartuffe* by Moliere, "The Overcoat" by Gogol, Egyptian love poems, *The Pillow Book* by Shonagon, "The Circular Ruins" by Borges, or "The Lay of Thrym," an ancient Icelandic poem, all organized into units with titles such as "Appearance and Reality," "The Quest," or "The Outsider." However, students' responses to such texts are likely to be similar to what we experience when we ask our students to read any piece of literature that is not in keeping with their life experiences: "Why do we have to read this? What does this have to do with me?"

World literature can be even more difficult than other standard texts of the English curriculum for high school readers to understand. Works considered as "classics" tend to be written about adult characters who have adult concerns. Additionally, classics of world literature—especially those from non-Western cultures—have foreign settings and characters with different values and belief structures who engage in different customs. We believe that pairing young adult (YA) literature—both from the United States and abroad—with world literature texts based on shared literary strengths can be a powerful teaching strategy in helping students not only understand the words on the page but enter into the often foreign worlds presented through those words.

In this chapter, we will outline goals for a unit centered on the theme of "The Clash of Cultures" with *Things Fall Apart*, a classic African text reflective of a non-Western culture. We will illustrate ways that contemporary YA literature—literature written specifically for an audience of young adults about young adult experiences—can be used as a bridge into the world of a text that is probably foreign to both teacher and student. We will provide a model for using YA novels as independent, out-of-class reading designed to enhance and supplement the study of a classic text and will describe how to use those novels in conjunction with that central text during a thematic unit. Finally, to illustrate that what we outline for *Things Fall Apart* can be applied to other unit situations, we will provide a brief list of additional YA titles that teachers may find useful for enhancing other thematically based units centered upon a classic of world literature.

An Overview of *Things Fall Apart*

In *Things Fall Apart*, first published in 1958, Chinua Achebe tells the story of Okonkwo, "a strong man ... well known throughout the nine villages and even beyond," whose life, nevertheless, is dominated by fear and anger. Through Okonkwo's story, Achebe dramatizes the clash of traditional Ibo life as it meets colonialism and Christianity at the turn of the century, illustrating how the arrival of the white man led to the destruction of the old ways.

Okonkwo lives in Umuofia, an Ibo village. The people of Umuofia believe in ancestor worship and ancient gods, engage in clandestine practices, and take pride in physical prowess and dexterity. Although Okonkwo's father leaves him only a small inheritance, Okonkwo is able to secure three wives and two barns full of yams through his own efforts. He attains a position of honor in Umuofia by "throwing the Cat," a famous wrestler from another village who had been unbeaten for seven years. In spite of his strength as a wrestler and his prowess in inter-tribal wars, Okonkwo lives in fear—fear of weakness and fear of future failure. His fear is heightened because of his father's failure; he lived a contemptible life and died a shameful death in debt and without a title. Spurred by these fears, Okonkwo desires to achieve the highest title of accomplishment. But, during Peace Week, he beats one of his wives, and he "inadvertently" kills the 16-year-old son of Ezcudu. As a result, Okonkwo is banished from the village for seven years.

When Okonkwo returns to Umuofia, "things fall apart." His clansmen no longer welcome him, and his former place in village life has been taken by others. Meanwhile, white men have come to bring Christianity to the tribe. Okonkwo recognizes the conflict between his fellow clansmen and these white men. He is angered by the increasing power of the Christian gods, an increase which means his own gods have lost importance and status. He seeks to organize his peers into battle against this new world order. Finally, bitter and saddened by the state of a world in which he no longer feels at home, he strikes out at the institution he perceives to have been inhumanly imposed upon his village and kills a Christian messenger sent to warn Umuofia not to war with the white men. Okonkwo's action is in vain because his clansmen let the other messengers escape; hence, their war council is disbanded. "They had broken into tumult instead of action. He discerned fright in that tumult. He heard voices asking, 'Why did he do it?'" (p. 188). Knowing that his world has, indeed, fallen apart, Okonkwo hangs himself—an attempt to die nobly, but an unsuccessful one because he has violated the beliefs that have guided his life: "It is an abomination for a man to take his own life. It is an offense against the Earth and a man who commits it will not be buried by his clansmen. His body is evil, and only strangers may touch it" (p. 190).

Things Fall Apart is useful for introducing high school readers to African writing, and perhaps to all non-Western writing in general, for several reasons. Achebe is an award-winning novelist, respected for his economic style, his use of irony, and his ability to tell a story that is very African in subject matter yet universal in theme. Okonkwo is a young man just beginning his adult life when the novel opens, and thus is somewhat accessible to older adolescents as he struggles to make a name for himself and to establish a niche in village society. The themes of clashing cultures and of the deterioration of a given culture through change over time are ones high school students experience almost daily as they seek to bridge the gap between adolescence and adulthood. Adolescents frequently feel the kind of outrage Okonkwo feels as they see the difficulties involved in creating a world order grounded in their youthful idealism.

Goals for a Unit Based upon *Things Fall Apart*

The goals for exposing students to non-Western literature and literature reflective of the world's cultural diversity fall into two categories: (1) goals important for any literary study, such as the study of the elements of narration and the author's use of language to create meaning, vocabulary goals, writing goals, speaking/listening goals, and so on; and (2) goals important for the study of literature reflective of a world view different from that experienced by the reader.

Things Fall Apart may profitably be used to achieve the following generic goals of the literature program:

1. Students will be able to define and identify the following literary elements used in the novel: allusion, archetype, characterization, foreshadowing, imagery, irony, plot, point of view, protagonist/antagonist, setting, and style.

2. Students will be able to develop their skill in using context clues to understand new vocabulary.

3. Students will practice classification, generalization, synthesis, and evaluation of concepts.

4. Students will be able to write comparison/contrast pieces, character sketches, critical analyses, and personal responses that connect their experiences to the world of the text.

5. Students will practice the speaking and listening skills necessary for participation in large and small group discussions, individual and group oral interpretations, and debate.

These goals reflect our sense of the literary strengths of Achebe's novel. Obviously, the specifics embedded in these goals would have to be adapted for another text.

Things Fall Apart may profitably be used to achieve the following goals that are specific to the study of literature reflective of a non-Western cultural perspective:

1. Students will be able to identify ways in which their own cultures and life experiences are similar to and different from Okonkwo's culture and resulting life experiences. Students will be able to better appreciate the richness of a contemporary culture woven from the threads of diverse heritages.

2. Students will be able to articulate the ways in which the clash of cultures described in Achebe's work affects the lives of the characters and the ultimate course of events.

3. Students who are themselves members of non-Western cultures will be able to find themselves in the text and will feel a sense of belonging; as a result, they will "enter into a new, unshakably proud relationship with their heritage" (Wigginton, 1992, p. 60).

4. Students will increase their tolerance for and appreciation of diverse values. When we give students literature reflective of only one culture's point of view to read, we are, in essence, telling them that there is only one kind of literature—and by implication one culture—of value (Smith, 1983, p. 7).

5. Students will be able to articulate the relationship between art and the culture in which it is produced. For example, *Things Fall Apart* is a Nigerian novel, reflecting that culture and, in some ways perhaps, contributing to its ongoing development. At the same time, students will note how non-Western books, with their use of imagery, symbolism, and style, are also works of art.

6. Students will develop a disposition to broaden their personal reading interests by choosing to read additional texts representative of other worlds because they are "just plain good."

Using Young Adult Literature to Introduce
Things Fall Apart

Edmund Farrell states, "If I were asked what the most serious shortcoming is of the student teachers I observe, I would reply, 'Their failure to motivate interest in a selection, to build bridges between students' concerns and experiences and the experiences recorded in the literature. Student teachers don't realize that assigning a selection and teaching it are not synonymous'" (1966, p. 44). To develop a bridge, the teacher could identify an element of the work that may be problematic for the students and then develop an activity to help the students understand that element more easily. Or, the teacher could determine what aspect of the book may be the most relevant to students' personal experiences and then develop an activity to help the students move into the text through examining that aspect of their own lives.

One of the most difficult aspects of *Things Fall Apart* for many American students to comprehend will be the thematic thread of "cultural clash" running throughout the entire novel. Many students may find it difficult to empathize with Okonkwo's pain which is caused by the arrival of the missionaries and the ways in which it disrupts life, changing it forever. After all, the white men bring to Umuofia a governmental and educational structure, as well as religious practices, which many U.S. students regard as the norm; the familiar is often regarded as superior to other options.

Discussing selections from YA literature in which characters of their own age confront the realities of cultural differences, and the ways in which clashes between cultures typically result in one culture gaining power and dominance over the other, may help prepare students to read Achebe's book. Many of the stories collected by Joyce Carol Thomas in *A Gathering of Flowers* provide useful bridges to *Things Fall Apart* because of their thematic connections. Rick Wernli's "Colony," for example, helps readers imagine what it might be like if America ceased to exist when school children in Omaha react to being taken over by "the colonists." Reiko, in "After the War" by Jeanne Wakatsuki Houston, must adjust to life upon his release after three years in a Japanese-American internment camp as he faces the violence intolerance can cause. The narrator in Gerald Vizenor's "Almost a Whole Trickster" reminds readers that the Native Americans were the first Americans—Americans who had to deal with the disruption of their way of life, just as the members of Okonkwo's Ibo village did.

Another possible bridge idea is to develop sections from the opening five chapters of the book *Number the Stars* by Lois Lowry into a readers' theater presentation. Although this novel is aimed at an audience younger than high school students, Lowry's portrayal of the ways in which Nazi soldiers disrupt daily life while occupying Copenhagen is graphic and touching. Through the dramatization, as students hear the voices of the people whose stories Lowry tells, the text develops an intensity and immediacy not always felt during independent, silent reading. The soldiers are described as having faces filled with anger and hatred and as having the power of numbers and firearms on their side. In the opening chapters, readers see the soldiers interrupt a schoolgirls' foot race between Annemarie and her best friend, Ellen Rosen, whose family is Jewish. We see the reaction of their mothers to the incident. We hear how the adults and children of the two families respond when they learn that shops run by Jewish owners have been closed by the soldiers. We tremble when, at 4:00 A.M., the soldiers, in search of Ellen and her family, burst into Annemarie's bedroom, where Ellen, masquerading as Annemarie's sister, is now staying. The way in which life is disturbed and changed forever by the presence of the Nazis is told through the words of children, particularly Annemarie, so that readers have a clear and immediate understanding of the clash of cultures and the struggle for power as they affect details of daily living more familiar to readers than the details of Okonkwovs life.

After participating in or witnessing such a presentation, students may be more able to discuss their own possible responses to an alien presence in their lives. What would they fear the most about having members of another culture take over control of their own towns? What small changes might occur in the routines of their daily lives? What customs would they miss that the intruders might not value and therefore might forbid? What kind of reactions would they have to this presence? Would there be any value in open resistance? In undercover resistance? Might there be any benefits to having someone else in charge? These questions then guide the students' reading of the more difficult, less easily accessible Nigerian text.

One of the easiest elements of *Things Fall Apart* for students to relate to is Okonkwo's anger and fear. The teacher can ask students to imagine that high school graduation has come and gone. The student has left whatever home he or she has had to date. Perhaps the student has gotten married, gone to college, or has been living with other recent graduates while working. During a holiday season, perhaps Christmas or Rosh Hashanna, the student decides to return home to be with family and participate again in familiar rituals associated with the season. Ask students to freewrite about the feelings they have as they anticipate this "return." As they share their responses, they may note that there is a mixture of trepidation and eagerness in their anticipation.

After sharing their responses, the teacher continues with the scenario. Students arrive home only to find that nothing of them remains in evidence. Perhaps their room has been taken over by a younger sibling or an older relative, their place at the dining table has been moved, and there is no longer any place for their coat or any of their belongings. Perhaps when they attempt to take part in what had been the routine of the house—drying the dishes, for instance—they find that the routine no longer exists. And, to top it off, there seems to be little interest in the returning family member—conversation is now dominated by attention to a new grandchild or to some impending and monumental change in family structure. The students then freewrite individually about their feelings, having "returned" only to find that the familiar family routine they anticipated does not exist anymore. How do they feel? Whom do they blame? What is their reaction? What do they imagine are the feelings of the others in the household about their return?

After the discussion, the teacher can read an excerpt from a YA novel such as Robert Kimmel Smith's *The War with Grandpa*, in which Pete describes his feelings when he learns that his bedroom is being given to his elderly grandfather who has moved into the family home; or, the ending of S.E. Hinton's *That Was Then, This Is Now*, where Bryon describes his inner struggles as he visits his former best friend, Mark, now in a reformatory because Bryon reported his drug dealing to the police. In these examples, both young men feel the pain of being unable to return to life as it once had been. There are parallels between their pain and the pain Okonkwo feels as he anticipates returning to Umuofia: "Seven years was a long time to be away from one's clan. A man's place was not always there, waiting for him. As soon as he left, someone else rose and filled it. The clan was like a lizard; if it lost its tail, it soon grew another... ." (p. 157).

By reading aloud Chapter 20 of Achebe's book, the teacher can guide students to listen for ways in which Okonkwo's village has changed and for how he responds to these changes. Teachers can help students draw parallels to their imagined reactions with their own return "home" after a long time away. After experiencing this bridge into the novel, students should be able to concentrate on the concept of how "things fall apart" as they read the book, noting ways in which Achebe foreshadows the dissolution of Okonkwo's life from the beginning of the story.

Using Young Adult Literature to Extend and Enhance In-Common Reading of *Things Fall Apart*

We are not going to outline day-by-day lesson plans for a thematic unit based on *Things Fall Apart*. The teacher can decide how to approach the text based on his or her knowledge of the students' reading skills, how much vocabulary priming is needed, how much their reading needs to be guided and directed, how much can be read at one time, what kinds of writing activities and in-class discussion and other activities might supplement the reading, and so on. We propose that whatever approach is taken to teaching *Things Fall Apart* to the entire class, students should also be asked to read, on their own, YA novels that relate in various ways to *Things Fall Apart*.

In the case of *Things Fall Apart*, we have chosen to focus on thematic concerns, characterization, and language use. The teacher introduces the supplemental titles through booktalks. (For a useful guide to developing booktalks, read *Booktalk! Booktalking and School Visiting for Young Adult*

Audiences by Joni Bodart.) Students choose one title to read independently, and, periodically throughout the unit, students come together in one of two ways based on their choices: (1) Students who have read the same supplemental novel work in small groups, drawing parallels between their book and *Things Fall Apart*, or (2) students who have chosen different books work in small groups to generalize about and synthesize these works with the core novel. Both groups will report their findings to the class at large.

In either case, the net result is that the students acquire a deeper understanding of the core novel and gain second-hand knowledge of many other titles while practicing higher-level thinking skills. For the purposes of this chapter, we have limited our discussion to possible YA novels that might be used in conjunction with *Things Fall Apart*. We could as easily have suggested other "classics" with similar themes. In *Hamlet*, for instance, Hamlet discovers his world is out of kilter, and *Native Son* by Richard Wright also describes the kind of fear and anger resulting from cultural clashes that Achebe explores. Since *Things Fall Apart* and similar world literature "classics" from *The Odyssey* to *A Doll House* to *The Stranger* are accepted fairly easily into the literature program, we wanted to focus on the use of YA novels in conjunction with a world literature text as one means of providing students an introduction to some of the best YA writers today. Our goal in this chapter is to provide a model the teacher can use while teaching whatever piece of world literature has been included in the curriculum.

Thematic Connections

Clash of Cultures

As noted earlier, the major theme of *Things Fall Apart* is the clash of cultures. One major thesis Achebe develops is that when two cultures clash, one tends to gain dominance—and thus the other slowly disintegrates. As they read the novel, students might keep a reading log in which they cite passages where the cultural clash is evident and record Okonkwo's responses to these clashes, the responses of others in his clan, and their own reactions. Must the two cultures, that of the Ibo village and that of the white man, have clashed? Must they still? What kind of relationships should and can exist when members of two cultures live side by side? What modern parallels exist? Students can explore race relations within their own school and community and make connections.

Students may also explore other kinds of cultural clashes in their logs. In what ways, if any, is the relationship between generations—between adolescence and adulthood—a "clash of cultures"? If it is, how is the clash typically resolved? How do they feel about entering adulthood and thus moving into "another culture"? Is it possible to describe the differences between genders as a cultural one, as Deborah Tannen suggests in *You Just Don't Understand*? Their daily lives are probably, upon reflection and exploration, filled with examples of the kinds of cultural clash that affect

Okonkwo. Students can examine newspaper articles relating to these topics if a more objective approach is preferred.

In *Things Fall Apart,* because Achebe immerses his readers in the Ibo tribal life before the missionaries come, the downfall of Okonkwo is striking and disturbing. As readers, we know what is important to him and what he has worked so hard to achieve. It is clear how he, as one individual, is affected when the clashes of the two cultures occur. Okonkwo is the tragic hero who carries within himself the seeds of his own destruction. Yet, in this story, as in all great tragedies, we wonder how much he is responsible for his own tragedy and to what extent he is the victim of events resulting from the colonization of Africa, specifically of Nigeria.

Examples of books written for young adults in which the central theme is the clash of cultures include Scott O'Dell's *Sing Down the Moon* (124 pp.), where the clash is between Native Americans and white settlers; Michael Dorris' *A Yellow Raft in Blue Water* (343 pp.), also about the clash of cultures experienced by a young native American; Katherine Lasky's *Night Journey* (150 pp.), where a Jewish family must flee from Czarist Russia; and Alicia Appleman-Jurman's *Alicia: My Story* (433 pp.), where another Jewish family is forced to flee from war-ravaged Poland. Additionally, *Nervous Conditions* (204 pp.) by Tsitsi Dangarembwa; *A Grain of Wheat* (280 pp.) by Ngugi; *Kaffir Boy* (350 pp.), an autobiography by Mark Mathabane; *Waiting for the Rain* (180 pp.) and the short story collection *Coming of the Dry Season* (61 pp.), both by Charles Mungoshi, are five titles by African authors about young people coping with the "clash of cultures" in their lives that could also be used to enhance the reading of *Things Fall Apart.*

Clash of Generations

The clash of cultures Okonkwo experiences later in his life is preceded by the clash of generations—first between Okonkwo and his father, then between Okonkwo and his son Nwoye. Okonkwo's fears result from his concern about who he is. His fear "was not external but lay deep within himself. It was the fear of himself, lest he should be found to resemble his father" (p. 17). His life is dominated by the question of identity, "Which I is I?" As a youth, he considered his father a failure and, as noted earlier, he purposefully tried to be everything his gentle and idle father was not. "He had no patience with unsuccessful men. He had had no patience with (Unoka) his father" (p. 9). Okonkwo knew it was possible to forge a different identity because "fortunately, among these people a man was judged according to his worth and not according to the worth of his father" (p. 11).

Okonkwo wants his son to be a great man and a great farmer, but Nwoye prefers the stories his mother tells to any show of strength and violence. More like his grandfather than his father, Nwoye is a contrast to Ikemefuna, Okonkwo's much loved adopted son. Nwoye is also different from Ezinma, Okonkwo's favorite daughter. "If Ezinma had been a boy I would have been happier. She has the right spirit," Okonkwo acknowledges (p. 63). Okonkwo's tenderness toward Ezinma is shown when he can refuse her nothing, when he worries over her illnesses, and when he hides in the dark to follow Ezinma and her mother Ekwefi to the priestess's cave.

Yet, Okonkwo shows no outward affection to any of his three children. To do so would be a sign of weakness: "the only thing worth demonstrating was strength" (p. 30). It is no surprise that when the missionaries come to Umuofia, Nwoye is attracted to the poetry of their words. He had been haunted by the ironic killing of Ikemefuna by his own father, Okonkwo, and by tribal beliefs, especially that the Earth decrees that twins be killed. Instead, to Nwoye, "the words of the [missionaries'] hymns were like the drops of frozen rain melting on the dry palate of the panting earth" (p. 37).

Okonkwo's brooding anger and inner fears cannot survive the encounter with the tremendously different way of life the missionaries bring to the village. His pain is intensified when he realizes his own son is among the missionaries. He asks his friend Obierika why nothing is being done about the white men. Why have his people lost the power to fight? Obierika tells him it is already too late. It would be easy to drive out the two white men in Umuofia, "but what of our own people who are following their way and have been given power?" (p. 161). One of the tribal villagers voiced his fears for the younger generation who "did not understand how strong is the bond of kinship. You do not know what it is to speak with one voice. And what is the result? An abominable religion has settled among you" (p. 155).

There are numerous books for young adults in which the clash of generations is also tied to the clash of cultures. The questions of identity ("Who am I?" or "Which I is I?") occur in a confusing mixture of conflicting cultural and social values and norms. In *The Lost Garden* (117 pp.), an autobiography by Lawrence Yep, the author conveys the difficulties of such a situation: "I was the Chinese American raised in a black neighborhood, a child who had been too American to fit into Chinatown and too Chinese to fit in elsewhere. I was the clumsy son of the athletic family, the grandson of a Chinese grandmother who spoke more of West Virginia than of China" (p. 91).

Many stories show young people who wonder what the role of the past and the family's traditions and expectations play in shaping identity. When the clash of generations is a part of the clash of cultures, the young person faces a difficult crossroad. Born in Eastern Nigeria, Chinua Achebe himself grew up at the crossroad that served as the background for *Things Fall Apart*. In an interesting twist from what Okonkwo and Nwoye experience, Achebe learned Christianity from his parents as he also heard the Ibo tales from the old men of his village.

One of the examples of the universality of *Things Fall Apart* is the exploration of young people's concerns about how to separate themselves from choices made by parents (as Okonkwo did) or from the expectations of parents (as Nwoye did). Similar clashes are experienced by Shabanu, and her Muslim father in *Shabanu, Daughter of the Wind*, Louise and her beloved sister in *Jacob Have I Loved*, by Sundara and her Cambodian aunt in *Children of the River*, and by Jeanne and her Japanese father in *Farewell to Manzanar*. In each story the protagonist wonders, "To find out who I am, do I have to leave behind who I was or who my parents expect me to be?" These four books are discussed below.

Shabanu: Daughter of the Wind by Suzanne Fisher Staples (240 pp.). Living in the Cholistan desert of contemporary Pakistan, Shabanu, the 11-year-old narrator of Staples' novel, wonders how she can obey her parents and honor the traditions of many centuries and still be who she seems to be. She has no patience with housework (folding quilts and sweeping sand from the tent), and feels cross if she is kept from the camels. She loves to mend their harnesses, spin their hair into twine, and sing as Guluband, her favorite camel, dances. Her beloved Dadi reminds her that she must abide by his rules, including his decision to sell Guluband and his arrangements for her marriage. Is she a child or an adult, a docile female or free spirit in the desert? Readers understand her character better because of the way she is contrasted to her beautiful sister, just as Nwoye in *Things Fall Apart* is contrasted to his adopted brother and to his sister, Ezinma.

Jacob Have I Loved by Katherine Paterson (175 pp.). Many young people experience feelings of sibling rivalry and think a brother or sister is the favored one who fulfills all of their parents' expectations. In *Things Fall Apart* Ezinma and Ikemefuna are what Nwoye is not, and Caroline in *Jacob Have I Loved* is all that Louise is not. In Katherine Paterson's story, Louise's pretty and delicate twin sister Caroline seems to have everything, including a beautiful voice. Thirteen-year-old Louise feels like the Biblical Esau, the despised elder twin of Jacob. Contrary to the cultural expectations for young women of the Chesapeake Bay, Louise learns the ways of the watermen, longing to be the son her father needs. "I would have given anything to be that son, but on Rass in those days, men's work and women's work were sharply divided, and a waterman's boat was not the place for a girl" (p. 23). Louise—like Shabanu who prefers to be outdoors doing men's work—loves to be on the water, collecting crabs and oysters. She knows what happens as crabs shed their shells; she identifies with the she-crabs: "Males ... always have a chance to live no matter how short their lives, but females, ordinary, ungifted ones, just get soft and die" (p. 133). Her search for identity takes her through clashes with her grandmother, who attempts to teach Louise by spouting Biblical verses at her. Much of her struggle, like Okonkwo's, is internal, which would allow for interesting comparisons to be made.

Children of the River by Linda Crew (213 pp.). *Children of the River* begins as Sundara, along with her aunt's family, must suddenly flee Cambodia to escape the Khmer Rouge army. Four years later, while living in Oregon, her clashes involve struggling between allegiance to her past life and culture and allegiance to Jonathan, the American boy who loves her. He cannot understand that she is forbidden to be with him because nice

Cambodian girls do not go on dates. She wonders who she is. Not only had she left her beautiful homeland—along with her parents, brother, sister, and boyfriend—behind, "she'd left her whole self behind, that laughing girl who had run along the sparkling sand beaches" (p. 57). Her aunt Soka, who feels responsible for bringing up Sundara in the traditional way, accuses her of being too American, while "at school she felt painfully aware of not being American enough. She didn't fit in anywhere" (pg. 81).

   Farewell to Manzanar by Jeanne Wakatsuki Houston and James Houston (177 pp.). Jeanne Wakatsuki and her family were part of the 120,000 people of Japanese ancestry living in the United States who were rounded up and held in detention camps from 1941 until the end of World War II. In *Farewell to Manzanar*, Jeanne tells how her coming of age occurs at the camp in Arizona where she and her family were forced to live for over three years. She struggles to define herself as an American citizen with a proud, well-educated Japanese papa who wants her to study Odori, traditional Japanese dancing. She wants desperately to be accepted, "and baton twirling was one trick [Jeanne] could perform that was thoroughly, unmistakably American" (p. 79). She yearns for things pictured in the Sears, Roebuck catalogue, sings "The Battle Hymn of the Republic" with the Glee Club, and participates in the Catholic Church. Back in California, the sting of internment has left her with the urge to disappear, yet she also wants to belong. Although the Girl Scouts reject her, Jeanne learns how to be noticed. Did she give away her identity when she was elected as her high school Homecoming Queen? Who was she then, she wonders.

   There are in these books, as in *Things Fall Apart*, issues of how young adults must craft a future out of a balance between traditional ways and the ways of the system in which they have been educated. Sundara and Jeanne, like Okonkwo, are keen observers of the culture that surrounds them. They all have to make decisions about what defines who they are. Yet, like Nwoye, they make choices that defy their families. Shabanu, the "daughter of the wind," also struggles, since what she would like to do conflicts with what her father dictates. Her struggle—as well as Louise's struggle—includes a reversal of the roles that males and females are expected to fulfill, something that permeates *Things Fall Apart* when Okonkwo is careful not to do "women's work" and where his disappointment in Nwoye results from his son's being too much like a woman.

Character Connections

   Okonkwo is clearly the main character in *Things Fall Apart*. And yet, because Achebe uses the third-person point of view, the reader at times enters into the mind of other characters, viewing the events of the plot and Okonkwo himself as others do. Students could work in groups to develop character charts about the various persons who inhabit Achebe's pages. As they read, they can add details about the characters' personalities, emotional reactions to events, views of others, others' responses to them, and physical traits, exploring in the process how a character is developed by an author. We learn a great deal about Okonkwo, for instance, during an incident in which one of his wives, Ekwefi, is the primary character as she reflects on her earliest impressions of her then husband-to-be and on how he has not changed much since she first ran away to be with him (pp. 90–103). *Beyond the Divide* by Kathryn Lasky, *We All Fall Down* and *After the First Death* by Robert Cormier, and *Celine* by Brock Cole are YA novels that could be paired with *Things Fall Apart* because of the methods of characterization used by the authors.

Beyond the Divide by Kathryn Lasky (254 pp.)

Beyond the Divide, like *Things Fall Apart*, is a story in which the main character is viewed against the backdrop of a changing nation. Much of the characterization is established through the characters' actions. In 1849, Meribah Simon and her father leave their Amish community in Pennsylvania after he is shunned for attending the funeral of a friend who was not a strict Amish. Will Simon, like Okonkwo, now can no longer stay in his native village. The difference is that Will and Meribah will never be able to return. Although the settings and characters are very different, readers will see many parallels with *Things Fall Apart*. Both stories, told in third-person point of view, are vivid portrayals of how characters react to a series of events, many of them the direct result of decisions based on the laws or "rules" that govern a group of people.

Beyond the Divide begins because of a clash based on differing beliefs. Clashes continue to occur as the wagon train journeys west, both among members of the wagon train community and with the Indians encountered along the way. The characterization of 14-year-old Meribah Simon is revealed first by her choice to leave her home with her father and subsequently by her reactions to a multitude of events as they travel west. She must face dangerous river crossings, mountain climbs, dwindling amounts of food and water, the threat of attack, the rape of her friend Serena, and most importantly, her father's illness. Will is always willing to stop and help others when their wagons break down. Yet, when he is too sick to travel, he and Meribah are abandoned in the desert, and Meribah has to cope with that fact.

Meribah must live with many fears, as did Okonkwo: "She was thinking about all the fears that people had had on the journey so far: fear of Indians, fear of drought, fear of massacring Mormons, fear of cholera, fear of bad water. Yet no one had spoken of this fear, the nameless one that was within, with the hollow square, within the wagons, within the people" (p. 116). Her greatest fear occurs when she must survive alone in the Sierra Nevada.

Also, like *Things Fall Apart*, this story includes a host of characters. A picture of each is established through the author's portrayal of their physical traits, their different personalities, contrasting emotional reactions to events, how they treat each other, what they say, and what is said to them. Meribah is a vivid contrast to many of the members of the wagon train, particularly to Serena Billings whose "refined" mother is both charmed by and appalled at Meribah's plain ways; Meribah, for example, does not wear a hat to protect her complexion. After Serena is raped by the evil Timm brothers, Meribah is the only one who will visit her. Others will not even use Serena's name. When Serena's dreamy world falls apart, Meribah's friendship with her is as strong as Obierika's, Okonkwa's best friend, when Okonkwo is an outsider.

We All Fall Down by Robert Cormier (193 pp.)

Young adults can read a variety of well-written books with very different settings and plots, stories with a host of characters who react in different ways when "things fall apart." Another example is *We All Fall Down*, a story about random violence. This story, also told in third person, shows how the various characters react to violence: the family whose home is vandalized, the various young men who committed the crime, and the strange observer who saw it happen. Cormier's story about the unexpected ways people's lives connect is another example of his craft, as is his use of the image of falling apart or falling down, which echoes Achebe's. Jane realizes how things have changed, and she wonders if her family can endure: "Jane got the shivers again as she had that day, but worse now. Middle-of-the-night worse. She shivered, not from the cold, but from a sense of dread. She remembered a poem from school: 'things fall apart, the center cannot hold.' Her family falling apart and her father, at the center. Could he hold them together? If he couldn't, who could?" (p. 76). At the end of the story, when the Avenger is threatening to kill her, Jane takes charge of the situation and does something—as Meribah does while in the desert and as Okonkwo does early in his life, when he, beginning with seed yams, gradually accumulates wealth.

What Lasky and Cormier share with Achebe is the craft involved in exploring theme through characterization. The question of identity, of who someone really is, cannot be explored if the author has not drawn well-developed characters. Buddy in Cormier's story struggles with achieving a masculine social role, as does Okonkwo. Buddy wonders if a young man has to be capable of inflicting violence on others, a question Nwoye certainly struggles with. Who is the real Buddy? Is he the one Jane sees, or is he the Buddy who is fighting alcoholism and who destroys the property of others? Students reading both the Cormier and Achebe texts should be able to discuss the ways in which character and theme are related in general and to compare the craft of these two authors in developing theme through character.

After the First Death by Robert Cormier (233 pp.)

Parents—what happens to them, what they do and expect, and the way young protagonists react to their expectations—are key parts of many young adult stories, as is true in *Things Fall Apart*. This Cormier novel also shows how theme is connected to characterization. The father-son relationships between Miro and Arkin and between Ben and his father, General Marchand, are as complex as those in Achebe's story, and the variety of characters is as well-developed. Is Arkin the real father of Miro? Who is alive at the end of the story—Ben or General Marchand? Parallels can be drawn in both stories about how the fathers are willing to sacrifice their sons for a cause or belief. Ultimately, neither Ben nor Miro can be all their fathers expect them to be. Kate is another fully developed character. When she and her busload of children are taken hostage by Miro, a chain of events is set in motion resulting in Kate's being a victim—just as Ikemefuna, Okonkwo's adopted son, is in Achebe's story.

Celine by Brock Cole

Who is Celine? Her family has fallen apart. In Brock Cole's novel, 16-year-old Celine is as concerned with her own identity as Okonkwo was at age 18, and she is as much alone in her struggle. She lives with her young, irresponsible step-mother. She does not have a parent who attempts to determine her identity—only the words of her father who tells her she must "show a little maturity" (p. 18) by the time he returns from a lecture tour in Europe. The changes in her feelings about her painting "Test Patterns," which serves as an analogy for who she is, mark her growing understanding about her own identity. *Celine* is an interesting novel to contrast with *Things Fall Apart* because it is told in first person and is more an example of irony than tragedy.

Language Connections

One of the interesting aspects of the way Achebe tells his tale, which is indicative of the oral traditions of the Nigerian culture, is the way he has different characters tell stories themselves. Through story, older clansmen teach the younger members, as Uchendu, Okonkwo's uncle, does in chapter 13 (pp. 122–125). In this passage, Uchendu tells about the clan custom of calling children Nneka, or "Mother is Supreme." Uchendu tells about bringing a woman who has died back to her own kinsmen, a story which, in context, serves to remind Okonkwo that, after all, seven years exile is not so much to bear. Through story, the clan is entertained and brought together in common experience, as is the case when Ekwefi tells the story of the tortoise and the birds (pp. 91–94).

Students could be asked to participate in storytelling activities for similar purposes. They might each prepare a short fable reflecting their own cultural background that they then "tell" to the rest of the class or to a small group. The audience members ask questions, as Ekwefi's daughter does, to prompt the storyteller into elaboration. Or, students might transcribe stories they have heard from a member of an older generation who was attempting to teach them a lesson of some sort.

There are other aspects of Achebe's writing that reflect his Nigerian heritage. Ask students to identify passages where the sentence structure or use of language seems different from their own language use. When Okonkwo is despairing about the choice of his son, Nwoye, to join the missionary school, he laments:

> He, Okonkwo, was called a flaming fire. 'How could he have begotten a woman for a son?'...He sighed heavily, and as if in sympathy the smoldering log also sighed. And immediately Okonkwo's eyes were opened and he saw the whole matter clearly. Living fire begets cold, impotent ash. He sighed again, deeply. (p. 143)

In this passage, for instance, Okonkwo uses an analogy between himself and the natural world to explain something he otherwise finds inexplicable. Achebe and his characters frequently use the tool of analogy to make a point. Students could record examples from the novel and attempt to write their reflections on some topic—perhaps a self-reflection—using this device.

Another frequent conversational element is Achebe's use of the rhetorical question, as when Okonkwo's friend Obierika is telling him about why the people of Umuofia have not fought the missionaries in Okonkwo's absence (p. 161). Also, Achebe's sentences tend to be short, of the subject-verb-completer variety. Students can discuss the effect these short sentences have on them as readers. The overall effect is almost fatalistic—the sentence structure in a way imitates the response of the people to the encroachment of the white men on their way of life. Students could attempt to write a descriptive piece of their own imitating Achebe's sentence structure, then using a more natural method, and finally comparing the effect of the two styles on the reader.

When readers explore an author's use of language, the focus must be on how stylistic choices have influenced the story. The exploration begins with how a reader's response is affected by the word and syntactic choices. The language must reflect the setting and be consistent with the characterization. For example, it would not have been authentic for Meribah and Will Simon in *Beyond the Divide* to speak the same way as the Billings from Philadelphia or as the other members of the wagon train speak. Meribah's use of the word "coupling" shocks Serena at first. Then Serena laughs and says, "Oh, farm girl! I forgot!" (p. 80). Their reaction to each other's speech reveals character traits and backgrounds. The way they use language also gives a more complete picture of who they are. *A Day No Pigs Would Die, A Hero Ain't Nothin' But a Sandwich*, and *The Moves Make the*

Man provide useful companions to *Things Fall Apart* because of the way language is used to reflect character, setting, and theme. Additionally, texts by Virginia Hamilton and Sandra Cisneros, as well as *Shadows across the Sun* by Likhanov, translated from Russian into English, could also be used.

A Day No Pigs Would Die by Robert Newton Peck (144 pp.)

This book is a fine example that shows how language and story are connected. Twelve-year-old Rob, through his dialogue and thoughts, reveals the Shaker culture of rural Vermont during the 1920s. As the story begins, Rob has left school because Edward Thatcher "made sport" of him. Someday, thinks Rob, he would "light into Edward Thatcher, and make him bleed like a stuck pig. I'd kick him from one end of Vermont to the other, and sorry him good" (p. 7). Other examples of colloquial expressions include "burdened" for carried, "don't cotton to" for dislike, and "owed up to silence" for being quiet. Rob lives with his elderly parents in a community where good friends "front name one another" (p. 135), and the nature around them is one measure of "richness."

Rob's descriptions reflect the setting and his youthful reactions to events. One day he watches a hawk as the clouds above him turn orange, "like when Mama poured peach juice on the large curds of white potcheese" (p. 61). In October, Rob and his beloved pet pig, Pinky, play outside, where the colors are "as pretty as laundry on the line" (p. 116). The understated way the characters express emotion and the words they use to show they will accept what must be done merits exploration.

A Hero Ain't Nothin But a Sandwich by Alice Childress (128 pp.)

Another outstanding example of how an author uses language to tell a story is *A Hero Ain't Nothin' But a Sandwich*. The viewpoints and voices of ten different characters are heard in various chapters, but the story, though, is primarily Benji's. He begins:

> Now I am thirteen, but when I was a chile, it was hard to be a chile because my block is a tough block and my school is a tough school. I'm not trying to cop out on what I do or don't do cause man is man and chile is chile, but I ain't a chile no more....My block ain't no place to be a chile in peace. Ain't no letrit light bulb in my hallway....You best get over bein seven or eight, right soon... (p. 9)

This book, challenging both emotionally and intellectually, provides several comparisons and contrasts to *Things Fall Apart* in addition to the language use. The protagonist's internal and external struggles are evident, along with considerations about who is responsible for things that happen around him.

The Moves Make the Man by Bruce Brooks (280 pp.)

Benji's life is very different from Jerome Foxworthy's, the precocious 13-year-old who tells the story of his friend Bix in this novel. Jerome not only speaks in a way that sounds authentic—"It's me gets to tell the truth" (p. 5)—he also comments about his skills in language: "I got seven straight grades of all A's in English, six in black schools that were harder than the white one, which nobody believes" (p. 6). Jerome prepares to tell the story with "plenty of pencils, number threes, all sharp and dark green enamel on the outside, and I have four black and white marble composition books" (p. 3). He "took right to the idea of French class, and I took right to the lingo itself too...I never realized before then how much my way of talking was what made me who I thought and other people thought I was" (p. 60). It is interesting to consider the effect on the reader of Brooks' decision to use no quotation marks and of his use of vivid sensory details: the smell of Bix's baseball glove, of mock apple pie, the "bammata" sounds of Jerome's basketball, the "Bawoomawett" rhythm of his favorite tune, and the color of the golden "spin light."

Bix's family has fallen apart—a vivid contrast to Jerome's close, loving family. Yet this serious story about the nature of truth, of prejudice, and of mental illness, contains light-hearted counterbalancing of stereotypes and many humorous passages. For example, Jerome describes what it would be like if he entered the white First Baptist church: "That would have been a sight, this skinny kid black as a clarinet wailing out a licorice tune right there on the light blue carpet aisle cutting off the organ with the fake pipes just as it wheezed into one of their wavery old hymns" (p. 4).

Whereas Okonkwo uses the natural world to understand himself, Jerome uses the game of basketball and the moves he has taught himself to explore who he is. The "spin light," a railroad lantern he wins with his basketball skill, is a symbol that brightens a dark basketball court and much more. Students could be guided to explore the use of symbolism in this text and *Things Fall Apart* as part of lessons focused on the authors' use of language.

Other Thematic Unit Topics and Related Young Adult Literature

The approaches we have outlined in these pages assist young adult readers in developing fairly deep understandings of *Things Fall Apart*. As they compare and contrast Achebe's book with YA texts written specifically for a young adult audience, texts to which they can more readily relate, they are able to connect on a more personal level to Okonkwo's life experiences. In a similar fashion, teachers can develop other thematic units based on a piece of non-Western literature and enhanced through the use of literature for young adults. Several resources useful in helping to choose books and develop activities for such units include the following: *Against Borders:*

Promoting Books for a Multicultural World by Hazel Rochman; NCTE's *Guide to World Literature* edited by Warren Carrier; "Glasnost in the Classroom," an article by Lois Stover and Rita Karr; and *Multicultural Teaching: A Handbook of Activities, Information and Resources* by the Tiedts. To end this chapter, we offer several possible thematic concepts and related titles as starting points for developing additional units centered on "classics" of world literature.

The Artist in Society

Classic Text: *Letters to a Young Poet* by Rainer Maria Rilke

Supporting YA texts: *Shizuko's Daughter* (227 pp.) by Kyoko Mori, *Come Sing, Jimmy Jo* (197 pp.) by Katherine Paterson, *In Summer Light* (160 pp.) by Zibby Oneal, *I Juan de Pareja* (180 pp.) by Elizabeth de Trevino, *Midnight Hour Encores* (263 pp.) by Bruce Brooks.

The Individual vs. the State

Classic Texts: *An Enemy of the People* by Henrik Ibsen, The Stranger by Camus, or *One Day in the Life of Ivan Denisovich* by Aleksandr Solzhenitsyn

Supporting YA texts: *Bless the Beasts and the Children* (205 pp.) by Glendon Swarthout, *The Sound of Dragons' Feet* (113 pp.) by Alki Zee, *A Handful of Stars* (195 pp.) by Rafik Schami, *Rice without Rain* (236 pp.) by Minfong Ho, *The True Confessions of Charlotte Doyle* (215 pp.) by Avi, *The Day They Came to Arrest the Book* (169 pp.) by Nat Hentoff, *After the First Death* (233 pp.) and *I am the Cheese* (233 pp.) by Robert Cormier.

The Quest

Classic Texts: *The Epic of Gilgamesh*, "The Lay of Thrym," *Les Miserables* by Victor Hugo, or *The Adventures of Tom Sawyer* by Mark Twain

Supporting YA texts: *The Leopard* (186 pp.) by Cecil Bodkir, *Dove* (199 pp.) by Robin Lee Graham, *Vision Quest* (128 pp.) by Pamela Service, *Tehanu* (226 pp.) by Ursula Le Guin, and *Park's Quest* (148 pp.) by Katherine Paterson.

Dealing with Death

Classic text: *Mother Courage and Her Children* by Bertolt Brecht

Supporting YA texts: *Bridge to Terabithia* (128 pp.) by Katherine Paterson, *Two Weeks with the Queen* (144 pp.) by Morris Gleitzman, *Remembering the Good Times* (181 pp.) by Richard Peck, *A Day No Pigs Would Die* (144 pp.) by Robert Newton Peck, *The Rain Catchers* (182 pp.) by Jean Thesman, *My Brother Stealing Second* (213 pp.) by Jim Naughton, *After the Rain* (291 pp.) by Norma Fox Mazer, and *A Ring of Endless Light* (332 pp.) by Madeleine L'Engle.

Survival

Classic texts: *Waiting for Godot* **by Samuel Beckett or** *All Quiet on the Western Front* **by Erich Maria Remarque**

Supporting YA texts: *Hatchet* (195 pp.) by Gary Paulson, *The Hostage* (171 pp.) by Anne Holme, *The Girl in the Box* (166 pp.) by Ouida Sebastyen, *The Goats* (184 pp.) by Brock Cole, *The Cigarette Sellers of Three Crosses Square* (166 pp.) by Joseph Ziemian, *The Faces of Ceti* by Mary Caraker (208 pp.), *So Far from the Bamboo Grove* (192 pp.) by Yoko Kawashima Watkins.

List of References

Achebe, C. (1991). *Things fall apart*. New York: Fawcett Crest.

Appleman-Jurman, A. (1990). *Alicia: My story*. New York: Bantam.

Avi. (1990). *The true confessions of Charlotte Doyle*. New York: Avon.

Beckett, S. (1987). *Waiting for Godot*. New York: Chelsea House.

Bodart, J. (1980). *Booktalk! Booktalking and school visiting for young adult audiences*. New York: H.W. Wilson.

Bodker, C. (1975). *The leopard*. Translated by Gunnar Poulsen. New York: Atheneum.

Brecht, B. (1963). *Mother Courage and her children: A chronicle of the Thirty Years' War*. Adapted by Eric Bentley. New York: Samuel French.

Brooks, B. (1986). *Midnight hour encores*. New York: Harper Keypoint.

Brooks, B. (1984). *The moves make the man*. New York: Harper & Row.

Camus, A. (1954). *The stranger*. New York: Random House.

Caraker, M. (1991). *The faces of Ceti*. Boston: Houghton Mifflin.

Carrier, W. (Ed.). (1980). *Guide to world literature*. Urbana, IL: National Council of Teachers of English.

Childress, A. (1973). *A hero ain't nothin' but a sandwich*. New York: Avon.

Cisneros, S. (1988). *The house on mango street*. Houston, TX: Arte.

Cole, B. (1989). *Celine*. New York: Farrar, Straus & Giroux.

Cole, B. (1987). *The goats*. New York: Farrar, Straus & Giroux.

Cormier, R. (1991). *We all fall down*. New York: Delacorte Press.

Cormier, R. (1979). *After the first death*. New York: Avon.

Cormier, R. (1977). *I am the cheese*. New York: Dell.

Crew, L. (1990). *Children of the river*. New York: Delacorte Press.

Dangarembwa, T. (1989). *Nervous conditions*. Seattle, WA: Seal Press.

de Trevino, E. (1965). *I, Juan de Pareja*. New York: Farrar, Straus & Giroux.

Dorris, M. (1988). *A yellow raft in blue water*. New York: Warner Books.

The Epic of Gilgamesh. (1960). Translated by N.K. Sandars. New York: Penguin Classics.

Farrell, E. (1966, January). Listen my children and you shall read. *English Journal*, 55 (1), 39–45.

Gleitzman, M. (1990). *Two weeks with the queen*. London: Macmillan.

Gordon, S. (1989). *Waiting for the rain*. New York: Bantam.

Graham, R.L. (1972). *Dove*. New York: Harper & Row.

Hamilton, V. (1985). *Junius over far*. New York: HarperCollins.

Hamilton, V. (1979). *Arilla sun down*. New York: Dell.

Hentoff, N. (1982). *The day they came to arrest the book*. New York: Delacorte Press.

Hinton, S.E. (1971). *That was then, this is now*. New York: Dell.

Ho, M. (1990). *Rice without rain*. New York: Lothrop, Lee, & Shepard.

Holme, A. (1980). *The hostage*. Translated by Patricia Crampton. London: Methuen.

Homer. (1963). *The odyssey*. Translated by Robert Fitzgerald. New York: Anchor Books.

Houston, J.W. & Houston, J.D. (1990). *Farewell to Manzanar*. New York: Bantam.

Hugo, V. (1938). *Les Miserables*. Translated by Lascalles Wraxall. New York: The Heritage Press.

Ibsen, H. (1951). *An enemy of the people*. Adapted by Arthur Miller. New York: Viking.

Ibsen, H. (1992). *A doll house*. In *Four Major Plays, Volume I*. New York: Signet Classics, 43–114.

Lasky, K. (1983). *Beyond the divide*. New York: Macmillan.

Lasky, K. (1981). *Night journey*. London: Puffin.

The Lay of Thrym. From the *Elder Edda*. (1969) Translated by Paul B. Taylor & W.H. Auden. New York: Random House.

Le Guin, U. (1990). *Tehanu*. New York: Atheneum.

L'Engle, M. (1980). *A ring of endless light*. New York: Dell.

Likhanov, A. (1983). *Shadows across the sun*. New York: Harper & Row.

Lowry, L. (1989). *Number the stars*. New York: Bantam.

Mathabane, M. (1986). *Kaffir boy: The true story of a black youth's coming of age in apartheid South Africa*. New York: Plume.

Mazer, N.F. (1987). *After the rain*. New York: William Morrow.

Mongoshi, C. (1972). *Coming of the dry season*. Nairobi: Oxford University Press.

Mongoshi, C. (1975). *Waiting for the rain*. London: Heinemann Educational.

Mori, K. (1993). *Shizuko's daughter*. New York: Fawcett Juniper.

Naughton, J. (1989). *My brother stealing second*. New York: Harper & Row.

Ngugi. (1967). *A grain of wheat*. Portsmouth, NH: Heinemann.

O'Dell, S. (1990). *Sing down the moon*. New York: Dell Laurel-Leaf.

Oneal, Z. (1986). *In summer light*. New York: Bantam.

Paterson, K. (1988). *Park's quest*. New York: E.P. Dutton.

Paterson, K. (1986). *Come sing, Jimmy Jo*. New York: E.P. Dutton.

Paterson, K. (1980). *Bridge to Terabithia*. New York: Avon.

- From 1985 to 2000, the U.S. youth population (0–18) will increase by 4.5 million minority youths—2.4 million Hispanics; 1.7 million blacks; 483,000 Asian or other—compared to 60,000 whites.

- By the year 2000, these states will have minority populations that will exceed more than half of the state's population: Washington, D.C. 93.2%, Hawaii 79.5%, New Mexico 76.5%, Texas 56.9%, California 56.9%, Florida 53.0%, New York 52.8%, and Louisiana 50.3%.

- By the year 2000, California, Texas, and Florida will gain enough seats in the U.S. House of Representatives to prevent any new piece of legislation from being passed.

Now examine that data in light of the following data (Kaywell, 1993, p. 161) about kids in school:

- More high school students said that they would join in or silently support a racial confrontation than said they would condemn or try to stop one. (Harris Poll, 1990)

- Klanwatch, a project of the Southern Poverty Law Center, documented more than 270 incidents of hate crimes in schools and colleges during 1992; more than half of them were committed by teenagers. (O'Neil, 1993)

- Approximately 20% to 25% of students are victimized by racial or ethnic incidents in the course of a school year. (National Institute Against Prejudice and Violence, 1992)

According to Applebee (1993), the curriculum is "dominated by familiar selections drawn primarily from a white (99%), male (86%), Anglo Saxon tradition...[and] the overall proportions of selections by minorities (1%) and women (14%) remain low in public schools" (pp. 60–64). It is not surprising that many middle and secondary teachers feel awkward and tentative about introducing literature they've never studied that is representative of countries they know little about. In fact, Applebee's study revealed that following "literary merit," the second most important criterion for selecting literature, cited by 80% of the teachers in the public school sample, was "personal familiarity with the selection" (p. 79).

Reader-Response Theory and Collaborative Groups

Current reader-response theory suggests that teachers need to help students learn how to interpret text and make meanings for themselves, rather than to interpret text for them. In many ways, the push for comprehensive world literature courses has presented a unique opportunity for teachers. Teachers can choose to follow the prescriptive "answer-the-questions-at-the-end-of-the-book" method inherent in most anthologies or model reader-response methods for students by experiencing the theory themselves.

As early as 1938, Louise Rosenblatt argued that it was important to consider the role of the reader when constituting meaning from a text. In 1978, she argued more forcibly that it was not as important that students get "correct answers" as it was that they experience literature for themselves. Reader-response theory is concerned with how readers make meaning from their transaction or experience with a text. According to Richard Beach,

> Knowledge is perceived not as a fixed, external entity to be imparted from teacher to student; rather it is mutually constructed and verified through social interaction. And within the context of the classroom as an "interpretive community," students learn to share certain common assumptions and strategies specific to the classroom as a social community. (p. 118)

Carlsen and Sherrill (1988) posit that the best atmosphere for the study of literature is one in which students have a vehicle for sharing personal responses. As it is now used, the traditional book report is too restrictive. Required readings should include both modern and classic works that permit a variety of interpretations (pp. 105–107). And above all, such an atmosphere should include, to the greatest extent possible, opportunities for freedom of choice in selecting literary works because it is "not necessary for everyone in the class to read the same book at the same time" (Purves, Rogers, & Soter; 1990, p. 65). Thus, the organization of the comprehensive world literature course described here emphasizes students' abilities to select, develop, and defend their interpretations of various literary selections from around the world.

Setting Up the Class

The design of this world literature course may be a unique experience for both you and your students because you will not choose the literature nor will you tell students what it means. Instead, part of the class's learning will be learning how to select representative, good pieces of literature and how to negotiate their interpretations with others. Using reader-response techniques and collaborative learning methods will help broaden students' understanding of themselves and of other cultures by appreciating their common bonds and celebrating their unique differences. Because world literature encompasses more than Western European literature, the course described here is designed to emphasize, but is not restricted to, the study of Eastern literature.

Objectives of the Course

Students Will Be Able To

1. Choose, read, and discuss representative literature from different cultures.

2. Engage in reader-response activities in order to enhance their own abilities to interpret literature.

3. Negotiate their own interpretations with peers in order to see that some interpretations are more true to the text than others.

4. Understand their own culture better by comparing and contrasting it with others.

5. Develop their multicultural perspectives by appreciating the common experiences we share and valuing the unique differences present in the world.

6. Acquaint themselves with all varieties of literature from around the world.

7. Improve their booktalking skills.

8. Develop their creativity by preparing alternative book reports.

Course Requirements

Individual Selection of Country and Representative Literature

Students must choose one country of interest to study other than their own. Because the United States is rich with people from different cultures, encourage your students to talk to someone they know whose family is from a different country. In their discussions, ask what literature—novels, poems, fairy tales, plays, and so forth—is representative of that country; where one can go to purchase such literature; and why certain works are more valued than others. If students don't know anyone from a different country and have no friends who know anyone from another country, have them note that fact for their own information and refer them to the prepared bibliography for suggestions (See Figure 6-1 on pages 123-136). For additional titles, refer to Lindgren's *The Multicolored Mirror: Cultural Substance Literature for Children and Young Adults* (195 pp.), Miller-Lachmann's *Our Family, Our Friends, Our World: An Annotated Guide to Significant Multicultural Books for Children and Teenagers* (710 pp.), and

Rochman's *Against Borders: Promoting Books for a Multicultural World* (288 pp.).

Another possibility is to have students choose a story from Janet Bode's *New Kids on the Block: Oral Histories of Immigrant Teens* (126 pp.). Bode presents the oral histories of 11 teenagers whose families emigrated to the United States from Cuba, El Salvador, India, Viet Nam, and other countries, often under harrowing circumstances. These teens share their feelings about leaving loved ones behind, feeling alone amidst a bunch of strangers, and wanting to fit in but not wanting to lose their cultural identities, and they talk about their dreams for the future. Exposure to these stories is likely to instill interest in students who do not have a compelling reason for studying a particular country.

Once students have selected their countries, group them according to the country they have chosen—not by ability—to formulate learning teams. Have students read and provide documentation of their reading of the equivalent of six representative novels of one country per learning team. Students' reading should not be limited to novels. Help students determine how many short stories equal a novel, how many combinations of poems and fairy tales equal a novel, and so on. During their reading, students should identify four outstanding works of literature that meet the following criteria:

1. One "novel" must be considered a classic piece of literature of the country they have chosen to study.

2. One "novel" must be a contemporary piece of literature of that country.

3. One "novel" must be nonfiction representative of that country.

4. One "novel" must deal with that country's infusion into the United States. For example, if students choose to study Vietnamese literature, then one novel must be written about a Vietnamese-American.

5. At least two of the four "novels" must have a young adult protagonist.

Students should type a plot summary of each of these four works on a single page and make copies for the rest of the class (See Figure 6-2 on page 137). Instruct students that their summaries should not spoil others' reading of the work, and teach students how to give a short booktalk on each of their selections in order to entice their classmates into reading at least one. By comparing "what you say during a booktalk" with "what you say when you want a friend to see a movie you're excited about," you can usually get across to students the message that they must not tell too much. Having students read six "novels," but only telling about four increases the likelihood that students will share selections they are genuinely excited about.

Each learning team tells why they selected their particular country (if pertinent), distributes the required handout to the class, gives a booktalk on each of the literary works, and tells how they found representative literature. Information about specialty stores where certain literature can be purchased should be mentioned if possible.

Expanding the Experience: Reading and Responding to a Selection from Each Country

After a learning team presents its booktalk, each individual in the class reads one of the four "novels" presented by that team and keeps a reader-response journal.   Students must accomplish two primary tasks in their response journals: (1) They must prove that they read the book in its entirety, and (2) they must connect it to their own lives in some meaningful way.   For classes that are unfamiliar with reader-response journals, it is advisable to give them starter questions such as the following: If the protagonist were your best friend, what advice would you give? Have you ever read, seen, or heard about someone in a similar circumstance? Who in the novel would you like to have as a friend? Why? Copy a passage you like and comment on it.

The learning team that selected the country and presented the literary works should be ready to share information about the country that will heighten the class's ability to discuss the literature.   The class's experience can be enhanced through guest speakers, maps, food, music, film, newspaper clippings, articles of clothing, and so forth.   The teacher and class should contribute as much as possible, but it is the role of the learning team to ensure a positive experience for the class.

Evaluation

For a Grade of C, all students must do the following:

1. Learning teams read the equivalent of six representative "novels" of a particular country and provide documentation of that reading.

2. Learning teams prepare a handout for the class about the four "novels" that meet the five criteria as described above; prepare one for the teacher about the other two books not mentioned.

3. Learning teams give booktalks on the four "novels."

4. Each member of the class reads and keeps a reader-response journal on a "novel" chosen from each learning team's presentation.

5. Each member of the class completes one alternative book report (See Figure 6-3 on pages 138–141) for any "novel" read as part of the class.

For a grade of B, all students must complete 1–5 and the following:

6. Learning teams prepare a presentation representative of their country (guest speakers, maps, food, music, film, newspaper clippings, articles of clothing, and the like).

For a grade of A, all students must complete 1–6 in a superior manner and ONE of the following (either individually or in learning teams):

7. Complete alternative book reports for all of the "novels" read.
    OR

8. Find, read, summarize, and respond to 20 newspaper, magazine, or journal articles about any country studied.
    OR

9. Write a literary analysis of any selection.
    OR

10. Write a short term paper about some aspect of any country studied. If someone chose African literature, a possible research topic might be "The Rise of Apartheid in South Africa."
    OR

11. Read and respond to three additional "novels" presented by a learning team of one country other than your own.
    OR

12. Develop a project related to a specific country that has been studied. Students should discuss their ideas with the teacher and are encouraged to work in their learning teams if possible.

When you let students develop their own projects, they often generate new ideas that you might never have considered. My favorite ones to date are from learning teams that studied Polynesian and South African literature. The learning team that studied Polynesian literature went to AAA and obtained a film that highlighted the beauty of Hawaii. They turned off the sound and, while the class watched, they read excerpts from the literature they had read. It was just beautiful! Another learning team set up a simulation of South Africa's apartheid, and then set up a conference call with an eloquent South African gentleman. His message: "Until everyone is free, no one is free."

Grading

I have found that grade contracts work well with this particular course. Students know exactly what they are expected to do for an "A," "B," or "C," and they can choose their own courses of action. I recommend grading all activities on a satisfactory and unsatisfactory basis. If they are deemed unsatisfactory, provide students an opportunity to redo them. Contracts determine their grades, but the teacher determines the quality. If students fulfill the requirements for an "A," but the work is shoddy and they choose not to redo various assignments, then lower their grades by one or two letters. To keep things simple, encourage students to fulfill the requirements of each assignment to the best of their abilities and have them complete weekly self-evaluations on their progress. Unexcused absences should have a negative impact on students' grades since this class is highly participatory in nature. In my experience, however, students usually exceed my expectations by reading way beyond the requirements; ownership has a way of getting people involved.

Conclusion

When you teach a world literature course using the model described here, "the reader seeks to participate in another's vision—to reap knowledge of the world, to fathom the resources of the human spirit, to gain insights that will make [the reader's] own life more comprehensible" (Rosenblatt, 1938, p. 7). Literature makes it possible to vicariously experience others' circumstances and to observe the myriad ways different people make meaning of their own lives. In 1938, Rosenblatt said that "in a turbulent age, our schools and colleges must prepare the student to meet unprecedented and unpredictable problems... . Young people everywhere are asking, 'What do the things that we are offered in school and college mean for the life we are living or going to live?'" (pp. 4–5). They've been asking for more than 50 years. Isn't it time that we heard our students' pleas?

Figure 6-1
World Literature: Annotated Fiction and NonFiction Books & Novels

African/African-American

    Classic Text: *Things Fall Apart* **by Chinua Achebe**
    Supporting YA Texts
    Song of Be by Lesley Beake (94 pp.). Love, courage, and dignity are universal themes that permeate this South African novel. Be, a young Bushman in Namibia, is sorting out her own coming-of-age issues against the backdrop of a country undergoing political reform.

    The Middle of Somewhere: A Story of South Africa by Sheila Gordon (152 pp.). Rebecca lives in constant fear and has nightmares about the white people coming to bulldoze her village for development purposes. All of the black families are supposed to be moved to "the middle of somewhere" where work, shelter, and food are difficult to come by. Rebecca's father, however, exposes the discriminatory nature of apartheid and helps her deal with her inner struggles.

    Winnie Mandela: Life of Struggle by Jim Haskins (173 pp.). The author presents the life of the wife of Nelson Mandela and outlines the couple's joint suffering. The biography begins in 1936 and traces the events of Winnie Mandela's life through her and her husband's efforts to abolish apartheid in South Africa.

    One More River to Cross by Jim Haskins (215 pp.). The author details the lives of 12 black Americans who overcame obstacles and created new opportunities for themselves despite racial discrimination.

    Go Well, Stay Well by Toeckey Jones (201 pp.). Becky is a Zulu from Soweto, South Africa, and Candy is a white girl from a privileged area of Johannesburg. The teenagers meet on a crowded street when Candy trips and sprains her ankle. They begin a friendship that grows and matures despite the social and legal obstacles facing them. Restricted by law and social custom, they can safely meet only in Candy's house. In Candy's room, they share their lives, their experiences, and their hopes. Through Becky, Candy comes to experience and hate the great injustices of the apartheid system. Through Candy, Becky emerges self-assured and determined to rise up out of her poverty and troubles.

    Voices of South Africa: Growing Up in a Troubled Land edited by Carolyn Meyer (244 pp.). Meyer has compiled several stories written by people growing up in a "troubled land."

    Chain of Fire by Beverly Naidoo (245 pp.). Fifteen-year-old Niledi and her friend Taolo are the leaders of a student resistance group against the evils of apartheid. The young people face unbelievable oppression and hardships: Their friends are beaten, Taolo's father is murdered, and their village is destroyed. In spite of their suffering, Niledi and Taolo stay strong in their conviction to fight for freedom.

    Somehow Tenderness Survives: Stories of Southern Africa edited by Hazel Rochman (189 pp.). This collection of 10 YA stories and autobiographical accounts shares several perspectives of what it was like growing up in the midst of apartheid.

Figure 6-1 Continued
World Literature: Annotated Fiction and NonFiction Books & Novels

Beyond Safe Boundaries by Margaret Sacks (156 pp.). Elizabeth, a young girl, is coming of age in South Africa during the Sixties. Her sister, Evie, joins an underground resistance group to oppose the racial policies that are enforced by the South African government. Elizabeth is concerned about how her sister's involvement is negatively affecting the family. The girls' father eventually helps Evie to find constructive, less damaging ways to fight for her cause.

Australian/Australian-American

Contemporary Text: *The Thorn Birds* **by Colleen McCullough Supporting YA Text**

Josh by Ivan Southall (179 pp.). Fourteen-year-old Josh leaves the city of Melbourne to stay with his aunt in the country. Not only does he have difficulty adjusting to his aunt's strict ways, but he finds it difficult fitting in with the country lifestyle.

Cambodian/Cambodian-American

Classic Text: *Cambodian Folk Stories from the Gatiloke* **retold by Muriel Paskin Carrison**

Supporting YA Texts

More than Meets the Eye by Jeanne Betancourt (176 pp.). Liz Gaynor volunteers to help Dary Sing, a new student who is a recent immigrant from Cambodia who can barely speak English. Additionally, Liz is falling for her science lab partner, Ben Lee, who is Chinese. Nobody takes Liz's feelings seriously, and she encounters prejudice in all of its forms.

To Destroy You Is No Loss: The Odyssey of a Cambodian Family by Joan D. Criddle & Teeda Butt Mam (304 pp.). This is the nonfiction account of Teeda Butt, a 15-year-old Cambodian schoolgirl, who is forced to leave her country because of the Khmer Rouge. She tells about her family and millions of other Cambodians just like them who flee amidst a nightmare of panic, horror, and death.

Children of the River by Linda Crew (213 pp.). Sundara, a teenage Cambodian-American, flees with her aunt's family from the Khmer Rouge terror in the mid-Seventies to a small Oregon town, only to find racial prejudice within the Cambodian community there. Additionally, Sundara faces the clash between American values and her own. (Honorable Mention, 4th Annual Delacorte Press Prize for Outstanding First Young Adult Novel)

Figure 6-1 Continued
World Literature: Annotated Fiction and NonFiction Books & Novels

Caribbean/Caribbean-American

> **Contemporary Text:** *Back Home* by Susan J. Wallace

> **Supporting YA Texts**

> *A Thief in the Village* by James Berry (148 pp.). This collection of nine short stories captures the wants, dreams, and desires of Jamaican children. From bicycles to pets (albeit mongooses perhaps aren't typical pets) children the world over have similar wants. Other stories deal with children's need for acceptance and self-identity issues.
> *Abeng* by Michelle Cliff (167 pp.). Twelve-year-old Clare Savage begins to consider what it means to be raised by multiracial parents in Jamaica.
> *For the Life of Laetitia* by Merle Hodge (213 pp.). Laetitia faces the pressure of being the first member of her Caribbean family to make it to high school. Although almost everyone is proud of her accomplishments, she struggles against her emerging identity.
> *The Cay* by Theodore Taylor (160 pp.). A prejudiced, blind, 11-year-old white boy gets stranded on a tiny Caribbean island with a black man. Eventually Timothy, an old sailor, becomes the key to Phillip's survival. (an American Library Association Notable Children's Book, Jane Addam's Children's Book Award, Lewis Carroll Shelf Award, Commonwealth Club of California Literature Award, Southern California Council on Literature for Children and Young People Award)

Chinese/Chinese-American

> **Classic Text:** *Three Kingdoms* by Lo Kuan-Chung

> **Supporting YA Texts**

> *Homesick: My Own Story* by Jean Fritz (163 pp.). Although the author was born and raised in China, she has always felt American. Her parents have frequently told her about their lives in the United States, and the letters from relatives in Pennsylvania have made her homesick for a land she has never visited. When her family announces that they will be returning to America in her 12th year, Jean wonders if she will be able to adjust to her new way of life.
> *In the Year of the Boar and Jackie Robinson* by Bette Bao Lord (169 pp.). Shirley Temple Wong, better known as Bandit, moves from China in 1947 to live with her parents in Brooklyn, New York. She knows very little English and has a difficult time making friends in her new school. When she gets a chance to play right field on a baseball team, she feels that she finally has an opportunity to participate in the American dream.

Figure 6-1 Continued
World Literature: Annotated Fiction and NonFiction Books & Novels

It's Crazy to Stay Chinese in Minnesota by Eleanor Wong Telemaque (118 pp.). Chig Wing's parents own the only Chinese restaurant in town. It is there that Wing waits on tables, takes in cash, and dreams of being able to attend the university. Wing struggles between her traditional Chinese heritage and her progressive non-traditional dreams; sometimes she wishes she were totally American. Through experiences with other Chinese-American friends, she is able to accept the fact that she does not have to retain all of her family's traditions, but her heritage is what adds to her uniqueness as an individual.

Dragonwings by Laurence Yep (248 pp.). Moon Shadow, a Chinese boy, goes to San Francisco to help his father, Windrider, make a fabulous dream into a reality. Yep has loosely structured this story around the actual events of a young Chinese man who built a biplane in the 1900's.

Sea Glass by Laurence Yep (215 pp.). After moving to San Francisco, Craig Chin learns that he is not accepted by his Anglo classmates. Ancient Uncle Quail is the only one who provides him with hope.

Child of the Owl by Laurence Yep (217 pp.). When Casey's American father has to be hospitalized, Casey is sent to live with her maternal Chinese grandmother in San Francisco. Casey learns about the Chinese side of herself through her experiences in Chinatown. Her grandmother tells Casey about Jeanie (the mother Casey never knew), her Chinese name, and the story of her family's owl charm.

The Star Fisher by Laurence Yep (150 pp.). Fifteen-year-old Joan Lee is caught in the middle of two battles. First, she is always in conflict between her family's traditional Chinese ways and the American way of doing things. And second, because she serves as an interpreter for her family, she directly hears the hurtful prejudicial slurs which force her to grow up faster than most.

Ethiopian/Ethiopian-American

Contemporary Text: *Ethiopia: The Roof of Africa* by Jane Kurtz

Supporting YA Text

The Return by Sonia Levitin (181 pp.). Desta, a black Ethiopian Jewish girl, grows up on a mountainside with others who keep the ancient laws of the Torah. She and others of her community know what it is like to face discrimination. When the state militia arrive, Desta and her family flee and end up in a refugee camp in Sudan. Eventually, through the covert evacuation effort of Operation Moses, she and several thousand other Jews reach the safety of the Promised Land of Israel.

Figure 6-1 Continued
World Literature: Annotated Fiction and NonFiction Books & Novels

Greek/Greek-American

    Classic Text: *Lysistrata* by Aristophanes

    Supporting YA Text

    Love Is Not Enough by Marilyn Levy (151 pp.). Delphi Decopolis is a beautiful, happy, 17-year-old girl who owes her copper-colored hair, tawny complexion, and green eyes to her mixed parentage; her mother is African-American and her father is Greek-American. Things are great until Delphi's white boyfriend, Nick Taylor, breaks up with her because of his family's disapproval of their relationship. Delphi had never thought of herself as black or white before, only a member of the gang. With the help of her next-door neighbor, Mr. Blaugrund, an elderly man who has his own stories of prejudice to tell, and her caring parents, Delphi is able to come to terms with her disappointing summer.

Haitian/Haitian-American

    Classic Text: *The Beast of the Haitian Hills* by Philippe Marcelin

    Supporting YA Texts

    The Happy Sound by Ruth Morris Graham (132 pp.). Dorlea is a young girl growing up on a banana plantation in the Haitian hills. Oblivious to all the chaos that exists in her country, hers is a pleasant but sheltered life.

    The Broken Bridge by Philip Pullman (218 pp.). Sixteen-year-old Ginny is a black girl living in a white family. Until now, living with her father has been all right. Now, Ginny is slowly learning about her family's real past. Ginny discovers that not only does she have a half brother, but also that her father spent time in jail when Ginny was a small child. Additionally, Ginny's mother, a Haitian artist, did not die when Ginny was born as Ginny had been led to believe.

India/Indian-American

    Classic Text: *Mano Majra* by Khushwant Singh

    Supporting YA Texts

    Daughters of the House by Indrani Aikath-Gyaltsen (199 pp.). Chchanda and her little sister live with their Aunt Madhulika. Everything is just fine until their aunt marries a man from across the river and brings him home to live with them. Disturbed by his presence, Chchanda decides that she must figure out a way to get rid of him. Things change again, however, when Aunt Madhulika becomes ill.

Figure 6-1 Continued
World Literature: Annotated Fiction and NonFiction Books & Novels

Jasmine by Bharati Mukherjee (214 pp.). Jasmine doesn't want her arranged marriage; she wants to become a doctor. When she was very small, an astrologer predicted that she would be widowed and exiled. With that added pressure, Jasmine Vidh struggles with her identity. She eventually emigrates illegally to America only to face more difficulty in rural Iowa as Jane Ripplemeyer.

Sumitra's Story by Rukshana Smith (168 pp.). Sumitra's family moves to Uganda when she is ten years old. She is amazed by the difference in treatment of the three groups: the British, the Africans, and themselves. When Idi Amin begins to threaten the Indians in Uganda, her family leaves their successful business and flees to England. Things aren't much better in England where she experiences much prejudice during her teen years.

Irish/Irish-American

Classic Text: *Gulliver's Travels* by Jonathan Swift

Supporting YA Text

The Commitments by Roddy Doyle (161 pp.). A group of Irish teenagers decide that they will bring "soul" to Dublin in the Eighties. Jimmy Rabitte, the group's leader, decides the band has to listen to James Brown, Otis Redding, and their contemporaries for hours at a time. The group experiences a brief period of fame but then pays a heavy price for their endeavors. (Note: Profanity abounds)

Italian/Italian-American

Classic Text: *Dante's Vita Nova* by Dante Alighieri

Supporting YA Text

Maria's Italian Springtime by Gillian Avery (265 pps.). This novel, set in the turn of the century, is the story of 12-year-old Maria and what she experiences when she leaves England to reside in Italy with her only living relative—a distant cousin. Maria tries to be optimistic about experiencing life in a different country, but she quickly discovers that things are more difficult than she could have possibly imagined.

Japanese/Japanese-American

Contemporary Text: *Kitchen* by Banana Yoshimoto.

Supporting YA Texts

Farewell to Manzanar by Jeanne Wakatsuki Houston & James D. Houston (160 pp.). This is the true story of Jeannie, the youngest daughter of the Wakatsuki family, and what she and her family experienced for four years in the Manzanar Internment Camp during World War II.

Figure 6-1 Continued
World Literature: Annotated Fiction and NonFiction Books & Novels

Kim/Kimi by Hadley Irwin (200 pp.). When 16-year-old Kim Andrews looks in the mirror, Kimi Yogushi looks back. Even though Kim feels American, she looks Japanese. Kim feels unsure of her true heritage, since she has never met any of her Japanese relatives; her Japanese father died before she was born. Kim searches for information about her father and ends up at Tule Lake in California, one of the Japanese-American concentration camps of World War II. Kim grows up when she stops running, confronts truth, and learns that "life is cause and effect—that what you do has consequences."

Breakaway Run by David Klass (192 pp.). During Tony's 16th year, he gets the opportunity of a lifetime. He gets to spend five months in the home of a Japanese family, the Maedas, as an exchange student. He tries to make friends with some of the local Japanese boys by showing off his soccer ability, but he quickly learns that life is drastically different in Japan. Things get more complicated as he develops feelings for the Maedas' daughter.

The War Between the Classes by Gloria D. Miklowitz (158 pp.). Amy Sumoto, the daughter of traditional Japanese parents, and Adam Tarcher, the son of a snobby upper-class mother, are determined to have a relationship with one another. At the same time, their school is participating in an experiment, the Color Game, where students are put into social classes according to specific rules in order to teach them about prejudice. Not only is Amy upset by the humiliation of it all, but she fears that the game is threatening her relationship with Adam. Amy plans to sabotage the game, but not without consequences.

Shizuko's Daughter by Kyoko Mori (208 pp.). Yuki Okuda is only ten years old when her mother, Shizuko, commits suicide. Her father hastily remarries, which places an additional burden on Yuki's development. Yuki must come to terms with her mother's death, adjust to stoic parents, and accept her own development.

Mop, Moondance, and the Nagasaki Knights by Walter Dean Myers (150 pp.). Mop, a teenage girl who can play baseball as well as any of the guys, is the protagonist who shares her insights during the play-offs. She and her teammates don't know what to make of the Japanese, Mexican, and French teams they must play. In spite of their cultural differences, each team wants to go to Nagasaki, Japan, and beat the Nagasaki Knights to prove they are the championship baseball team of the world.

Pacific Crossing by Gary Soto (126 pp.). Lincoln Mendoza is selected to represent his high school in an exchange program where he will get to go to Japan for the summer. There, he stays with Mr. and Mrs. Ono and their son, Mitsuo, who teach him about Japanese culture and family values. When the three men of the "family" go on a camping trip, Lincoln learns about cultural similarities when Mr. Ono is bitten by a poisonous spider and nearly dies.

Figure 6-1 Continued
World Literature: Annotated Fiction and NonFiction Books & Novels

Korean/Korean-American

Contemporary Text: *Modern Korean Literature: An Anthology* **edited by Peter H. Lee**

Supporting YA Texts

Year of Impossible Goodbyes by Sook Nyui Choi (169 pp.). Based on the author's life, this story recounts what life was like during the Japanese occupation of Korea during World War II. Sookan and her family endure much hardship under the tyranny of the Japanese. Sookan is forced to attend a Japanese school, and her family is told to give up their Korean ways. Things get worse when the Russian Red Army invades North Korea, and they decide to risk their lives to escape from their wretched existences.

Finding My Voice by Marie G. Lee (165 pp.). Ellen, a Korean-American, struggles to find her identity as the only non-white teenager in a small town in Minnesota.

Mexican/Mexican-American

Contemporary Text: *The Monkey Grammarian* by Octavio Paz

Supporting YA Texts

Bless Me, Ultima by Rudolfo Anaya (262 pp.). Antonio Marez is growing up in New Mexico during the Forties. He is torn between the traditions of his family and the American ways of his classmates in school. Ultima serves as his curandera, or mentor, in this coming-of-age story.

The House on Mango Street by Sandra Cisneros (102 pp.). In a beautiful and intense series of vignettes, Esperanzo shares her coming-of-age trials and tribulations as a Mexican-American growing up in Chicago. She describes her Hispanic neighborhood along with her dreams of a real house in which to live.

Journey of the Sparrows by Fran Leeper Buss & Daisy Cubias (155 pp.). Maria is an extraordinary teenager who barely manages to escape from the political unrest occurring in El Salvador. Her mother gets Maria to flee to Mexico with her pregnant sister and her frail brother. From there, Maria and her siblings hide in a vegetable crate and are shipped to Chicago, where Maria must find work in order to support herself and her family. In spite of the hardships placed on her, Maria manages to survive and does it well.

Coyotes by Ted Conover (264 pp.). This is a nonfiction account of the author's travels with Mexican illegal aliens who immigrate into the United States. These people endure many hardships and work at the most menial of jobs for low pay in the hopes of finding better lives.

Figure 6-1 Continued
World Literature: Annotated Fiction and NonFiction Books & Novels

Kathleen, Please Come Home by Scott O'Dell (196 pp.). Kathleen's life is pretty regular until she befriends Sybil, a rebellious teenager, and falls in love with Ramon, an illegal immigrant from Mexico. Kathleen's mother disapproves of their relationship and actually contributes to Ramon's eventual death. Kathleen cannot believe her mother's prejudice and decides to run away with Sybil to Baja, California.

The Crossing by Gary Paulsen (128 pp.). Manny Bustos, a homeless Mexican teenager, fights for his daily existence on the streets of Juarez, Mexico. He sees the possibility for a better life in America but first has to pass across the border, which is guarded by Sergeant Locke. Locke himself fights daily against memories of dead comrades from the Viet Nam War. Through several chance encounters, these two eventually push each other to improved conditions. (Literary Merit)

Famous All Over Town by Danny Santiago (285 pp.). Fourteen-year-old Rudy is part of the Shamrock gang and goes by the name of Chato. Being part of a gang is "machismo," and being a Shamrock makes Rudy feel like a kingpin. His family disapproves of this gang but really doesn't do anything concrete to help Rudy to get out of it. His father just says things like "and this is the thanks I get for putting a roof over your head," his sister says he's going to wind up dead, and his mother says nothing. There is a part of Rudy that wants to do well in school, but to do so would bring intense criticism from his father. Rudy is aware of other Mexicans who do well academically and are not criticized for their success. Rudy lives the consequences of his decisions.

Living Up the Street by Gary Soto (159 pp.). The author recounts what it was like for him growing up in the barrios of Fresno, California. Soto experienced many hardships on his way to becoming a successful author and poet, and he shares how he overcame those obstacles. Soto has a second work, *Small Faces* (126 pp.), that continues his life's recollections, beginning with his marriage to his Japanese wife and continuing through the raising of his daughter.

Native American

Classic Text: *Native American Stories* **edited by Joseph Bruchac**

Supporting YA Texts

The Education of Little Tree by Forrest Carter (216 pp.). The author recounts what it was like growing up in the Appalachian Mountains during the Depression. He shares the prejudice displayed to the Cherokee Indians and the pride they managed to maintain in spite of their treatment.

A Yellow Raft in Blue Water by Michael Dorris (384 pp.). Three women on a Montana reservation tell their stories. Rayona describes what it is like being the 15-year-old daughter of a Native American mother and a black father. Her mother, Christine, tells about the difficulties she had with her own mother, the confinement of the reservation, her brother's death in Viet Nam, and her husband's desertion. Finally, Grandmother Ida tells how difficult it was for her to raise two children alone during difficult times.

Figure 6-1 Continued
World Literature: Annotated Fiction and NonFiction Books & Novels

The Owl's Song by Janet Campbell Hale (144 pp.). Fourteen-year-old Billy White Hawk lives alone with his alcoholic father on an Indian reservation. After his best friend commits suicide, Billy leaves the reservation in search of a better life. He goes to a school in the city but faces difficult discrimination by prejudiced students. He survives and returns to the reservation determined to work things out with his father.

Rising Voices: Writings of Young Native Americans edited by Arlene B. Hirschfelder & Beverly R. Singer (115 pp.). The editors have compiled several short essays and poems written by young Native Americans. These 19th- and 20th- century literary pieces are personal in nature, yet reflect concerns relative to most people today.

The Brave by Robert Lipsyte (195 pp.). As a sequel to *The Contender*, this novel is about George Harrison Bayer, better known as Sonny Bear, and his pursuit of a better life away from his reservation home in upstate New York. Sonny Bear wants to make it as a heavy-weight boxer, and Alfred Brooks, the boxer from *The Contender* who has become a police officer, is just the person to help. Sonny Bear's Great Uncle Jake instructs Sonny in the ways of the Moscondaga Running Braves in preparation for his biggest fight against the white man.

Sing Down the Moon by Scott O'Dell (128 pp.). This novel is based on a historic event—the forced migration of the Navaho Indians from their original homeland in 1864. Fifteen-year-old Bright Morning tells the story from her Indian point of view. She tells the story of her capture by Spanish slave traders, her escape, her return to her clan, and the spirit-breaking effects of the relocation. (a Newbery Honor Book and a *New York Times* Outstanding Book of the Year)

The Night the White Deer Died by Gary Paulsen (105 pp.). After her parents' divorce, Janet moves with her mother to Tres Pinos in New Mexico. There, the boys are intrigued by her appearance, but the girls are envious. Finding she doesn't seem to fit in anywhere, Janet chooses to be a loner. Janet begins to have a recurring dream in which an Indian brave stands poised to shoot a white deer drinking from a pool of water. Every night, just as the arrow is about to strike the deer, she wakes up. One day, she meets Billy Honcho. It is through this old, alcoholic Indian that Jenny begins to make sense of her dream in the context of this culture so foreign to her.

A Woman of Her Tribe by Margaret A. Robinson (148 pp.). Fifteen-year-old Annette has an Indian father and an English mother. Having been raised as a Nakotah Indian in her father's village for most of her life, she finds that her cultural values are challenged when she wins a scholarship and attends an English school in British Columbia. Not only are people's attitudes about life different, but all of a sudden she has to deal with stereotypes and prejudicial treatment. Katie, a Ukranian classmate, seems to understand, and they become friends. Annette can hardly wait for break so she can return to the village, but once she gets there, she no longer seems to fit into that world.

Tisha by Robert Specht (352 pp.). This is the story of 19-year-old Anne Hobbs and her struggles as a teacher in a tiny community in the Alaskan wilderness. She sees a frightful side of the community, but she treats the local Indians with respect and dignity. (an American Library Association Best Book for Young Adults)

Figure 6-1 Continued
World Literature: Annotated Fiction and NonFiction Books & Novels

Pakistan/Pakistan-American

> **Contemporary Text:** *God's Own Land: A Novel of Pakistan* **by Shaukat Siddiqi**

> **Supporting YA Text**

Shabanu: Daughter of the Wind by Suzanne Fisher Staples (240 pp.). Shabanu is the 11-year-old daughter of a camel breeder who survives in the harsh desert of Pakistan. In a very male-dominated society, she must contend with issues surrounding her sister's upcoming wedding and her own betrothal. (a Newbery Award Winner)

Polish/Polish-American

> **Classic Text:** *On the Field of Glory* **by Henryk Sienkiewicz**

> **Supporting YA Texts**

Alicia: My Story by Alicia Appleman-Jurman (448 pp). This autobiography is Alicia's account of Germany's invasion of Poland during World War II. As a young Jewish girl growing up in Buczacz, Poland, Alicia's life went from normal to horrific as she survived the deaths of her entire family. (1989 Christopher Award Winner)

The Cage by Ruth Minsky Sender (224 pp.). Riva Minska recalls what it was like for her growing up in the Lodz ghetto in Poland during the Holocaust. After her mother is taken away to a concentration camp, Riva is left to care for her younger brothers. Eventually, she and her siblings are taken to the death camps but she survives. (an NCSS-CBC Notable Children's Book in the Field of Social Studies)

Puerto Rican/Puerto Rican-American

> **Classic Text:** *Borinquen: An Anthology of Puerto Rican Literature* **edited by Maria Teresa Babin & Stan Steiner**

> **Supporting YA Texts**

Gaucho by Gloria Gonzalez (144 pp.). Gaucho lives with his mother in El Barrio in New York City. It is Gaucho's hope and dream to be able to someday return to Puerto Rico with his mother.

Nilda by Nicholasa Mohr (292 pp.). This story, set in the early Forties, is about Nilda Ramirez's growing up in El Barrio in New York City. Nilda not only has to contend with the prejudicial attitudes from all of the authority figures in her life but also has to deal with gender issues associated with her four brothers.

Figure 6-1 Continued
World Literature: Annotated Fiction and NonFiction Books & Novels

Russian/Russian-American

Contemporary Text: *The Image of Women in Contemporary Soviet Fiction* edited by Sigrid McLaughlin

Supporting YA Texts

Sworn Enemies by Carol Matas (132 pp.). Aaron is revered in his Russian community for his academic ability, but Zev is jealous of Aaron's success. The two Russian Jews have numerous confrontations until both are forced to work together if they want to escape forced military service.

Face to Face: A Collection of Stories by Celebrated Soviet and American Writers edited by Thomas Pettepiece & Anatoly Aleksin (230 pp.). This American and Soviet short story collection is designed to remind teenagers of the common humanity our two countries share. (Note: Philomel is donating $.50 to the U.S. Committee for UNICEF for each copy sold in the United States.)

We Were Not Like Other People by Ephraim Sevela (1989). A Russian Jewish teenager is separated from his parents at the onset of World War II. His life is a test of survival as he wanders in search of his parents for six years.

Thailand/Thai-American

Contemporary Text: *Ten Lives of the Buddha* by Elizabeth Wray, Clare Rosenfield, & Dorothy Bailey

Supporting YA Text

Rice Without Rain by Mingfong Ho (236 pp.). This novel—which is dedicated to those killed at Thammasart University on October 6, 1976—addresses the problems of rural Thailand in conflict with its military dictatorship. Seventeen-year-old Jinda lives with her father in a poor rice-farming village where they are required to pay half of their harvest for rent. Four university students from Bangkok visit the village in hopes of getting these poor people to resist such payments. Jinda's father agrees, and his decision disrupts her life forever.

Vietnamese/Vietnamese-American

Classic Text: *Under the Starfruit Tree: Folktales from Vietnam* edited by Alice M. Terada

Supporting YA Texts

The Voyage of the Lucky Dragon by Jack Bennett (149 pp.). After a Vietnamese family endures much hardship in a Communist re-education camp, they seize an opportunity to escape by embarking on a fishing boat that will take them away from their oppressed country. The suffering they endure is a fair exchange for freedom once they reach Australia.

Figure 6-1 Continued
World Literature: Annotated Fiction and NonFiction Books & Novels

Our Love by Fern Brown (119 pp.). During Suzy Belkowski's senior year at East High, after racial tensions were noted, Suzy is assigned to write a story about how the Vietnamese feel about being students at her school. She interviews Daniel Lu, a thin Vietnamese refugee who is also a senior. Through the interviews, she is able to write a spectacular human interest series about the contrast between life in America and in Viet Nam. She eventually falls in love with Daniel, much to the chagrin of Travis Brennan, another writer for the school newspaper, who has been courting Suzy for some time.

Shadow of the Dragon by Sherry Garland (314 pp.). Sixteen-year-old Danny Vo lives with his extended family in the United States. Life changes dramatically when Sang Le, a cousin, comes to America to live with them. Sang Le gets involved with a dangerous Vietnamese gang, while Danny is more interested in getting involved with Tiffany Schultz. Unbeknownst to Danny, however, Tiffany's older brother is a member of a white supremist skinhead gang.

Song of the Buffalo Boy by Sherry Garland (249 pp.). Seventeen-year-old Loi loves Khai, the herder of the water buffalo, and he loves her. Unfortunately, the ugly Officer Hiep wants to marry Loi and offers her Vietnamese mother the monetary dowry to make Loi his wife. In Romeo and Juliet style, Loi and Khai plan for her fake death and an escape to America.

Hello, My Name Is Scrambled Eggs by Jamie Gilson (159 pp.). Harvey Trumble's family is hosting a Vietnamese family, and Harvey tries to help 12-year-old Tuan adjust to the American way of doing things. Although Tuan learns a lot about American ways, things don't always turn out as Harvey plans; they're often "scrambled."

When Heaven and Earth Changed Places by Le Ly Hayslip (362 pp.). The author shares her life's story about growing up as a young Vietnamese woman during the Viet Nam War. Le Ly was 12 years old when the war started. By the time she was 16 years old, Le Ly had first-hand experience of the tragedy of war. She nearly starved, was imprisoned, tortured, and raped, and lived through the deaths of family members. Le Ly tells her story in flashbacks as she returns to visit her family 20 years after the war.

Jason's Women by Jean Davies O'Kimoto (224 pp.). Jason, an awkward and shy 16-year-old, decides he wants a job. He answers an ad in the newspaper and finds himself working for an eccentric 80-year-old woman named Bertha Jane Filmore. Bertha has a young Vietnamese refugee girl staying with her who stretches Jason's ability to communicate. (an American Library Association Best Book for Young Adults)

Park's Quest by Katherine Paterson (148 pp.). The only thing Park knows about his father is that he died in the Viet Nam War. Park's mother offers little information because she doesn't want him to know that she and his father were divorced prior to his father's death. When Park meets 12-year-old Thanh, a Vietnamese immigrant whose American father also fought in the war, the two develop a friendship based on their mutual interest.

Figure 6-1 Continued
World Literature: Annotated Fiction and NonFiction Books & Novels

My Name Is San Ho by Jayne Pettit (149 pp.). Growing up in Viet Nam during the Viet Nam War, San Ho has witnessed the destruction of his village, the murder of his honored teacher, and the loss of his father. His mother, fearing for his safety, sends him to Saigon, marries an American soldier, and moves to the United States. She eventually gets permission for him to leave Viet Nam and come to America to live with her and his new stepfather. In America, he must learn how to be accepted by others at his school. San Ho struggles with English and the need for friends but makes some progress through his athletic abilities.

The Vietnamese in America by Paul Rutledge (70 pp.). This nonfiction book depicts the struggles the Vietnamese have faced as "boat people" trying to adapt to the American way of life. Information is included about Viet Nam and its condition after the war.

New Kid on the Block by Karen Sommer (127 pp.). Satch, Spinner, Pete, and A.J. have been the "Fearless Foursome" of the 6th grade for quite some time. Things change when a new kid comes to their school from Viet Nam. The best thing about this boy is that he's a great soccer player; the worst thing is that A.J. can't stand him. Satch likes the new kid but feels torn by his loyalty to A.J. Things would be so much easier if everybody could just get along.

The Girl in the White Ship by Peter Townsend (171 pp.). Townsend interviewed family members, friends, and officials in writing a historically accurate account of one family's struggle to escape from Communist rule. Hue Hue, a young Vietnamese girl, not only experienced the loss of her country but also managed to survive being shipwrecked for four months during her family's escape.

A Boat to Nowhere by Maureen Crane Wartski (160 pp.). Kien, an orphan boy, discovers the meaning of family when he helps two Vietnamese children and their sickly grandfather, Thay Van Chi, escape from the Vietcong. As "boat people," they experience rejection that contemporary Americans will have difficulty imagining. *Publisher's Weekly* says, "Wartski's moving story, mirroring actuality in today's tragic climate, creates an indelible memory while it teaches a hard lesson." (a Children's Book Council Notable Book in the Field of Social Studies)

A Long Way from Home by Maureen Crane Wartski (144 pp.). This realistic story is Wartski's sequel to *A Boat to Nowhere* and recounts Kien's struggles adjusting to American life.

Figure 6-2
African/African-American Literature

Something Old (classic)

    Things Fall Apart **by Chinua Achebe (191 pp.)**

        Set in an Ibo Village in Nigeria in the early 1900s, the novel presents an interesting perspective concerning the colonialization of Africa by the white man. Okonkwa, a self-made leader of the Ibo Tribe, tells the story of the brutal clash between Christianity and a tribe with its own gods and belief system.

Something New (contemporary)

    Waiting For the Rain **by Sheila Gordon (214 pp.)**

        Tengo, a black, and Frikkie, an Afrikaner, grow up together as childhood friends on a farm in South Africa. As tensions over apartheid grow, the boys find their friendship in jeopardy amidst the ongoing tragedy of South Africa. Finally, violence seems the only solution that can bring about the necessary changes in an unjust system. (an American Library Association Best Book for Young Adults)

Something Nonfiction

    Kaffir Boy: The True Story of a Black Youth's Coming of Age in Apartheid South Africa **by Mark Mathabane (350 pp.)**

        Growing up amidst poverty and violence in Alexandra, South Africa, this author beats the odds and writes about his experience as a kaffir boy under apartheid.

Infusion of Culture (African-American)

    Blue Tights **by Rita Williams-Garcia (138 pp.)**

        Joyce Collins, an adolescent black girl, is devastated when Miss Sobol forbids her from trying out for an upcoming ballet because her "butt is too big." Joyce has always had self-esteem problems, especially since her mother gave birth to her out of wedlock and fears Joyce will make the same mistake. When Joyce joins an African dance troupe and gets the lead for the Kwanzaa Celebration, the change in Joyce is wonderful.

Figure 6-3
Thirty-Four Alternative Book Reports

From *Ideas for Teaching English in the Junior High and Middle School* edited by Candy Carter & Zora Rashkis (1980). Urbana, IL: National Council of Teachers of English. Reprinted by permission of the publisher.

1. Design an advertising campaign to promote the sale of the book you read. Include each of the following in your campaign: a poster, a radio or TV commercial, a magazine or newspaper ad, a bumper sticker, and a button.

2. Write a scene that could have happened in the book you read but didn't. After you have written the scene, explain how it would have changed the outcome of the book.

3. Create a board game based on events and characters in the book you read. By playing your game, members of the class should learn what happened in the book. Your game must include the following: a game board, a rule sheet and clear directions, events and characters from the story on cards or on a game board.

4. Make models of three objects which were important in the book you read. On a card attached to each model, tell why the object was important in the book.

5. If the book you read involves a number of locations within a country or geographical area, plot the events of the story on a map. Make sure the map is large enough for us to read the main events clearly. Attach a legend to your map. Write a paragraph that explains the importance of each event indicated on your map.

6. Complete a series of five drawings that show five of the major events in the plot of the book you read. Write captions for each drawing so that the illustrations can be understood by someone who did not read the book.

7. Design a movie poster for the book you read. Cast the major characters in the book with real actors and actresses. Include a scene or dialogue from the book in the layout of the poster. Remember, you are trying to convince someone to see the movie that is based on the book, so your writing should be persuasive.

8. Make a test for the book you read. Include ten true-false, ten multiple choice, and ten short answer essay questions. After writing the test, provide answers to your questions.

Figure 6-3 Continued
Thirty-Four Alternative Book Reports

9. Select one character from the book you read who has the qualities of a heroine or hero. List these qualities and tell why you think they are heroic.

10. Imagine that you are about to make a feature-length film of the novel you read. You have been instructed to select major characters in your novel from your English classmates and tell why you selected each person for a given part. Consider both appearance and personality.

11. Plan a party for the characters in the book you read. In order to do this, complete each of the following tasks: (a) Design an invitation to the party which would appeal to all of the characters. (b) Imagine that you are five of the characters in the book and tell what each would wear to the party. (c) Tell what food you will serve and why. (d) Tell what games or entertainment you will provide and why your choices are appropriate. (e) Tell how three of the characters will act at the party.

12. List five of the main characters from the book you read. Give three examples of what each character learned or did not learn in the book.

13. Obtain a job application from an employer in your area, and fill out the application as one of the characters in the book you read might do. Before you obtain the application, be sure that the job is one for which a character in your book is qualified. If a resume is required, write it. (A resume is a statement that summarizes the applicant's education and job experience. Career goals, special interests, and unusual achievements are sometimes included.)

14. You are a prosecuting attorney, putting one of the characters from the book you read on trial for a crime or misdeed. Prepare your case on paper, giving all your arguments and supporting them with facts from the book.

15. Adapt the prosecuting attorney activity outlined above to a dual-role project: in one role, present the prosecuting case, and in the other present the case for the defense. If a classmate has read the same book, you might make this a two-person project.

16. Make a shoebox diorama of a scene from the book you read. Write a paragraph explaining the scene and attach it to the diorama.

17. Pretend that you are one of the characters in the book you read. Tape a monologue (one person talking) of that character telling of his or her experiences. Be sure to write out a script before taping.

Figure 6-3 Continued
Thirty-Four Alternative Book Reports

18. Make a television box show of ten scenes in the order that they occur in the book you read. Cut a square from the bottom of a box to serve as a TV screen and make two slits in opposite sides of the box. Slide a butcher paper roll on which you have drawn the scenes through the two side slits. Make a tape to go with your television show. Be sure to write out a script before taping.

19. Make a filmstrip or slideshow picturing what happened in the book you read. You can make a filmstrip by using Thermofax transparency material, but be sure it is narrow enough to fit through the projector. You will have to work carefully on a script before making your tape.

20. Tape an interview with one of the characters in the book you read. Pretend that this character is being interviewed by a magazine or newspaper reporter. You may do this project with a partner, but be sure to write a script before taping.

21. Make a book jacket for the book you read. Include the title, author, and publishing company of the book on the cover. Be sure the illustration relates to an important aspect of the book. On the inside flap or on the back of your book jacket, write a paragraph telling about the book. Explain why this book makes interesting reading when writing this "blurb."

22. Write a letter to a friend about the book you read. Explain why you liked or did not like the book.

23. Make a "wanted" poster for a character in the book you read. Include the following: (a) a drawing of the character (you may use a magazine cutout), (b) a physical description of the character, (c) the character's misdeeds, (d) other information about the character that you think is important, (e) the reward offered for the capture of the character.

24. In *The Catcher in the Rye*, Holden Caulfield describes a good book as one that "when you're done reading it, you wish the author that wrote it was a terrific friend of yours and you could call him up on the phone whenever you felt like it." Imagine that the author of the book you read is a terrific friend of yours. Write out an imaginary telephone conversation between the two of you in which you discuss the book you read and other things as well.

25. Imagine that you have been given the task of conducting a tour of the town in which the book you read is set. Make a tape describing the homes of the characters and the places where important events in the book took place. You may use a musical background for your tape.

Figure 6-3 Continued
Thirty-Four Alternative Book Reports

26. Make a list of at least ten proverbs or familiar sayings. Now decide which characters in the book you read should have followed the suggestions in the familiar sayings and why. Here are some proverbs to get you started: He who hesitates is lost. All's fair in love and war. The early bird catches the worm. A stitch in time saves nine.

27. Write the copy for a newspaper front page that is devoted entirely to the book you read. The front page should look as much like a real newspaper page as possible. The articles on the front page should be based on events and characters in the book.

28. Make a collage that represents major characters and events in the book you read. Use pictures and words cut from magazines in your collage.

29. Make a time line of the major events in the book you read. Be sure the divisions on the time line reflect the time periods in the plot. Use drawings or magazine cutouts to illustrate events along the time line.

30. Change the setting of the book you read. Tell how this change of setting would alter events and affect characters.

31. Make a paper doll likeness of one of the characters in the book you read. Design at least three costumes for this character. Next, write a paragraph commenting on each outfit; tell what the clothing reflects about the character, the historical period, and events in the book.

32. Pick a national issue. Compose a speech to be given on that topic by one of the major characters in the book you read. Be sure the contents of the speech reflect the character's personality and beliefs.

33. Retell the plot of the book you read as it might appear in a third-grade reading book. Be sure that the vocabulary you use is appropriate for that age group. Variation: Retell this story to a young child. Tape your story-telling.

34. Complete each of these eight ideas with material growing out of the book you read: This book made me wish that, realize that, decide that, wonder about, see that, believe that, feel that, and hope that.

References

Achebe, C. (1988). *Things fall apart.* New York: Fawcett Crest. (ISBN: 0-449-20810-9) (originally published in 1958)

Aikath-Gyaltsen, I. (1991). *Daughters of the house.* New York: Ballantine. (ISBN: 0-345-38073-8)

Alighieri, D. (1973). *Dante's vita nova.* Translated by Mark Musa. Bloomington: Indiana University Press. (ISBN: 0-253-20162-4)

Anaya, R. (1992). *Bless me, Ultima.* New York: Warner Books. (ISBN: 0-89229-002-1)

Applebee, A.N. (1993). *Literature in the secondary school: Studies of curriculum and instruction in the United States.* Urbana, IL: National Council of Teachers of English.

Appleman-Jurman, A. (1990). *Alicia: My story.* New York: Bantam. (ISBN: 0-553-28218-2)

Aristophanes. (413 B.C.). *Lysistrata.* Translated by Charles T. Murphy. *The Norton anthology of world masterpieces.* New York: Norton.

Avery, G. (1964). *Maria's Italian springtime.* New York: Simon & Schuster. (ISBN: 0-671-79582-1)

Babin, M.T. & Steiner, S. (Eds.). (1974). *Borinquen: An anthology of Puerto Rican literature.* New York: Alfred A. Knopf. (ISBN: 0-394-47462-7)

Beach, R. (1993). *A teacher's introduction to reader-response theories.* Urbana, IL: National Council of Teachers of English.

Beake L. (1993). *Song of Be.* New York: Henry Holt & Company. (ISBN: 0-8050-2905-2)

Bennett, J. (1985). *The voyage of the Lucky Dragon.* New York: Prentice Hall. (ISBN: 0-139-44165-4)

Berry, J. (1987). *A thief in the village.* New York: Orchard Books. (ISBN: 0-531-05745-3)

Betancourt, J. (1990). *More than meets the eye.* New York: Bantam. (ISBN: 0-553-05871-1)

Bode, J. (1989). *New kids on the block: Oral histories of immigrant teens.* New York: Franklin Watts. (ISBN: 0-531-10794-9)

Brown, F. (1986). *Our love.* New York: Ballantine/Fawcett-Juniper. (ISBN: 0-449-70034-8)

Bruchac, J. (1993). *Native American stories.* Colorado: Fulcrum Publishing. (ISBN: 1-55591-094-7)

Buss, F.L. & Cubias, D. (1991). *Journey of the sparrows.* New York: Lodestar. (ISBN: 0-525-67362-8)

Carlsen, R.G. & Sherrill, A. (1988). *Voices of readers: How we come to love books.* Urbana, IL: National Council of Teachers of English.

Carrison, M.P. (1987). *Cambodian folk stories from the Gatiloke.* Translated by The Venerable Kong Chhean. Rutland, VT: Tuttle. (ISBN: 0-8048-1518-6)

Carter, F. (1986). *The education of Little Tree.* New Mexico: University of New Mexico Press. (ISBN: 0-826-30879-1)

Choi, S.N. (1991). *Year of impossible goodbyes.* New York: Dell. (ISBN: 0-440-40759-1)

Cisneros, S. (1988). *The house on mango street*. Houston, TX: Arte. (ISBN: 0-934770-20)

Cliff, M. (1991). *Abeng*. New York: Penguin. (ISBN: 0-140-15314-4)

Conover, T. (1987). *Coyotes*. New York: Vintage Books. (ISBN: 0-394-75518-9)

Crew, L. (1990). *Children of the river*. New York: Delacorte Press. (ISBN: 0-385-29690-8)

Criddle, J.D. & Mam, T.B. (1989) *To destroy you is no loss: The odyssey of a Cambodian family*. New York: Anchor/Doubleday Books. (includes an eight page photo insert) (ISBN: 0-385-26628-6)

Dorris, M. (1988). *A yellow raft in blue water*. New York: Warner Books. (ISBN: 0-446-38787-8)

Fritz, J. (1982). *Homesick: My own story*. New York: Dell. (ISBN: 0-440-73683)

Garland, S. (1993). *Shadow of the dragon*. New York: Harcourt, Brace, & Company. (ISBN: 0-152-73530-5)

Garland, S. (1992). *Song of the buffalo boy*. San Diego: Harcourt, Brace, & Jovanovich. (ISBN: 0-152-77107-7)

Gilson, J. (1985). *Hello, my name is Scrambled Eggs*. New York: Lothrop, Lee, & Shepard Books. (ISBN: 0-688-04095-0)

Gonzalez, G. (1977). *Gaucho*. New York: Alfred A. Knopf. (ISBN: 0-394-83389-9)

Gordon, S. (1990). *The middle of somewhere: A story of South Africa*. New York: Orchard Books. (ISBN: 0-531-05908-1)

Gordon, S. (1989). *Waiting for the rain*. New York: Bantam. (ISBN: 0-553-27911-4)

Graham, R.M. (1970). *The happy sound*. Chicago: Follett.

Hale, J.C. (1991). *The owl's song*. New York: Bantam. (ISBN: 0-553-28829-6)

Haskins, J. (1988). *Winnie Mandela: Life of struggle*. New York: Putnam. (ISBN: 0-399-21515-8)

Haskins, J. (1992). *One more river to cross*. New York: Scholastic. (ISBN: 0-590-42896-9)

Hayslip, L.L. (1990). *When heaven and earth changed places*. New York: Plume. (ISBN: 0-452-26417-0)

Hirschfelder, A.B. & Singer, B.R. (Eds.). (1992). *Rising voices: Writings of young native Americans*. New York: Charles Scribner's Sons. (ISBN: 0-684-19207-1)

Ho, M. (1990). *Rice without rain*. New York: Lothrop, Lee, & Shepard. (ISBN: 0-688-06355-1)

Hodge, M. (1993). *For the life of Laetitia*. New York: Farrar, Straus, & Giroux. (ISBN: 0-374-32447-6)

Hodgkinson, H. (1993, April). American education: The good, the bad, and the task. *Phi Delta Kappan, 74* (8), 619–623.

Houston, J.W. & Houston, J.D. (1990). *Farewell to Manzanar*. New York: Bantam. (ISBN: 0-553-27258-6)

Irwin, Hadley. (1988). *Kim/Kimi*. New York: Viking/Penguin. (ISBN: 0-140-32593-X)

Jones, T. (1980). *Go well, stay well*. New York: Harper & Row. (ISBN: 0-060-23061-4)

Kaywell, J.F. (1993). *Adolescents at risk: A guide to fiction and nonfiction for young adults, parents, and professionals*. Westport, CT: Greenwood Press.

Klass, D. (1987). *Breakaway run*. New York: E.P. Dutton. (ISBN: 0-525-67190-0)

Kuan-Chung, L. (1976, 1320). *Three kingdoms*. Translated by Moss Roberts. New York: Pantheon. (ISBN: 0-394-73393-2)

Kurtz, J. (1991). *Ethiopia: The roof of Africa*. New York: Dillon Press. (ISBN: 0-875-18483-9)

Langer, J.A. (1989). *Literature instruction: A focus on student response*. Urbana, IL: National Council of Teachers of English.

Lee, M.G. (1992). *Finding my voice*. Boston: Houghton Mifflin. (ISBN: 0-395-62134-8)

Lee, P.H. (Ed.). (1990). *Modern Korean literature: An anthology*. Honolulu: University of Hawaii Press. (ISBN: 0-824-81321-9)

Levitin, S. (1987). *The return*. New York: Ballantine. (ISBN: 0-449-70280-4)

Levy, M. (1989). *Love is not enough*. New York: Ballantine/Fawcett Juniper. (ISBN: 0-449-70313-4)

Lindgren, M.V. (Ed.). (1991). *The multicolored mirror: Cultural substance literature for children and young adults*. Fort Atkinson, WI: Highsmith Press. (ISBN: 0-917846-05-2)

Lipsyte, R. (1991). *The brave*. New York: HarperCollins. (ISBN: 0-060-23916-6)

Lord, B.B. (1986). *In the year of the Boar and Jackie Robinson*. New York: Harper & Row. (ISBN: 0-064-40175-8)

Marcelin, P. (1986). *The beast of the Haitian hills*. San Francisco, CA: City Lights Books. (ISBN: 0-87286-189-9)

Matas, C. (1993). *Sworn enemies*. New York: Bantam. (ISBN: 0-440-21900-0)

Mathabane, M. (1986). *Kaffir boy: The true story of a black youth's coming of age in apartheid South Africa*. New York: Plume. (ISBN: 0-452-26471-5)

McCullough, C. (1977). *The thorn birds*. New York: Harper & Row. (ISBN: 0-060-12956-5)

McLaughlin, S. (Ed.). (1989). *The image of women in contemporary Soviet fiction*. New York: St. Martin's Press. (ISBN: 0-312-02823-7)

Meyer, C. (Ed.). (1986). *Voices of South Africa: Growing up in a troubled land*. San Diego: Harcourt, Brace, & Jovanovich. (ISBN: 0-152-00637-0)

Miklowitz, G.D. (1986). *The war between the classes*. New York: Dell Laurel-Leaf. (ISBN: 0-440-99406-3)

Miller-Lachmann, L. (Ed.). (1992). *Our family, our friends, our world: An annotated guide to significant multicultural books for children and teenagers*. New Providence, NJ: Bowker. (ISBN: 0-8352-3025-2)

Mohr, N. (1973). *Nilda*. New York: Harper & Row. (ISBN: 06-024331-7)

Mori, K. (1993). *Shizuko's daughter*. New York: Fawcett Juniper. (ISBN: 0-449-70433-5)

Mukherjee, B. (1989). *Jasmine*. New York: Fawcett Crest. (ISBN: 0-449-21923-2)

Myers, W.D. (1992). *Mop, Moondance, and the Nagasaki Knights*. New York: Delacorte Press. (ISBN: 0-385-30687-3)

Naidoo, B. (1990). *Chain of fire*. Philadelphia: J.B. Lippincott. (ISBN: 0-397-32426-X)

O'Dell, S. (1990). *Sing down the moon*. New York: Dell Laurel-Leaf. (ISBN: 0-440-97975-7)

O'Dell, S. (1978). *Kathleen, please come home*. Boston: Houghton Mifflin Company. (ISBN: 0-395-26453-7)

O'Kimoto, J.D. (1990). *Jason's women*. New York: Dell. (ISBN: 0-440-20000-8)

Pace, B.G. (1992, September). The textbook canon: Genre, gender, and race in U.S. literature anthologies. *English Journal*, **81** (5), 33–38.

Paterson, K. (1988). *Park's quest*. New York: E.P. Dutton. (ISBN: 0-525-67258-3)

Paulsen, G. (1990). *The crossing*. New York: Dell Laurel-Leaf. (ISBN: 0-440-20582-4)

Paulsen, G. (1978). *The night the white deer died*. New York: Dell. (ISBN: 0-440-21092-5)

Paz, O. (1990). *The monkey grammarian*. New York: Arcade Publishing. (ISBN: 1-559-70135-8)

Pettepiece, T. & Aleksin, A. (Eds.). (1990). *Face to face: A collection of stories by celebrated Soviet and American writers*. New York: Philomel. (ISBN: 0-399-21951-X)

Pettit, J. (1992). *My name is San Ho*. New York: Scholastic. (ISBN: 0-590-44172-8)

Pullman, P. (1992). *The broken bridge*. New York: Alfred A. Knopf. (ISBN: 0-679-81972-X)

Purves, A.C., Rogers, T., & Soter, A.O. (1990). *How porcupines make love II: Teaching a response centered literature curriculum*. New York: Longman.

Robinson, M.A. (1990). *A woman of her tribe*. New York: Ballantine. (ISBN: 0-449-70405-X)

Rochman, H. (Ed.). (1988). *Somehow tenderness survives: Stories of Southern Africa*. New York: HarperCollins. (ISBN: 0-06-025022-4)

Rochman, H. (1993). *Against borders: Promoting books for a multicultural world*. Chicago: American Library Association.

Rosenberg, D. (Ed.). (1991). *World literature*. Lincolnwood, IL: National Textbook Company. (ISBN: 0-844-25482-7)

Rosenblatt, L. (1978). *The reader, the text, the poem: The transactional theory of the literary work*. Carbondale, IL: Southern Illinois University Press.

Rosenblatt, L. (1938). *Literature as exploration*. New York: Modern Language Association.

Sacks, M. (1989). *Beyond safe boundaries*. New York: Penguin. (ISBN: 0-525-67281-8)

Santiago, D. (1983). *Famous all over town*. New York: American Library. (ISBN: 0-452-25974-6)

Sender, R.M. (1990). *The cage*. New York: Bantam. (ISBN: 0-553-27003-6)

Sevela, E. (1989). *We were not like other people*. Translated by Antonin Bouis. New York: Harper & Row. (ISBN: 0-06-025507-2)

Siddiqi, S. (1991). *God's own land: A novel of Pakistan*. Translated by David J. Matthews. Kent, England: Paul Norbury/UNESCO. (ISBN: 0-904-40499-4)

Sienkiewicz, H. (1906). *On the field of glory*. Cambridge: The University Press. (LCCN: 06-2341)

Singh, K. (1956). *Mano majra*. New York: Grove Press. (LCCN: 56-5725)

Sommer, K. (1987). *New kid on the block*. Elgin, IL: Chariot Books/David C. Cook Publishing Company. (ISBN: 0-89191-746-2)

Soto, G. (1992). *Pacific crossing*. San Diego: Harcourt, Brace, & Jovanovich. (ISBN: 0-152-59187-7)

Soto, G. (1986). *Small faces*. Houston: University of Houston. (ISBN: 0-934770-49-2)

Soto, G. (1985). *Living up the street.* San Francisco: Strawberry Hill Press. (ISBN: 0-894-07064-9)

Southall, I. (1988). *Josh.* New York: Macmillan. (ISBN: 0-02-786280-1)

Specht, R. (1990). *Tisha.* New York: Bantam. (ISBN: 0-553-26596-2)

Staples, S.F. (1989). *Shabanu: Daughter of the wind.* New York: Alfred A. Knopf. (ISBN: 0-679-81030-7)

Swift, J. (1960). *Gulliver's travels.* New York: Penguin. (ISBN: 0-451-52219-2)

Taylor, T. (1990). *The cay.* New York: Doubleday. (ISBN: 0-385-07906-0)

Telemaque, E.W. (1978). *It's crazy to stay Chinese in Minnesota.* Nashville: Thomas Nelson. (ISBN: 0-8407-6613-0)

Terada, A.M. (Ed.). (1989). *Under the starfruit tree: Folktales from Vietnam.* Honolulu: University of Hawaii Press. (ISBN: 0-8248-1252-2)

Townsend, P. (1983). *The girl in the white ship.* New York: Holt, Rinehart, & Winston. (ISBN: 0-0305-7787-X)

Wallace, S.J. (1992). *Back home.* Essex, England: Longman Carribean. (ISBN: 0-582-10030-5)

Wartski, M.C. (1988). *A boat to nowhere.* New York: Signet Books. (ISBN: 0-451-16285-4)

Wartski, M.C. (1982). *A long way from home.* New York: Signet Books. (ISBN: 0-451-16035-5)

Williams-Garcia, R. (1988). *Blue tights.* New York: E.P. Dutton. (ISBN: 0-8335-4109-9)

Wray, E., Rosenfield, C. & Bailey, D. (1972). *Ten lives of the Buddha.* New York: Weatherhill. (ISBN: 0-834-80067-5)

Yep, L. (1991). *The star fisher.* New York: William Morrow. (ISBN: 0-688-09365-5)

Yep, L. (1990). *Child of the owl.* New York: Harper & Row. (ISBN: 0-064-40336-X)

Yep, L. (1975). *Dragonwings.* New York: Harper & Row. (ISBN: 0-060-26737-2)

Yoshimoto, B. (1988). *Kitchen.* New York: Grove Press. (ISBN: 0-671-88018-7)

For additional ideas regarding the teaching of multicultural literature, teachers may wish to refer to the following references:

Blair, L. (1991, December). Developing student voices with multicultural literature. *English Journal,* **80** (8), 24–28.

Carey-Webb, A. (1991, April). Auto/Biography of the oppressed: The power of testimonial. *English Journal,* **80** (4), 44–47.

Cross, B.E. (1993, May). How do we prepare teachers to improve race relations? *Educational Leadership,* **50** (8), 64–65.

Heath, S.B. & Mangiola, L. (1991). *Children of promise: Literate activity in linguistically and culturally diverse classrooms.* Washington, D.C.: National Education Association.

Higuchi, C. (1993, May). Understanding must begin with us. *Educational Leadership,* **50** (8), 69–71.

O'Neil, J. (1993, May). A new generation confronts racism. *Educational Leadership,* **50** (8), 60–63.

Pine, G.J. & Hilliard, A.G. (1990, April). Rx for racism: Imperatives for America's schools. *Phi Delta Kappan,* **71** (8), 593–600.

Polakow-Suranski, S. & Ulaby, N. (1990, November). Students take action to combat racism. *Phi Delta Kappan*, **71** (8), 601–606.

Slade, L.A., Jr. (1991, spring). Growing up as a minority in America: Four African-American writers' testimony. *The ALAN Review*, **18** (3), 9–11.

Smagorinsky, P. (1992, December). Towards a civic education in a multicultural society: Ethical problems in teaching literature. *English Education*, **24** (4), 212–228.

Stover, L. (1991, spring). Exploring and celebrating cultural diversity and similarity through young adult novels. *The ALAN Review*, **18** (3), 12–15.

Trimmer, J. & Warnock, T. (Eds.). (1992). *Understanding others: Cultural and cross-cultural studies and the teaching of literature*. Urbana, IL: National Council of Teachers of English. (ISBN: 0-814-15562-6)

Vann, K.R. & Kunjufu, J. (1993, February). The importance of an Afrocentric, multicultural curriculum. *Phi Delta Kappan*, **74** (6), 490–491.

CHAPTER 7

Relationships and Identity: Young Adult Literature and *The Tragedy of Julius Caesar*

PATRICIA L. DANIEL

Introduction

In our sixth grade play, I played the part of Marc Antony, and I became that character. I was passionate as I delivered my speeches. My social studies and English teachers thought both disciplines would be enhanced if we performed *The Tragedy of Julius Caesar*. I am still indebted to them for introducing me to the Bard and his works; of course, I became an English teacher. Although I did not understand all that was in the play, I knew that I was eager to read more of Shakespeare's plays because I had connected with my character; the play touched me deeply. But, what of my other classmates who were not a part of the production? Did I overhear a peer saying that Shakespeare was stupid?

Today we have the benefit of quality young adult (YA) literature which helps more students make connections with Shakespeare's universal themes. Many students first encounter Shakespeare with inadequate reading preparation. Reading numerous Shakespearean lines aloud can become drudgery, both for students and teacher. The language is difficult, and his plays are seemingly so distant from students' experiences. YA literature helps to bridge that gap because students can first relate to the contemporary realistic fiction and then see the relevance of Shakespeare today.

Relationships in *The Tragedy of Julius Caesar*

Examining the relationships among the characters in *The Tragedy of Julius Caesar* is a valuable and relevant approach for teenagers to pursue. Relationships help us know ourselves more completely and enable us to see situations from another's vantage point, a skill most teenagers need to develop. For purposes of this chapter, I will briefly address only two characters in *Julius Caesar*, Brutus and Marc Antony, and then thoroughly examine how different YA literature might be used to enhance students' understanding of the play.

Brutus

Brutus is righteous, noble, and idealistic—the embodiment of integrity. Brutus' character flaw is that he believes other people share his characteristics. He is not suspicious of Cassius' motive for assassinating Caesar; after all, Cassius is a colleague. Brutus has colleagues and limited relationships, but he does not have any real friends. After Cassius approaches Brutus about joining the conspiracy, Brutus has only his own counsel to consider. He falls prey to Cassius as a "false friend" because he is able to rationalize Cassius' point of view. Brutus understands books and intellectual matters; his head rules his heart. If Brutus were a "people person," things would not have turned out as they did. A person with friends might seek others' counsel or perhaps talk to Caesar personally in order to investigate the possibility of Caesar's ambition being detrimental to Rome. Brutus does not even discuss the situation with his wife, Portia. Even in his closest relationship, he has boundaries.

Marc Antony

By contrast, Marc Antony is fun-loving, easy-going, and passionate; he understands people. He is capable of making and maintaining intimate relationships with others. He is a loyal friend, willingly subjecting himself to Caesar. Antony is able to assess people as they really are and is not deceived by how they portray themselves in public. He has a better balance between "head and heart" matters than Brutus.

Using *Killing Mr. Griffin* as an Introductory Core Novel

The purpose of reading a core novel before the study of *Caesar* is to provide a common background experience before undertaking the more difficult Shakespearean work. Lois Duncan's *Killing Mr. Griffin* (243 pp.) works well because young adult readers can identify with the characters and the problems presented. Students recognize themselves and their friends in Duncan's well-developed characters; hence, students are able to make connections to the characters in *The Tragedy of Julius Caesar* as they experience literature that reflects life as they know it.

In *Killing Mr. Griffin*, Mark manipulates other teens and gets them to engage in a dangerous prank that none of them would have seriously considered on his or her own. Mark is like Cassius because Cassius is the chief conspirator who systematically convinces Brutus to join the conspiracy. Mark's friend, Jeff, is exasperated with Mr. Griffin, the strict English teacher, and whispers, "He's the kind of guy you just want to kill." Mark challenges Jeff to live up to those words by concocting a plan to scare Mr. Griffin into passivity and submission. Mark's farfetched plan becomes more and more believable as each of the other characters voices why it cannot be implemented. In the same way, Brutus questions Cassius. Mark systematically answers each of the excuses until all involved submit to the plan.

Main Characters in *Killing Mr. Griffin*

Mark

Mark has been living with his aunt and uncle since his father's death and his mother's nervous breakdown. Mark is a psychopath, but readers do not learn this until the end of the story. He exhibits all of the characteristics, but no one really believes that Mark is really "crazy" and in need of professional help.

Jeff

Jeff is the high school's star athlete and a loyal friend. He has been friends with Mark since the 7th grade and is Mark's mainstay. Jeff enjoys working on cars and extends his help to other friends who have cars in need of repair. His parents see a bright future for their son.

Betsy

Betsy is a vivacious, popular cheerleader. She is going steady with Jeff but is fascinated and infatuated with Mark. Her father is a local politician, and her mother is a socialite. Betsy is indulged by her parents and expects preferential treatment from everyone. She is jealous of anyone else who might be in the spotlight.

Susan

Susan is a homely, serious student. She feels alienated from her classmates at school so she tries to compensate by excelling academically. She also feels isolated at home, where she is surrounded by dominating males, a father and three younger brothers, and a mother who is submissive and doting. Susan is vulnerable to anyone who shows interest in her and is a year younger than the other characters.

David

David is the senior class president. He lives with his mother and paternal grandmother because his father walked out on them when he was very young. David is very responsible to his family and has a limited social life. He desperately wants to go to college and knows he must earn a scholarship to be able to afford it. All of his decisions are controlled by his responsibility to his family and his goal of obtaining a scholarship.

Mr. Griffin

Mr. Griffin is a dedicated English teacher who takes a cut in pay and prestige by resigning his university position in order to teach at the high school level. He is recently married, even though he is in his mid-thirties, and his wife is expecting their first child. Mr. Griffin also has an angina, a heart condition for which he regularly takes medication. Mr. Griffin has noble intentions, but he may be going overboard as far as zeal and dedication are concerned. A similar case can be made for Julius Caesar; he is zealous in his attempt at making life better for Roman citizens.

Making Connections between the Core and the Classic

By my reading *Killing Mr. Griffin* aloud to the class, everyone is privy to the spontaneous discussions that occur. I intentionally think out loud so students can hear how an experienced reader transacts with a story, but I also encourage them to volunteer their ideas and questions to specific dilemmas: "What do you think you would you do if you were in Susan's situation? Jeff's? Who is letting their 'heart rule their head'? Explain."

Students discuss and record their ideas in reader-response journals. Teachers can point out Duncan's use of foreshadowing by asking students to predict what they think will happen next. Students gain by hearing how different people, besides the teacher, interpret a text. Speculations are valued, pondered, and tested by other members.

Reader-response methods help students make personal connections with the more difficult play's characters, setting, and themes. Much time is devoted so that students can discuss the literature among themselves and with the teacher. Because I tend to dominate whole class discussions, I have my students work in small groups so that they can do most of the talking. I also try to ask questions that stimulate their thinking and extend their responses, rather than telling them what I think. The important part is their active involvement, their exploration of the works.

Character Connections

As Duncan's characters are introduced, have students write their names and brief descriptions for each one. They need to check their descriptions daily, making sure the present description is in keeping with what they know of the characters. As the story progresses, the descriptions may change or become more clear. The earlier descriptions should not be erased so that students are able to see how the author develops the characters. The following list is one possible result:

Susan — bookworm, no real friends, low self-esteem
David — responsible, studious, few friends
Mark — selfish, manipulative, evil

Jeff — loyal friend, easy-going, star athlete
Betsy — popular, snobbish, expects preferential treatment
Mr. Griffin — strict, dedicated, demanding, caring

Next, have students keep a continuum of teenagers ranked according to their moral conduct, and have them justify their placements:

Mark   Betsy   Jeff   David   Susan

Only near the end of the book do readers see the characters so clearly. Throughout the reading experience, students will shift the characters' positions. A sample explanation for the continuum above might include the following:

Mark is evil and manipulative. He wants revenge because Mr. Griffin flunked him for cheating the previous year. Betsy wants Mark to like her in a special way, even though Jeff is her boyfriend. Because Jeff is Mark's best friend and Betsy's boyfriend, he is easily swayed out of blind loyalty to each of them. David is a reluctant participant but is shamed into participating for the thrill of doing something other than taking care of his mother and grandmother. Susan acts as the decoy but refuses to go and watch. It is Susan's convictions that give the reader any hope for a "good" solution to the madness.

These lists are used to compare the characters of *Killing Mr. Griffin* to the characters of *The Tragedy of Julius Caesar* and eventually to the characters of other books the students will read. Once students have become familiar with the core novel and the classic, have them develop a chart comparing the characters from the core novel to those in Shakespeare's play. Discussions get lively as students defend their opinions in their small groups. An example follows:

Killing Mr. Griffin	*Tragedy of Julius Caesar*
Mark	Cassius
Susan	Brutus
Jeff	Antony
David	Portia
Mr. Griffin	Caesar

Setting Connections

The setting in *Killing Mr. Griffin* is similar to *The Tragedy of Julius Caesar*. Because of a southwest wind, a bird is swept into a window at school and dies. The wind creates an unsettled feeling, a setting of chaos. The wind is in contrast to the inscription on Mr. Griffin's and David's Dad's rings, "The winds of freedom blow..."

In *Caesar*, the setting is tumultuous as Brutus agonizes over joining the conspiracy. The candles are blown out by the strong wind, and the rain beats against the conspirators as they seek out Brutus under the cover of darkness. These are not "winds of freedom" that are blowing. Ask students to notice the use of setting in the core novel so they can make other observations in the classic.

Extending the Learning through Other Young Adult Novels

There are many different ways for teachers to set up this extension activity, but I prefer ones that give the teacher and students a lot of choice and flexibility. I group various YA novels into four categories: character novels, identity and self-discovery novels, protagonists' writing in order to understand and explain, and isolated protagonists. Students participate in a book pass (Tchudi & Mitchell, 1989, pp. 139–140) in which they read from each of the books for five minutes in order to make their book selections. Students are then grouped according to their choices, not to exceed five in a group.

Students individually read their books and keep double-entry reading logs. Have students divide their papers in half vertically with "Reading Notes" on the left side and "Discussion Notes" on the right side. Students individually record their ideas, questions, thoughts, and discoveries on the left side of the paper. Students discuss their books with other students who are reading books from the same category. Students log their new insights or thoughts sparked by the discussion on the right side of the paper. Additionally, each group keeps a group list of all characters and their characteristics.

Character Novels

I Know What You Did Last Summer by Lois Duncan (199 pp.)

Four teenagers—Julie, Ray, Barry, and Helen—are involved in an automobile accident that kills a young boy on a bicycle. Someone has discovered their identities and their crime and wants revenge.

Julie acquiesces when the group votes not to help the boy and not to report the incident, but she is tragically wounded. She breaks all ties with the three other teens, quits the cheerleading squad, and becomes an antisocial bookworm. She has aged, carrying the weight of guilt on her shoulders.

Ray sells his vote to his best friend, Barry, believing Julie will submissively go along. Ray is bothered by the group's decision, but he is more bothered by Julie breaking up with him afterward. He goes away for several months and tries to forget about the incident, but he realizes he must return and face himself and those he really cares about.

Barry is untouched by the accident because "guilt" is not in his vocabulary. He attends the local university, makes the football team, spends time in a fraternity, and enjoys being popular with beautiful women; he is flippant about all of his relationships. He is "a big man on campus" but is juvenile in his development.

Helen "lives life in the fast lane" and has made the big time as the "Golden Girl" for Channel 5. She enjoys the money she is making, the good life it affords, the clothes she sports, and her model lifestyle. She fantasizes about Barry marrying her in the near future.

The following list and explanation might be one student's interpretation of the characters:

Julie — responsible, moral, strong character, a doer
Ray — kind, sensitive, loyal friend, smart
Barry — selfish, conceited, womanizer
Helen — shallow, pretty, low self-esteem, devoted to Barry
Bud (Collie) — Vietnam veteran, loner, physically strong,
            out for revenge

Unlike Brutus, Julie does not have to agonize over her decision. She is forthright and steadfast in her decision to help the boy and call the police. Her agony of spirit is the result of her agreeing to abide by the group's vote, which went against her decision.

Like Brutus, Julie wants to be responsible—but what constitutes responsibility? Brutus is faced with this dilemma: His beloved Rome is in jeopardy unless Caesar is stopped. Cassius asks him to consider a possible solution: "Wouldn't it be better to crush the snake in the shell than to live with the poisonous destruction that would surely transpire if the snake hatched?"

Julie lives in pain as the result of abiding by the decision she did not want to make, knowing in her heart it was wrong. Brutus is in pain during the decision-making process, weighing the possibilities against each other in cold detachment. Brutus, however, is able to go forth with a clear conscience once he makes his decision to join the conspirators for "the good of Rome." He, alone of the assassins, acts unselfishly.

Downriver by Will Hobbs (204 pp.)

Jessie is a spoiled teenager who does not want to deal with her Dad's remarriage. He sends her off to Discovery Unlimited, an outdoor education program for nine weeks. As Al, the leader, explains, "Sometimes self-reliance is the key to survival, but other times cooperation is" (p. 5). When is asserting oneself best and when is going along with others best? Did Brutus make the wisest choice?

Jessie must see through the manipulative, attractive Troy to stay alive. Jessie sells everyone else short, discounting Freddy and his quiet strength in order to follow the turbulent, demanding Troy. Troy needs to control others even though he is out of control most of the time. He throws the map of the mile-by-mile river guide away, knocks Rita into the rapids, and puts the poisonous scorpion in Freddy's sleeping bag.

Freddy, on the other hand, is quietly confident. He is the dependable person with knowledge of the earth and wisdom of the ages. Freddy always has to be asked for his knowledge; he does not flaunt what he has. He pulls Jessie to safety when she freezes with fright and falls when mountain climbing, he stitches Rita's forehead, he recognizes and explains the Hopi Indian shrine and prayer stick that he and Jessie discover, and he sets Adam's dislocated shoulder.

At the beginning of the novel, Jessie "could see nothing but the frightening dark tunnel that was my [her] future. I saw no images there, no hopes, only blackness" (p. 2). At the end of the novel, Jessie tells her Dad, "I really do love this place [their new home], Dad. Especially all the light" (p. 200). Jessie eventually discovers her inner strength, and her view of her world is enlightened. She is able to make meaningful relationships because she discovers her own identity, and her intense experiences expose the true characteristics in others. She will probably be a better judge of characters in the future.

A student's list of characters and their characteristics might include the following:

Jessie — spoiled and has an attitude, survivor, smart,
    reflective thinker, determined
Freddy — quiet, confident, dependable, resourceful, common
    sense, respectful of nature
Troy — attractive, natural leader, controlling, demanding,
    undependable, unpredictable, mean
Star — quiet, superstitious, serene, accepting
Adam — funny, never serious, comedian, actor
Pug — obnoxious, always hungry, a follower
Rita — loud-mouthed, opinionated, rebellious, sassy
Al — leader, adult authority, laid-back, loved outdoors,
    double-crosser

Through discussions, students will discover similarities between the characters of the different books by fully describing each character. Eventually students will come to know the characters from *Killing Mr. Griffin*, *I Know What You Did Last Summer*, *Downriver*, and *Julius Caesar*, and develop a chart comparing the characters like the one below:

Killing	I Know	Downriver	*Caesar*
Mark	Barry	Troy	Cassius
Susan	Julie	Jessie	Brutus
Jeff	Ray	Freddy	Antony
David	Helen	Star	Portia?
Mr. Griffin	Bud (Collie)	Adam	Caesar

Of course the analogous relationships between characters in different texts are not judged on their "correctness" but rather on the explanation of how students see the connections. The richness of this activity is in the discussion of students' insights.

Using analogies to compare characters may be taken one step further by having students compare the characters to any medium. What if the characters in **Killing Mr. Griffin** were compared to types of advertisements? An example follows:

Susan:newspaper::David:*Newsweek*::Jeff:television::
Betsy:telephone::Mark:pornography

Comparing these characters to a mineral might result in the following:

Susan:14ct gold::David:silver::Jeff:aluminum::
Betsy:plastic::Mark:steel

Characters in different books may be compared in terms of what they trust and hold most dear:

Susan:books::Julie:morals::Jessie:perception::Brutus:intellect

Characters can be compared to musical instruments:

Susan:piano::Julie:guitar::Jessie:drums::Brutus:violin

Identity/Self Discovery Novels

Adolescents are searching for their own identities and are persuaded sometimes by "false friends" to sell themselves short. Coming of age, developing individual convictions, and having the fortitude to stand up for personal convictions are difficult challenges. Young adult readers admire characters who demonstrate the strength to stand up for their own convictions even if they are not completely successful.

Brutus is a strong character who does not see that Cassius is a "false friend." After Brutus decides to join the conspiracy, he never looks back. He endures the hardships his decision creates: battling Octavius and Antony, accepting Portia's suicide, and falling upon his own sword. He maintains his dignity and respect even in death.

The Contender by Robert Lipsyte (167 pp.)

Alfred Brooks is an orphan and a high school dropout who lives with his aunt and cousins. Nonetheless, he wants to be a boxing champion; he wants to be somebody. Mr. Donatelli tells him, "Everybody wants to be a champion. That's not enough. You have to start by wanting to be a contender, the man coming up, the man who knows there's a good chance he'll never get to the top, the man who's willing to sweat and bleed to get up as high as his legs and his brains and his heart will take him. It's the climbing that makes the man. Getting to the top is an extra reward" (p. 25).

In order to achieve his goals, Alfred must break away from the "false friends" who surround him. Major and Hollis resent Alfred's working for the white Jewish Epsteins. As Alfred begins training and working out at Mr. Donatelli's gym, they harass him and try to get him to come back to their way of life, which involves drugs, women, and stealing. Alfred has a genuine interest in James, who was once his best friend, but does not know how to relate to him when he is stoned on drugs.

Alfred has setbacks along the way. He is temporarily distracted from his goal of becoming a contender by his "false friends," but he is not permanently hindered. Alfred—unlike Brutus, who does not even realize he is being used by Cassius and other "false friends"—seeks others to provide him with good advice. Alfred emerges as an adolescent who respects himself, and his strength of character enables him to really help his friend James. Before Alfred can be successful in building relationships, he must develop his own identity.

The Friends by Rosa Guy (185 pp.)

Phyllisia surrounds herself with "false friends" because she chooses her friends based on their appearance. Her one real friend is Edith Jackson, but Phyllisia wants to reject her because of how she looks. The friends Phyllisia wants do not give her the time of day, and some are downright abusive. Edith adopts Phyllisia as her friend-in-need and protects her from being attacked again by Beulah. By contrast, Phyllisia is ashamed to be seen with such a "ragamuffin as Edith."

Phyllisia is too selfish and shallow to be able to be a friend to Edith. Phyllisia betrays Edith's friendship just as Brutus betrayed Caesar's leadership. Unlike Brutus, Phyllisia has more time and opportunities to make amends. It takes many events for Phyllisia to mature enough to risk her pride to embrace Edith's friendship on a full-time basis.

Phyllisia must first realize that she entertains the same prejudices that she hates in her father. As difficult as it is for any adolescent to realize, Phyllisia must recognize that she, not her father Calvin, is a fraud. She must be true to herself before she can be a friend. At the end of the book, the first of a trilogy, Phyllisia appears to be ready to be a real friend to Edith.

Tex by S.E. Hinton (194 pp.)

Tex is persuaded by Lem to sell drugs, an activity he would never participate in of his own accord. Tex is experiencing self-doubt and low self-esteem when he is swept into the action of a drug deal gone bad. His older brother, Mason, had sold Tex's horse in order to pay the utilities and get money for groceries. Their mother died years ago, and Pop is only an itinerant father. Mason develops ulcers trying to manage for the two of them while keeping up his grades. Mason wants to earn a basketball scholarship so that he can attend college, which would mean leaving Tex. Furthermore, Tex learns that Pop is not his real father.

Lem, like Cassius (and Mark and Troy), preys on Tex's vulnerability. It is Mason who understands Tex and serves as Antony in explaining Tex's behavior. Tex's character is dynamic because of his relationship with Mason.

He is able to let Mason go to college, realizing that Mason is one of those people who will go places and that he is the one who must stay behind.

The Chocolate War by Robert Cormier (191 pp.)

After the death of his mother, Jerry Renault is willing to pay his dues for acceptance into the school's secret society—the Vigils. Like Brutus, Jerry does not question the social structure of his society—in Jerry's case, school. In the case of Brutus, he works to preserve the society, decides to assassinate Caesar for "the good of Rome," and dies for his actions. Similarly, Jerry pays. *The Chocolate War* is considered a YA tragedy even though Jerry does not physically die. The tragedy lies in the death of Jerry's inner strength, his moral character.

In order for acceptance into the Vigils, Jerry must complete "the assignment" Archie Costello delegates. Jerry's first assignment is to refuse to sell chocolates for ten days; selling chocolates is the school's major fund raiser. Throughout the story, Jerry asks the question posed by J. Alfred Prufrock, "Do I dare disturb the universe?" Jerry wants to find his place in the world, and in doing so, disturbs the society created by the Vigils. He "disturbs the universe" by ignoring the second assignment of selling the chocolates after 10 days of refusing to sell them.

Jerry, like Alfred Brooks in *The Contender*, wants to be somebody. He wants to stand his own ground. He witnesses Gregory Bailey being true to himself when Brother Leon accuses him of cheating, but Jerry sits passively, unable to do anything to stop the unfair inquisition.

Jerry has a friend in Goober but, like Brutus, he does not talk through the details with him. Jerry does not break the secrecy of the assignment; like Brutus, he keeps the conspiracy a secret. Goober, however, assumes what the truth is and tries to get Jerry to quit going against the Vigils. When Jerry realizes that his peers want him to lose the fight, he retreats and surrenders. The crowning blow occurs when he realizes he is Archie's pawn, and the decision is not his own. He suffers a moral wound.

Like Cassius, Archie manipulates the other boys by calculating each one's vulnerability. Archie is a cold character who does not seem to care about anything except controlling others; Archie is amoral.

Continuing with the analogies of characters from Robert Lipsyte's *The Contender*, Rosa Guy's *The Friends*, S.E. Hinton's *Tex*, and Robert Cormier's *The Chocolate War*, students from each group might develop a chart similar to the one that follows. (Note: Even though I am presenting the charts separately here, they actually make one large chart that serves as a lead into the classic.)

Contender	Friends	Tex	Chocolate War	Caesar
Major/Hollis	Calvin	Lem	Archie	Cassius
Alfred	Phyllisia	Tex	Jerry	Brutus
Mr. Donatelli	Edith	Mason	Goober	Antony
James	Mother	Pop	Obie	Caesar

The following compares the characters to weather:

> Mr. Donatelli:sunshine::Phyllisia:thunderstorm::
> Pop:cloud::Archie:hurricane::Brutus:snow

Protagonists' Writing in Order to Understand and Explain

Antony respects Brutus. He understands that Brutus willingly murdered Caesar only because Caesar was a perceived threat to Rome. Brutus sacrificed the one for the benefit of the many. Antony explains, as he delivers Brutus' eulogy, that Brutus represented mankind at its very best.

Ponyboy in *The Outsiders*, Charlotte Doyle in *The True Confessions of Charlotte Doyle*, and Jerome Foxworthy in *The Moves Make the Man* write their stories. But in a sense, Ponyboy is writing Johnny's story and Jerome is writing Bix's. They are acting as Antony did in explaining the complex characters of the people they admire, even if they disagree with them. Charlotte writes her own story for vindication, knowing her story will not be told unless she tells it herself. She accepts that society misunderstands her because she does not accept society's standards.

The Outsiders by S.E. Hinton (156 pp.)

In S.E. Hinton's *The Outsiders*, Ponyboy Curtis is like Brutus. Ponyboy is persuaded by the gang and is loyal to the society he knows. He is a thinker and often a loner. He shares some of his passion for movies, books, poetry, and sunsets with his fellow gang member, Johnny, and the female Soc, Cherry. He writes his thoughts in a journal which becomes the book. He, like Brutus, believes he is misunderstood but that his actions are just.

The True Confessions of Charlotte Doyle by Avi (232 pp.)

Charlotte is a proper young lady, groomed in high society and schooled in European manners. She accepts society's understanding of the world without question. On a voyage to America during which she is the only female and the only passenger on board, Charlotte must confront her learned prejudices of class, status, and ethnicity. She is suspicious of the friendship and kindness Zachariah offers her because he is black and merely a crewmember, a person quite beneath her status. Meanwhile, she witnesses Captain Jaggery blatantly abuse his power and authority.

Charlotte records the actions and emotional highs and lows she experiences in a journal to show her father upon her arrival. She trusts his judgment to be like hers, just as Brutus thinks the citizens of Rome will see the validity of the assassination once they know the facts. Charlotte believes her father will use his authority to bring justice. Charlotte arrives a changed person, much to her father's disapproval. He does not tolerate the truth she has written in her journal, forbids her to talk about her voyage, and isolates her in her room. Because he is in complete control of the household, no one questions his decisions.

Charlotte is too confined by the orderliness of such a way of life after having experienced the "winds of freedom" (from *Killing Mr. Griffin*) and the responsibilities of a sailor and crew member. She rejects the society she inherited so that she can develop her potential as a person within the society she chooses, the society of a ship's crew.

Like Brutus, Charlotte was also born into nobility and is well-schooled. Brutus accepts the hierarchical society and willingly participates in maintaining its order. Charlotte allows herself to become emotionally involved whereas Brutus relies on his intellectual reasoning of the entire situation.

What might have happened if Brutus had rejected Cassius' invitation to participate or if he had consulted with someone? Why did he agree to Cassius' solution even if he agreed with Cassius' statement of the problem? Brutus is a static character; he does not change or grow. He dies the noble Roman.

The Moves Make the Man by Bruce Brooks (280 pp.)

Jerome writes Bix's story in order to make sense of what happens. Jerome admires Bix even though he does not understand why Bix cannot learn to put the moves on an opponent in basketball. Bix is an excellent baseball player who is learning the basics of basketball. But, Bix refuses to even try to fake his moves. As Jerome recounts what he knows about Bix, he realizes that Bix had been caught up in one big move his entire life—his mother's mental illness—and he was determined not to live that way.

Bix, like Brutus, is a narrow character. Things are either black or white; neither of them see shades of gray. Bix is a respected leader on the baseball field, and Brutus is a respected leader in the Roman senate. Neither Bix nor Brutus can tolerate people who do not share their high standards of behavior. They are surrounded by less competent people, and yet they do not understand people well enough to be able to lead them effectively. In this sense everyone loses.

Students continue to develop the chart as they share their descriptions of the characters from these books. Please note that there is not a one-to-one correspondence of characters in these books:

Outsiders	Charlotte	Moves	Caesar
	Capt. Jaggery		Cassius
Ponyboy/Johnny	Charlotte	Bix	Brutus
Ponyboy	Charlotte and Zachariah	Jerome	Antony
Johnny/Bob	Cranick		Caesar

Isolated Protagonists

The character of Brutus is interesting because students expect the smart guys to know better, to understand. People who are intellectually detached and emotionally underdeveloped seem to be the most vulnerable when it comes to getting caught in others' webs of deceit.

No Kidding by Bruce Brooks (207 pp.)

Few protagonists have the cold intellectual detachment that Brutus demonstrates, but Sam in Bruce Brooks' *No Kidding* is a close match. Twelve-year-olds may commit their parents to alcohol rehabilitation centers in this 21st-century society. Sam committed his mother when he was 13, but after one year he is having her released into his custody. Sam feels obligated to consider all aspects in regards to his mother's release and her affect on the family. He takes care of the details: gets her a job, buys her clothes, and rents an apartment.

Fourteen-year-old Sam methodically collects data, reading the latest research published in the *Journal of Secondary Education Methodology* so that he stays current with anything that might relate to his younger brother, Ollie. Sam desperately wants Ollie to have a stable, non-alcoholic childhood. Alcohol abuse is so widespread in this novel that schools have Alcohol Offspring Programs, and alcohol rehabilitation is the second-largest organization in the country—only the postal service is larger. Sam's big decision is whether or not to sign the papers so Ollie's foster parents can legally adopt him.

The cold detachment creates the climax of this story. Families, even in the 21st century, must communicate even when their emotions are not calm, harmonious, or comfortable. No one can be sheltered from pain completely. Sam tries to protect Ollie from his mother and from the truth. Ollie, however, needs the truth and seeks it on his own without the benefit of the family who loves him.

It is a dangerous thing when Sam and Brutus make their decisions in an intellectual vacuum. They both have the best intentions, but they rely solely on their own rationalizations. Neither of them trust anyone enough to listen to their counsel. In this world, people need friends and practice in making and keeping friends.

I Am the Cheese by Robert Cormier (233 pp.)

Adam Farmer is isolated. The Witness Protection Program completely strips witnesses of their friends in order to protect them. But then what happens when your only connection to the "good guys" is a double agent?

There are times when we must not talk to others. Brutus perceives that the decision regarding Caesar is his alone. Knowing when to speak and how much to say is a lifelong learning process for many. Adam Farmer displays tremendous strength of character because he must keep his own counsel or be destroyed if he tells all that he knows. Adam Farmer is the cheese, "and the cheese stands alone." What worse fate is there? Cormier makes readers face the cruel possibilities of our realistic world. What might life be like without an identity and without friends?

Students add the characters of these books to the class chart. As in the last group of books, these books' characters do not match with a one-to-one correspondence.

No Kidding	*I Am the Cheese*	*Caesar*
	Mr. Black/government	Cassius
Sam	Adam	Brutus
		Antony
Ollie	Adam's parents	Caesar

Conclusion

As a culminating activity, each group presents an "I Am" poem of each of the different characters and analogous comparisons. An "I Am" poem is a formula poem that provides the first two words of each sentence (Mee, 1986). The first sentence is repeated at the end of each stanza. Students must be able to identify with the character's point of view to write it. Two student examples are included (see Figure 7-1). As classmates listen to each group's description of the characters in different books, they often volunteer their insights: "Oh, Barry sounds like Mark." "Yes, and Troy sounds like Mark and Barry."

All of the reading of the YA literature and the discussions and activities provide students with common background knowledge which the teacher can activate when everyone is reading *The Tragedy of Julius Caesar*. As students see common characteristics between and among characters in the YA literature, they will also identify these characteristics in the characters in Shakespeare's play. "Oh, Cassius is like Mark." The teacher facilitates discussion by asking the students to extend their responses, "How are they alike?"

Figure 7-1
From *Killing Mr. Griffin*

David's "I Am" Poem

I am responsible and dependable.
I wonder what it would be like to have a social life.
I hear Gram asking, "Davey, is that you?"
I want Mom, Gram, and I to have a better life.
I am responsible and dependable.
I pretend it doesn't bother me to be a loner.
I feel like a fraud: Senior Class President and King of the Sink.
I touch Mr. Griffin's hand and I take his ring.
I worry about Mom, Gram, Mr. Griffin, getting caught, and not getting a
      scholarship.
I cry because Gram and Mr. Griffin died needlessly.
I am responsible and dependable.
I understand we cannot bring them back to life and that our lives will never
      be the same.
I say, "I'm sorry. I'm ashamed."
I dream that Dad never left, Mark never talked all of us into kidnapping Mr.
      Griffin, and that I receive a scholarship to college.
I try to be strong and take it like a man.
I hope Mom, Mrs. Griffin, her baby, and Susan will be all right.
I am responsible and dependable.

Mark's "I Am" Poem

I am cold and manipulative.
I wonder how everyone can be so stupid.
I hear my dad and the cat scream, and I want to hear Mr. G. scream.
I am cold and manipulative.
I pretend to care about others.
I feel no remorse for my actions.
I touch the fire of the houses I torched.
I worry Susan and David will blow the whistle.
I cry never.
I am cold and manipulative.
I understand I am smarter than the others.
I say, "I'll take care of it; leave it to me."
I dream of revenge with fire.
I try to keep everyone on course and under my control.
I hope I see the people who have gotten in my way hurt.
I am cold and manipulative.

Having invested the time in reading and discussing these YA novels, students will be much better prepared to understand the character development, setting, and themes of *The Tragedy of Julius Caesar*. By asking students to remember the characteristics of the characters in the YA novels and comparing them to each other, students are more apt to continue that same process with more difficult, "remote" literature.

List of References

Avi. (1990). *The true confessions of Charlotte Doyle*. New York: Avon.

Brooks, B. (1989). *No kidding*. New York: Harper & Row.

Brooks, B. (1984). *The moves make the man*. New York: Harper & Row.

Cormier, R. (1977). *I am the cheese*. New York: Dell.

Cormier, R. (1974). *The chocolate war*. New York: Pantheon.

Duncan, L. (1978). *Killing Mr. Griffin*. Boston: Little, Brown & Company.

Duncan, L. (1973). *I know what you did last summer*. New York: Archway Paperbacks.

Guy, R. (1983). *The friends*. New York: Bantam.

Hinton, S.E. (1989). *The outsiders*. New York: Dell.

Hinton, S.E. (1979). *Tex*. New York: Delacorte Press.

Hobbs, W. (1991). *Downriver*. New York: Bantam.

Lipsyte, R. (1987). *The contender*. New York: Harper & Row.

Mee, S. (1986, September 8). I am. *Scholastic Voice*.

Shakespeare, W. (1969). *Julius Caesar*. London: Cornmarket.

Tchudi, S. & Mitchell, D. (1989). *Explorations in the teaching of English*. New York: Harper & Row.

CHAPTER 8

Friendships and Tensions in *A Separate Peace* and *Staying Fat for Sarah Byrnes*

LYNNE ALVINE AND
DEVON DUFFY

Introduction

First published in 1959, *A Separate Peace* was on its way to becoming a modern classic long before the appearance of *The Outsiders*, *The Pigman*, and *Mr. and Mrs. Bo Jo Jones* signaled the beginnings of young adult (YA) literature. For over three decades, classroom sets of John Knowles' tragic story of Finny and Gene and the accident at the river have been on the shelves of teachers interested in having young readers connect with books.

We have both taught *A Separate Peace* as a whole class assignment—Lynne as an experienced teacher of senior English in Virginia in the late 1970s, and Devon as a student teacher of sophomore English in Pennsylvania in the early 1990s. Although our classroom interactions with the novel were over 15 years and several hundred miles apart, we both found ways to assist our young readers in connecting World War II prep school students' experiences with their own lives.

Shortly after Devon completed her student teaching under Lynne's supervision, we each read Chris Crutcher's *Staying Fat for Sarah Byrnes*. Lynne told Devon she saw connections between it and *A Separate Peace*, and Devon immediately began listing the ones that came to mind for her. In this chapter, we share the parallels we see between the two novels and suggest a teaching strategy for both. Although many teachers have found ways to use a YA novel as a thematic bridge to a classic, we recommend having students begin with *A Separate Peace*. Its themes are accessible to most young readers. They can then further connect the experiences of Finny and Gene to their own lives through Crutcher's very contemporary characters.

To extend the unit, we have selected five additional YA choices for collaborative group reading and discussion. We provide thematic connections between the various novels and offer interrelated follow-up activities for each. Finally, we suggest titles for further independent reading.

A Separate Peace by John Knowles (186 pp.)

In *A Separate Peace*, narrator Gene returns to Devon School 15 years after the end of World War II and recalls the unnatural "peace" experienced there by boys who were on the brink of going to war. His most poignant memory is of his love and jealousy for the brash, daredevil Phineas who eventually died from injuries sustained in a fall onto the river bank from their "jumping" tree. Suspecting that Finny had really been trying to undermine his academic success, Gene thinks he may have caused the fall by jiggling the branch ever so slightly. He is ridden with guilt for years but, in the retelling of the story, is able to realize Finny's forgiveness and achieve absolution.

Staying Fat for Sarah Byrnes by Chris Crutcher (216 pp.)

In *Staying Fat for Sarah Byrnes*, a teenage girl who was severely disfigured in a childhood "accident" is best friends with an overweight member of the high school swim team who calls himself Moby. Believing their differences are the basis of their friendship and that Sarah will abandon him if he loses weight, Moby continues to eat great quantities of food. Then, Sarah becomes catatonic out of fear of her abusive father's return. While Sarah is hospitalized, Moby investigates and learns what caused Sarah's burns. Out of concern for Sarah's safety, he confides in a teacher, Mrs. Lemry. Moby also has to deal with his friend Steve, who is grieving his brother's death, and a Fundamentalist Christian classmate named Mark, who is unable to reconcile forcing his girlfriend Jody to have an abortion. Eventually, Mrs. Lemry and Moby's mother's boyfriend Carver sort out the confusion and offer the young people the support they need.

Friendships and Tensions in the two Core Novels

What do the two central books in this unit plan have in common? At first glance, perhaps very little. In *A Separate Peace*, the focus is on two young men at a boys' prep school who are very popular. One of them struggles with jealousy and guilt. In Chris Crutcher's latest work, *Staying Fat for Sarah Byrnes*, the main characters, a boy and a girl at a public high school, are social isolates. They both struggle with self-esteem and self-actualization issues.

Despite the obvious differences, these two novels have several interesting parallels that can be brought out when they are read together as the central books of a unit on friendship. Human beings seek out friendships and create bonds with others at all ages and phases of life, but never so much as during the teenage years.

Exploring Friendship on the Brink of Adulthood

Both of these novels explore the nature of friendship through very serious subjects. *Staying Fat for Sarah Byrnes* deals with eating disorders, child abuse, oppression, depression, and abortion. *A Separate Peace* takes on war and death. In both stories, the characters make discoveries about themselves and others, discoveries about the very essence of human experience that age them beyond their chronological years.

A Separate Peace presents the tensions of competition and jealousy in a close friendship. Finny is accomplished in the areas of sports and social interaction; he is a star athlete and a star trickster as well. Gene is nearly as good as Finny at sports and is in line to finish at the top of their class in academics. Finny enjoys being identified as Gene's friend and makes several overt statements about their good friendship. Gene, however, who is uncomfortable with Finny's talk about their relationship, has a need to separate from Finny, to become his own person. Gene's feelings of jealousy for Finny's sports ability lead him to suspect that Finny is similarly jealous of his academic prowess. Because Gene, who is the narrator, is unable to discern whether "the accident" was an accident, the reader can never know what really happened in that tree. What is clear is Gene's response to the guilt and shame he feels and the behaviors that reveal his conflicted sense of loyalty to Finny.

When Finny is away convalescing, Gene both embraces and rejects his feelings for Finny. In some ways his actions suggest that he is trying to convince himself that he is a good friend to Finny; he wears Finny's clothes. It is as if he thinks Finny's injuries will go away if he can just show that he is a good enough friend. In other ways, Gene reacts to the accident by changing his identity at Devon. He abdicates his role as sports leader, opting instead for the lesser job of crew manager. By refusing to compete in sports, he does not have to "defeat" Finny's legend. It was Finny who was injured and who died from his injuries, but it is Gene who is in need of healing. Only through Finny's forgiveness is Gene able to become whole.

In *Staying Fat for Sarah Byrnes*, Moby and Sarah are initially drawn together because they believe their physical ugliness sets them apart from others in their school. Moby comes to know what Sarah has known all along—that difference is a state of mind, that what is important is how they feel about their difference, and that they do not have to stay different to remain friends.

Moby also learns quite a lot about the dynamics of human relationships and that the lines between friendship and enmity can become blurred. Dale, who has been Moby's enemy, becomes his friend and rescuer. Mark and Moby clash throughout the novel, yet it is Moby who ironically gives Mark the power to go on at his darkest moment. A central theme of the novel, then, is that there comes a time to put enmity aside and to find a meeting place. When Moby and Mark meet in the hospital, Moby reaches out, and Mark responds. Moby's life models acceptance of self. He says,

"Look at me. I call myself 'Moby.' You have a problem? Deal with it. Get on with your life." Moby also comes to a fuller appreciation of Steve, seeing beyond the facade to the sensitive person that Steve is beneath all the rebellion he projects. Moby discovers that Steve feels much more deeply than Moby had given him credit for.

Sarah Byrnes learns that other people also have scars, though theirs may not be as visible as hers; other people also have walls they hide behind. Steve uses rebellion to cover the pain of losing his brother. Jody and Mark have been scarred by the external imposition of fundamentalist religious values and by the emotional pain of Jody's abortion. When Sarah learns that her internal beauty can be seen by others, she learns that she is worthy. She learns that she can be Sarah without being Sarah BYRNES. Once she has learned to accept herself, she can accept the friendship extended by Moby and Ms. Lemry and can, in turn, extend her hand to others. Earlier, she had expected some favor from Dale in exchange for her friendship. Later, she can reach out to Jody without expectation of something in return.

Character Connections

Another way the two novels come together is through the characters. Moby, in *Staying Fat for Sarah Byrnes*, is a complex young man. He is often quite reserved and introspective—hanging around the edges of classroom and social interactions—offering his commentary on what he sees. At other times, he is outgoing. He excels in swimming events and draws attention to himself. These two parts of Moby's character offer interesting parallels with the two main characters in *A Separate Peace*. Gene is introspective, reserved. Finny, however, may be said to represent the other part of Moby, the part that excels in athletic events and is the center of attention as a result. When Moby confronts Sarah's dad, Moby takes the best of the "Gene" and "Finny" traits and merges them into an integrated whole.

Both Sarah Byrnes and "Leper" Lepellier have physical and emotional problems. Sarah's face was burned severely in a childhood "accident." Leper is not athletic and labeled as "crazy." Both have serious problems adjusting to their lot in life. Whereas Sarah is rescued—through the support of Moby, Dale, and the teacher, Mrs. Lemry—Leper is without support and is not saved from himself. Although at one point Gene reaches out to Leper, he has a greater need to save himself and, thus, is unable to save Leper.

The characterizations of both the Christian Fundamentalist Mark in *Staying Fat for Sarah Byrnes* and the army enthusiast Brinker in *A Separate Peace* have elements of Fascism. Both believe they have a privileged access to the "Truth." In the end, they both learn that their "truths" are lies, forced onto them by someone whom they thought they could trust. In Mark's case it is his father and the Assistant Principal, Mr. Mautz. For Brinker, it is his father and the other "old men" who send boys off to fight their wars.

Adolescents often perceive adults as adversaries. In reading *Staying Fat for Sarah Byrnes*, kids see that some adults can be enemies to each other.

Sarah's dad, Virgil Byrnes, and the Assistant Principal Mr. Mautz are everyone's enemies. By contrast, this novel also shows that some adults are friends to adolescents. Near the end of the story, Moby sighs and says, "Boy, ain't it a trip where heroes come from." He is referring ostensibly to Carver. But there are many heroes in this novel: Mrs. Lemry, Steve's dad, and Carver are all friends and heroes to the young people. Several of the young people also develop heroic qualities. Sarah and Dale, along with Mark and Jody, survive their various abusive situations. Steve lets down some of his defenses so that others may see him more clearly. Sarah's wounds heal as she lets go of her pain. When Moby stands up to Virgil Byrnes, he also becomes a hero. With the merging of the two aspects of his personality, he becomes whole.

Using a Themes Carousel with the Core Novels

After the students discuss the events of *A Separate Peace*, a cooperative learning strategy called "the carousel" is an effective way to get students more deeply involved with the themes of the novel. We suggest using the themes carousel with *A Separate Peace* while laying the ground work for reading *Staying Fat for Sarah Byrnes*.

Day One

Briefly review the literary element of theme. Have each student discuss with a partner the themes they see in the novel. Each pair should hand in a list of a minimum of five themes. Using the group lists, produce a list of the seven or eight most important themes generated by the class. Print each of these themes on the top of a large sheet of poster board and hang the boards around the room before the next day's class. Divide students into groups of three or four and list group members' names on the board prior to class. For example, Devon's students identified *Jealousy, War, Competition, Confusion, Loyalty, Death, Forgiveness,* and *Friendship* as the major themes in *A Separate Peace*.

Day Two

Have each group choose a marking pen of different color, and note each group's color on the board. Each of the seven or eight groups moves to a different theme board to begin and works with one theme at a time. The students are to identify a passage from the novel that represents the theme named on the board. They must write the quotation, identify the speaker responsible for it (narrator or character), and note the page number. For example, under "Death", one of Devon's groups wrote, "This is something I think boys of your generation are going to see a lot of" (Dr. Stanpole, p. 185). The groups move around the room, focusing on each important theme and writing their quotation in their group's color of ink. The teacher should keep the carousel turning, allowing a bit longer at each board so that students can read what others have written and avoid duplication.

Day Three

In a large group, have students discuss each theme with a group spokesperson reading each of the quotations and explaining why the group chose that quotation and how it fits into the novel. As students begin to associate the various ink colors with the groups' members, they will direct their questions to the appropriate people and generate a student-directed discussion.

The themes carousel activity is amazing to watch. Students in Devon's class were intense in their search for quotations, sometimes discussing which of three quotations was the best to represent the theme. The large group discussion brings to light the different ways students read and interpret a text and its themes.

Sometimes the quotations don't seem to fit the themes. When given the opportunity to explain their connections, however, the groups are able to take the entire class and the teachers to new levels of understanding and insight. On a day when Lynne was observing Devon's class, the yellow group had written the following on the *War* theme board: "That night I slept easily, and it was only on waking up that this illusion was gone, and I was confronted with myself, and what I had done to Finny" (Gene, p. 54). The rest of the quotations on this board were directly related to the part World War II plays in the novel. The discussion came to a halt; students were confused about how this particular quotation fit into the theme. Allison, the group spokesperson, explained that Gene was fighting an inner war fueled by guilt over his role in Finny's injury. She gave several examples from the text that were further evidence of Gene's inner war, and the class erupted into an extended discussion of the nature of internal war and its role in the novel. That day we watched the students learning and growing as readers right before our eyes.

The carousel activity is an especially effective way for students to prepare for writing about a novel. It asks that they synthesize events, characterizations, and issues from the novel. It also helps them become familiar with what is located where so that they are more able to find evidence to support various points in their essays.

The carousel poster boards can also be used for other explorations of a novel that involve looking for evidence from the text such as literary elements, characterizations, or symbols. Have fun with this activity. The students enjoy the game aspect of it, and they will come to understand and defend the novel on much deeper levels.

After the class has read *Staying Fat for Sarah Byrnes*, pull out the poster boards again and ask the class to determine which of the themes is also important in the second novel. And, of course, ask them to identify additional themes and find support for them.   The extent to which the carousel activity is repeated with the second novel will depend on the needs of the class. Save those poster boards! We will refer to them again later.

Selected Novels for Student Choice and Group Reading

We have selected five novels that may be used to help students extend their exploration of how adolescent characters handle the complexities and tensions of friendship.   Some of the novels have themes and/or situations that relate directly to the two core novels. Because there are many connections between these novels, students reading different novels can be brought into the same discussion. For each, we have given a brief synopsis that can be used as a book talk to help students with their selections.   We have also listed the themes we see in the novels and several suggestions for student activities.   In many cases, the same activity is adaptable to several of the novels.

The Moves Make the Man by Bruce Brooks (280 pp.)

Jerome Foxworthy, who prides himself on his dedication to academics and to basketball, has recently transferred to an all-white school where he has difficulty fitting in. The "Jayfox" is teaching his strange new friend, Bix, how to play basketball until the lesson on "faking" brings up bad memories for Bix of having been tricked.   Jerome teaches Bix about basketball; Bix teaches Jerome about life.

There are several themes possible for study: *Friendship, Lying, Racial Prejudice, Responsibility, Dealing with Mental Illness,* and *Running Away.*

The Nature of Friendship

Discussion: How would you describe the friendship between Bix and Jerome?   What does each contribute to the friendship?   What does each receive from it?

Writing: Write a scene that is set 10 years after the end of the novel. What might happen if the two friends were to meet again? How has each of them changed?

The Nature of Truth

Discussion: How is the truth as Bix sees it different from the truth as Jerome sees it?   Where does the line between the truth and a lie fall?   Is it ever okay to tell a lie?   Is "faking" in basketball the same as lying?   How would you convince Bix (or Jerome) to change his mind on this matter?

Writing: Write a scene for the book in which Jerome is able to convince Bix that faking in basketball is not the same as lying.

The Nature of Racial Prejudice

Video: Have students view a videotape of Martin Luther King's "I Have a Dream" speech in terms of its relevance to *The Moves Make the Man*.

Discussion: Have you ever been the target of prejudice? Or have you ever witnessed prejudicial behavior toward others? How did you handle the situation? How would you advise others to handle prejudice?

Writing: Rewrite the "I Have a Dream" speech, inserting some dream for the future that you have. Perhaps you might focus on treatment of the mentally ill.

Princess Ashley by Richard Peck (208 pp.)

Chelsey has a lot to deal with: a new school, a guidance counselor for a mom, and a burning desire to be just like Ashley, who is everything Chelsey could hope to be. During her high school years, Chelsey discovers much about her mother, herself, and the nature of true friendship.

Some themes possible for study: *Friendship; Journey of Adolescence; Parents, Step-Parents and Teens; Substance Abuse;* and *Social Class Difference*.

The Nature of Peer Pressure

Discussion: Peer pressure, however subtle, exists in everyone's life. How did Chelsey and her friends handle it? How do you handle it?

Writing: Write a scene that is set 10 years after the end of the novel. What might happen if Chelsey and Ashley were to meet again? How has each of them changed?

The Journey of Adolescence

Charting a Lifeline: As a group, plot Chelsey's journey through adolescence on a lifeline that reflects the major high and low events. What were the turning points for her? Plot your own journey through adolescence on a similar lifeline. What events have represented your personal highs and lows, your turning points?

The Nature of Parent-Child Relationships

Discussion: What are some of the problems Chelsey and her mother have? How does her relationship with her mother affect Chelsey's life? Discuss some of the typical problems teens have with their parents and vice versa.

The Effects of Substance Abuse

Discussion: Substance abuse plays a major role in the novel. How did it affect the lives of the various characters? Investigate ways to curb the use of alcohol and other drugs around your school. "Just Say No" appears not to be a solution to this important social problem. What might be a more effective strategy for reducing the abuse of illegal substances?

Jacob Have I Loved by Katherine Paterson (175 pp.)

Although Louise and Caroline are twins, they could not be more different. Living in the 1940s on a small Atlantic coastal island, Louise finds herself at odds with her family and the social expectations of her times. In order to discover her own path in life, Louise must overcome her jealousy of her beautiful and talented sister.

Some possible themes include: *Friendship and Personality, Sibling Rivalry, Mental Illness, Love/Infatuation, Guilt,* and *Responsibility.*

Similarity and Difference

Discussion: How are Louise and Caroline different from each other? Are there any ways they are alike? How are you alike or different from one of your siblings, cousins, or friends?

Art Activity: Make a collage from pictures that represent the different aspects of your personality.

The Nature of Sibling Rivalry

Discussion: After reading an account of the Biblical story of Jacob and Esau, discuss how the title alludes to the relationship between Louise and Caroline. What does Louise's grandmother say about the Biblical characters? Can you name any other famous siblings from literature, pop culture, or current events who are very different from each other?

The Nature of Mental Illness

Discussion: What are some of the causes and current treatments of mental illness? How have these people been abused by society? What are our responsibilities toward those who are mentally ill?

Writing: Create mental illness awareness pamphlets for distribution around your school and community.

Memory by Margaret Mahy (288 pp.)

Jonny has lost his sister and his childhood acting career. He is also in danger of losing himself to alcohol when he meets Alzheimer victim,

Sophie. In his struggle to care for her, he learns much about himself and finds absolution for his guilt over his sister's death.

Various themes that could be explored include the following: *Mental Illness, Substance Abuse, Surviving Losses, Friendship, Responsibility, Love/Infatuation,* and *Guilt.*

The Nature of Alzheimer's Disease

Discussion: What are believed to be some of the causes, and what are the current treatments of Alzheimer's disease? What are our responsibilities for those who develop Alzheimer's disease?

Writing: Create Alzheimer's disease awareness pamphlets for distribution around your school and community.

The Nature of Substance Abuse

Discussion: What role does alcohol play in Jonny's descent into his new life? How do you think alcohol affected his feelings of guilt? How does Jonny's "affliction" compare and contrast with Sophie's situation?

The Loss of a Loved One

Discussion: How does the loss of a loved one affect members of the family? How does Jonny feel about his sister's death?

Writing: Write a letter to Jonny expressing how you feel about his loss. Is there anything you might say to help him get over his feelings of guilt?

Searching for Lost Children

Video: Play the video for the song "Runaway Train" by Soul Asylum, which shows pictures of lost children. This video, the TV show "America's Most Wanted," and pictures on milk cartons are ways the public gets information about lost children. What other ideas do you have for helping to find lost children?

Writing: Write letters to corporations and non-profit agencies urging them to participate in the efforts to rescue lost children.

All Together Now by Sue Ellen Bridgers (192 pp.)

Casey thinks the summer at her grandparents' home will be the most boring ever, until she meets Dwayne, an adult with the mental capabilities of a child. Because she wants to be his friend, even though she knows he hates girls, Casey lets him think she is a boy. Her struggle to keep her secret and her new position within the family add interest to her summer.

Themes that could be studied include *Friendship and Family, Lying or Misrepresentation, Mental Deficiencies, Love/Infatuation, Responsibility,* and *Guilt.*

The Nature of Friendship

Discussion: How would you describe the friendship between Casey and Dwayne? What does each contribute to the friendship? What does each receive from it?

Writing: Write a scene that is set 10 years after the end of the novel. What might happen if the two friends were to meet again? How has each of them changed?

The Nature of Family Relationships

Creating Family Trees: Work with your group to create a family tree that shows the connections between Casey and the various other characters in the novel. Talk about how the relationships change over time. Create your own family tree to show how you are related to other members of your family.

The Nature of Truth

Discussion: Casey lets Dwayne continue to believe that she is a boy because she knows he "hates girls." Do you consider Casey's actions to be lying? Is it ever okay to misrepresent the truth?

Writing: Write about a time when you had to decide whether it was justifiable to misrepresent the truth or to let someone go on thinking what they thought.

The Nature of Mental Deficiencies

Investigate mental deficiencies. What are some causes? How often do mental deficiencies occur at birth? Do they occur more or less frequently than in the past? What special activities and schooling opportunities exist for the mentally impared today?

Volunteer to assist with the Special Olympics the next time they are held in your community.

Culminating Activities for the Five Novels

One way of having a reading group share a synopsis of their novel with the rest of the class is to have them select one important scene from each third of the text for dramatization before the large group. Encourage students to select representative scenes or turning points so that the essence of characterization and plot comes through for those who have not read the novel. This activity is best done as improvisational role play rather than as scripted, rehearsed scenes.

The carousel activity is a great way to conclude this unit on friendship. Again, post the theme carousel boards around the room. Ask each reading group to identify major themes in their novels and prepare to present them to the class. Throughout this unit on friendship, various activities have asked students to examine personal friendships in relation to the situations of the characters in the novels. Have students shape the bits of writing and the various insights from the reading and discussion into a personal essay on the role of friendship in their own lives. By personalizing the literature, students may find that reading books is a valuable way to spend their time.

Other YA titles dealing with friendship that you can recommend to students wishing to engage in additional independent reading include the following: *Tiger Eyes* (221 pp.) by Judy Blume, *Permanent Connections* (264 pp.) by Sue Ellen Bridgers, *Lizard* (198 pp.) by Dennis Covington, *It's an Aardvark Eat Turtle World* (144 pp.) by Paula Danziger, *The Summer of my German Soldier* (199 pp.) or *The Drowning of Stephan Jones* (217 pp.) by Bette Greene, *Peace Breaks Out* (178 pp.) by John Knowles, *Bright Days, Stupid Nights* (194 pp.) by Norma Fox & Harry Mazer, *The Truth About Alex* (176 pp.) by Anne Snyder, and *The Pigman* (176 pp.) by Paul Zindel.

List of References

Blume, J. (1982). *Tiger eyes*. New York: Dell.

Bridgers, S.E. (1990). *All together now*. New York: Bantam.

Bridgers, S.E. (1987). *Permanent connections*. New York: Harper & Row.

Brooks, B. (1984). *The moves make the man*. New York: Harper & Row.

Covington, D. (1991). *Lizard*. New York: Delacorte Press.

Crutcher, C. (1993). *Staying fat for Sarah Byrnes*. New York: Greenwillow.

Danziger, P. (1986). *It's an aardvark eat turtle world*. New York: Dell Laurel-Leaf.

Greene, B. (1991). *The drowning of Stephan Jones*. New York: Bantam.

Greene, B. (1973). *The summer of my German soldier*. New York: Dial Press.

Head, A. (1968). *Mr. and Mrs. Bo Jo Jones*. New York: Signet Books.

Hinton, S.E. (1989). *The outsiders*. New York: Dell.

Knowles, J. (1982). *Peace breaks out*. New York: Bantam.

Knowles, J. (1959). *A separate peace*. New York: Macmillan.

Mahy, M. (1989). *Memory*. New York: Dell Laurel-Leaf.

Mazer, N.F. & Mazer, H. (1992). *Bright days, stupid nights*. New York: Bantam.

Paterson, K. (1981). *Jacob have I loved*. New York: Avon Flare.

Peck, R. (1987). *Princess Ashley*. New York: Delacorte Press.

Snyder, A. (1987). *The truth about Alex*. New York: Signet Books.

Zindel, P. (1983). *The pigman*. New York: Bantam.

CHAPTER

9

PATRICIA P. KELLY

The Miracle Worker
**and Young Adult Literature
about Disabilities**

Introduction

Each of us is disabled in some way to a lesser or greater degree. We are not as tall as we would like to be, as strong as we want, find reading difficult because of a particular visualization problem, hear less well than we should, or suffer from a host of differing physical or medical problems. We adjust to our limitations because that is the way we are, that is the way we know ourselves.

As more and more physically and/or emotionally disabled students become part of the regular classroom setting as a result of the 1990 Individuals with Disabilities Education Act, it is even more important that we develop ways to help both disabled students and their peers relate to and appreciate each other. Of course, interacting and working together on a daily basis usually helps students understand another's feelings. But they may also need some direct guidance in managing physical interactions. For example, people often do not know how to relate to someone in a wheelchair or someone who is blind or deaf. Most of us are not intentionally insensitive, but our ignorance of how to react to or help another person with a disability creates uncomfortable situations for everyone involved. How better to raise such awareness than through adolescent novels of young people with disabilities, coupled with the study of one of the most profoundly disabled but highly successful people in modern times, Helen Keller.

Prereading for *The Miracle Worker*

As an introduction to *The Miracle Worker*, I like to use *The Cay* by Theodore Taylor as a read-aloud. The novel begins in 1942 on the Netherlands Antilles off the coast of Venezuela. The German submarines are getting close, so Phillip and his mother set out for safety in Norfolk, Virginia. Their ship is torpedoed, and Phillip suffers a severe head injury as they abandon the sinking ship. While Phillip and Timothy, a West Indian deck hand, drift together toward an unnamed, uncharted island, the head injury results in Phillip's blindness. On the cay, Phillip and Timothy overcome their cultural and age differences so that they can survive, but in the process come to care about each other as well. Timothy, both old and wise, knows that he must make Phillip self-sufficient because they might never be rescued, and Phillip could likely end his days alone on the island. After Timothy dies, Phillip is able to live alone for nearly five months before being rescued because of what Timothy has taught him. A discussion of the comparisons between Annie Sullivan's "tough love" teaching approaches in *The Miracle Worker* and Timothy's teaching of Phillip makes a good conclusion to the reading of both works.

The West Indian dialect brings Timothy's character to life and enhances the book as a real-aloud. Students also enjoy the Robinson-Crusoe-like way that Timothy builds huts, feeds the two of them, and arranges various signals. Some students even compare his ingenuity to television's McGyver. In addition to our general discussion of events and characters, I periodically have students respond to passages that deal with blindness as we come to them in our reading. They first do a quick-write in their journals and then use their reactions as the basis for a short large-group discussion.

Selected Passages about Blindness from *The Cay*

1. I got down on the hot boards, blinking my eyes again and again, trying to lift the curtain of blackness. I touched them. They did not feel any different. Then I realized that the pain had gone away. It had gone away but left me blind. (p. 45)

2. I'll never forget that first hour of knowing I was blind. I was so frightened that it was hard for me to breathe. It was as if I'd been put inside something that was all dark and I couldn't get out. (p. 46)

3. I remember that at one point my fear turned to anger. Anger at Timothy for not letting me stay in the water with my mother, and anger at her because I was on the raft. I began hitting him and I remember him saying, 'If dat will make you bettah, go 'ead.' (p. 46)

4. During those first few days on the island, the times I spent alone were terrible. It was, of course, being unable to see that made all the sounds so frightening. I guess if you are born blind, it is not so bad. You grow up knowing each sound and what it means. (p. 64)

5. I liked the rain because it was something I could hear and feel; not something I must see. (p. 74)

6. If you are blind, the sensation of falling can be terrifying. (p. 95)

7. I was learning to do things all over again, by touch and feel. (p. 96)

8. I also think that had I been able to see, I might not have been able to accept it all. But strangely, the darkness separated me from everything. It was as if my blindness were protecting me from fear. (p. 114)

9. Without Timothy's eyes, I was finding that in my world, everything had to be very precise; an exact place for everything. (p. 117)

In presenting *The Cay* as a read-aloud, I usually briefly summarize the first two chapters, relate the situation, and begin reading with "We were torpedoed at about three o'clock in the morning...," which begins Chapter 3. The beginning of the book introduces characters who either do not appear again in the story or are unimportant to the plot. Chapter 3 puts students immediately into the action. The book takes approximately three weeks if read aloud 10 to 15 minutes at the beginning of each class, followed then by other curriculum activities. In that way the reading serves as a long-range introduction to *The Miracle Worker* and related young adult (YA) novels. The read-aloud, of course, can be done on a more intensive basis, or the novel can be assigned as out-of-class reading. I have used all three methods, depending on the individual needs of my classes.

Once students have encountered Phillip's feelings and fears about his blindness and his enormous courage in surviving alone in *The Cay*, they usually want to try an activity in which they can experience to a small degree those sensations. I form triads of students; in that way they can select the ways in which they want to participate. One student chooses to be blindfolded, another becomes the assister, and the third observes the action. Students may switch roles during the activity or not as they wish. The first task is to guide the blindfolded person to a destination, for example the cafeteria. The guider quickly learns the best methods for offering assistance—for example, letting the seeing-impaired person hold the arm of the person who is guiding rather than trying "to steer" someone by the elbow. The observer should be noting the processes that are tried and their effectiveness.

With new roles or the same, as the group wishes, the second task is to guide the blindfolded person to a different destination, but with voice directions only. There are variations of tasks that students might devise, but they should be aware that it is important to maintain a safe environment for the tasks. Once students have experienced the role or roles they would like to try, they like to share their feelings and observations in a large-group discussion. We conclude that discussion with thinking about how difficult it would be to learn new tasks if one were both blind and deaf.

Reading *The Miracle Worker*

I like to have the play read aloud in small groups because more students are actively involved; however, the reading is equally effective if done readers' theater style in the front of the room. I have also used the film version of the play as the text, because students need to learn how "to read" performances. Starring Anne Bancroft as Annie Sullivan and Patty Duke as Helen Keller, *The Miracle Worker* is available in video format in black and white, running 105 minutes. Another way of using the film that I have found very effective is to use clips of the lengthy scenes described in the play. These scenes contain extensive and intensive action but no dialogue; therefore, they are sometimes hard for students to visualize. It is easy to insert these video clips into the students' reading of the play. I do not, however, read the play and then see the film version, because I do not want students to believe that seeing a movie is a reward for having read a text or that seeing a movie is easier than reading a text. The two "readings" are different; one is not preferable or better or easier than the other. On the other hand, plays are meant to be performed, whether by students or by professionals; so I always have the play performed in some manner. Whether students are reading and performing the play or we are seeing the film, the class activities can be the same.

First Impression/Last Impression

Characters frequently change throughout the course of the action either because they undergo a transformation or because we get to know them better and our attitude toward them changes. To chart these changes, students list these major characters in their journals—Arthur Keller, Helen's father; Kate Keller, her mother; James, her half-brother; Annie Sullivan, her teacher; and Helen—leaving room for writing about their first impressions of each character and their last impressions.

The first entries can be made at the end of Act One or about one-third through the film. After they write, I then ask them to write two adjectives or nouns that describe or name the characters as they have written about them. On a large sheet of butcher paper on a bulletin board, I have a "skeleton web" for each character: The name is printed in a circle with several lines emanating from the circle. On these lines students write in red some of the words that represent their first impressions. At the conclusion of studying the text, they write in their journals their last impressions. Students again write two words and put those words in blue on lines that extend out from the characters' circles.

Students, of course, do not agree on the exact nature of the changes, but they are usually amazed at how much their feelings toward all the characters have changed. The "evidence" on the webs generates an excellent discussion. For example, Arthur Keller, who initially comes across as cold, distant, and uncaring, clearly loves Helen and touchingly communicates that in the end; and James, who appears weak and lazy (students call him a "nerd" or a "dweeb"), eventually stands up to his father in a way that is decisive for Helen's development.

Dramatic Freeze Frames

Whether students have read the play or have seen the film, I use dramatic freeze frames as one of the culminating activities. In groups of four or five (I use my regular cooperative learning groups), students have the task of selecting key scenes (with *The Miracle Worker* I assign four scenes) that show the progress of the story. All members of the group must be in every scene, but each student decides how he or she will contribute to the action. The groups have 15 minutes to select the scenes, decide the order, discuss the possibilities for portraying the action, and practicing. After a one-minute "curtain time" call, students assemble their desks in theater style for the show.

Usually groups volunteer, but I sometimes have them draw numbers for the order of presentation. The first group goes to the front, and the students in the audience close their eyes for the few seconds it takes the performing group to arrange the first scene. I signal the students to open their eyes, and they look at the scene for about 10 seconds. They close their eyes again while the group arranges the second scene, and then the students view the new scene for a few seconds. We continue this process until the four scenes are performed. The next groups follow the same procedure. Completing all the presentations in a single class period is important to the success of this activity; otherwise, students lose their "edge," the excitement that builds during the exercise.

All is not quiet during the performances: Students clap and laugh, show their appreciation and approval of particular interpretations, and even point out effective aspects of the depictions they are viewing. We use the time at the end of the class to discuss the differences in interpretations. Almost always, at least one key scene will be performed by all groups, which furnishes a good focus for exploring these variations. The varied views presented in the same freeze frame scene offer a good lesson in the efficacy of multiple literary interpretations, and students begin to trust and to enjoy a wide range of interpretive options.

Individual or Group Projects

I offer a variety of extension activities that students may do as a group. As an option, many students may prefer to read or investigate something on their own. Students are encouraged to develop their own project ideas as well.

1. Read the first four chapters of Helen Keller's autobiography, *The Story of My Life*, and compare the account with that contained in the play. How are they different? Why do you think the differences occur? Are the differences significant?

2. Read *The Helen Keller Story*, a biography by Catherine Owens Peare, which covers not only the period in the play but also Helen's learning to read, write, and talk, all particularly difficult tasks for someone who is deaf and blind. The story follows Helen as she goes to college, writes books, makes speeches, and works for the deaf-blind.

3. Read the biography of Anne Sullivan, *The Touch of Magic*, by Lorena A. Hickok. Annie's early difficulties and visual problems were alluded to in the play, but this biography brings Annie's story to life. Called "Teacher" by Helen, she became Helen's eyes and ears for the remainder of her life. How does the additional information about Annie's early years illuminate the scenes in *The Miracle Worker* where she is remembering her brother and her own blindness?

4. Research modern advances in addressing disabilities as a result of collaboration between engineering and medicine—for example, voice computers for the blind that not only take voice directions but also read aloud written material in their memories; various technologies for aiding the deaf; and new breakthroughs in helping people walk after spinal injuries. Share your work with your classmates in some way.

5. Learn sign language, and prepare a project in which you demonstrate your knowledge.

6. Learn about the Braille alphabet, and prepare a project to share that knowledge with your classmates.

7. Research the various ways that print media and art forms are presented for the blind today. Bring examples to class if possible.

8. Volunteer at a nursing home to assist in reading to a sight-impaired person, writing for someone who needs it, going on a walk with someone in a wheelchair, or generally helping a disabled person. Write a letter to the person explaining what you learned from the experience.

9. Read a play written by teenagers about teenagers with disabilities, such as "The Invisible Room" by Risa Yanagisawa, in which a girl

struggles to understand the dyslexia that is affecting her life, or
"In the Dark" by Max Moore, which centers on a blind student in
a multicultural high school. These and other plays are published
each year by the Young Playwrights Program, which encourages
students to think about disabilities in modern society and write
stage scripts expressing those ideas. After reading one of these
plays, you or your group may want to try writing a short play
that concerns a disability.

Young Adult Novels about Disabilities

As a final activity, students are asked to read and respond to an
individual YA novel of choice in their reader-response journals. To help
students decide which book they want to read, I give brief book talks on
several YA novels that center on disabilities. In addition, I make other novels
available about other disabling conditions such as diabetes, epilepsy, mental
illness, and learning disabilities. Some students prefer nonfiction accounts.
(An excellent source for identifying resources on disabilities as well as other
subjects is *Adolescents at Risk: A Guide to Fiction and Nonfiction for
Young Adults, Parents, and Professionals* by Joan Kaywell.) Here is a
thumbnail sketch of the books I always introduce to students because they
represent a range of reading interests.

Of Such Small Differences by Joanne Greenberg (272 pp.)

This novel is good parallel reading for *The Miracle Worker* because,
like Helen, John cannot see or hear. His everyday struggle as well as his love
for someone who is not handicapped makes readers see their own lives
differently.

Belonging by Deborah Kent (200 pp.)

Meg decides she wants to attend a regular high school rather than
the special school for the blind. The novel is a first-person account of her
struggle, fears, problems, and successes as she works toward being accepted
as a person rather than being pitied. Both Helen Keller's autobiography and
biography report many of the same issues when she enters Radcliffe to
study.

One Step at a Time by Deborah Kent (208 pp.)

Tracey Newberry, having been told during her freshman year in high
school that she is going blind, struggles to cope with the situation and to
build a new life.

Annie's World by Nancy Smiler Levinson (97 pp.)

Annie finally gets to go to public school but there she encounters the cruelty of her classmates because she is deaf. Despite her family's help, Annie's alienation grows.

Belonging by Virginia M. Scott (200 pp.)

Life for Gustie Blaine was wonderful: She was a cheerleader, an honor student, and popular. When she loses her hearing because of meningitis, her life changes dramatically. Her friends do not understand her deafness, but neither does Gustie understand her isolation and how it is causing her to act. Two new friends and a special education teacher help her learn to communicate with others and to learn the real meaning of belonging. (Note: Because this book is published by Gallaudet College Press, it reflects an accurate account of adjusting to deafness.)

Alice by Sara Flanigan (306 pp.)

Kept caged like an animal in a hut, Alice, a teenager, is unable to communicate with her family because she is deaf. They do not understand her and literally shut her out. Neighborhood teenagers, Louellen and Sammy Perkins, discover Alice and secretly begin teaching her. The young people stand up for what they know is right, and Alice flourishes as the result of care and attention.

The Unfrightened Dark by Isabelle Holland (120 pp.)

Jocelyn, blinded at 12 in an accident that also killed her parents, has adapted well and moves freely about town with her dog Brace. There are excellent descriptions of how this confident girl manages in a dark world. Also realistic is the portrayal of some people who think that having a "working" dog is cruel, which leads to the mysterious action in the story.

The Young Unicorns by Madeleine L'Engle (224 pp.)

Emily, recently blind, encounters the Austins, who have just moved to New York City. The Austins, trying to help Emily adjust to her blindness, become involved in a frightening gang plot to take over the city.

Listen for the Fig Tree by Sharon Bell Mathis (175 pp.)

Muffin Johnson, a black teenager who is blind, manages to cope quite well despite considerable complications resulting from her father's murder and her mother's alcoholism.

Twink **by John Neufeld (128 pp.)**

Sixteen-year-old Harry Walsh is unprepared for his reaction to his new stepsister Twink, who has cerebral palsy and is blind. Through Twink's bravery and strong will, Harry comes to understand the joy of living.

Deenie **by Judy Blume (144 pp.)**

Deenie Fenner's mother has aspirations that her daughter will be a model. When Deenie is diagnosed with adolescent idiopathic scoliosis, a lateral curvature of the spine, she must wear a brace for four years to prevent being permanently crippled.

The Girl in the Plastic Cage **by Marilyn Levy (190 pp.)**

Also diagnosed with scoliosis, Lori had wanted to be a gymnast. Those aspirations are gone, but she also fears that a developing relationship with Kurt, whom she has met at the doctor's office, will suffer now that Kurt is getting out of his brace.

Winning **by Robin Brancato (211 pp.)**

Paralyzed from the shoulders down as a result of a football injury, Gary Madden becomes angry and depressed. Faced with having to build a life he had not imagined, he turns to friends but finds that they are not always supportive. He discovers the help he needs from an English teacher who has suffered her own tragedy.

Head over Wheels **by Lee Kingman (224 pp.)**

After a terrible car accident, one 17-year-old twin boy will never walk again, but both must come to terms with the effect on their lives.

Killing the Kudu **by Carolyn Meyer (208 pp.)**

Eighteen-year-old Alex is a paraplegic, the result of an accidental shooting. One summer, while visiting his grandmother, he encounters Scott, the cousin responsible for the tragedy. The boys struggle with the circumstances but manage to come to a resolution.

Wheels for Walking **by Sandra Richmond (176 pp.)**

The physical and emotional trials of Sally, paralyzed from the chest down in a car accident at 18, is the heart of this story. Although she has friends for support, the answer to her bitterness must come from within.

Izzy, Willy-Nilly by Cynthia Voigt (262 pp.)

Excited about being asked out by a senior, Isobel "Izzy" Lingard gains her parents' reluctant consent, much to their regret. Her drunk-driving date causes a car accident that results in the amputation of Izzy's right leg below the knee. Although Izzy's friends knew he was too drunk to drive, no one intervened. As Izzy examines her life and her disability, she redefines friendship and its meaning for her.

Never Look Back by Alida Young (144 pp.)

A high school long-distance runner, Heather Ames begins to experience severe pain. She continues her school activities despite the pain and despite the fact that, because doctors are unable to readily diagnose her problem, people do not believe she is in pain. Ultimately, she is diagnosed with juvenile rheumatoid arthritis. With treatment, Heather is determined to carry on as before.

Conclusion

There's an old saying that reflects how difficult it is to truly understand another's life: "How do I know how you feel unless I've walked in your shoes?" One way to gain that understanding and empathy about disabilities, "to walk in another's shoes," is through reading, for we can experience vicariously the feelings, difficulties, and courage of characters' struggles. Not only are we allowed to enter their minds—something that cannot happen during real encounters—but also we can use their stories as a mirror to view our own lives. Adolescent novels provide just that mirror for their teenage readers.

List of References

Blume, J. (1973). *Deenie*. New York: Dell Laurel-Leaf.

Brancato, R. (1988). *Winning*. New York: Alfred A. Knopf.

Flanigan, S. (1988). *Alice*. New York: St. Martin's Press.

Gibson, W. (1956). *The miracle worker*. New York: Tamarack Productions, Ltd.

Greenberg, J. (1989). *Of such small differences*. New York: Signet Books.

Hickok, L.A. (1961). *The touch of magic*. New York: Dodd, Mead & Company.

Holland, I. (1990). *The unfrightened dark*. New York: Fawcett Juniper.

Kaywell, J.F. (1993). *Adolescents at risk: A guide to fiction and nonfiction for young adults, parents, and professionals*. Westport, CT: Greenwood Press.

Keller, H. (1954). *The story of my life*. New York: Doubleday & Company.

Kent, D. (1989). *One step at a time*. New York: Scholastic.

Kent, D. (1978). *Belonging.* New York: Ace Books.

Kingman, L. (1985). *Head over wheels.* New York: Dell Laurel-Leaf.

L'Engle, M. (1989). *The young unicorns.* New York: Dell Laurel-Leaf.

Levinson, N.S. (1990). *Annie's world.* Washington, D.C.: Kendall Green.

Levy, M. (1982). *The girl in the plastic cage.* New York: Ballantine.

Mathis, S.B. (1990). *Listen for the fig tree.* New York: Puffin.

Meyer, C. (1990). *Killing the kudu.* New York: Margaret K. McElderry.

Moore, M. (1993). "In the dark." Young Playwrights Program. Washington, D.C.: John F. Kennedy Center for the Performing Arts.

Neufeld, J. (1971). *Twink.* New York: Signet Books.

Peare, C.O. (1959). *The Helen Keller story.* New York: Thomas Y. Crowell.

Penn, A. (1962). *The miracle worker.* Playfilm Productions, Inc. (VHS video by United Artists, 1987), 105 mins.

Richmond, S. (1988). *Wheels for walking.* New York: Signet Books.

Scott, V.M. (1986). *Belonging.* Washington, D.C.: Gallaudet College Press.

Taylor, T. (1990). *The cay.* New York: Doubleday.

Voigt, C. (1987). *Izzy, willy-nilly.* New York: Fawcett Juniper.

Yanagisawa, R. (1993). "The invisible room." Young Playwrights Program. Washington, D.C.: John F. Kennedy Center for the Performing Arts.

Young, A. (1988). *Never look back.* Worthington, OH: Willowisp Press.

CHAPTER

10

Exploring the Horror Within:
Themes of the Duality of Humanity in
Mary Shelley's *Frankenstein* and
Ten Related Young Adult Novels

TERI S. LESESNE

Introduction

In the summer of 1816, so the story goes, Mary Shelley and a group of her contemporaries discussed the possibility of writing horror stories. Among this distinguished group was Shelley's husband, the poet Percy Bysshe Shelley; another poet, Lord Byron; Byron's physician, Polidori; and Jane Clairmont. Each person in this assemblage was either an important writer of the Romantic movement (particularly Shelley and Byron), was a close friend of these writers, or was a less influential writer of the time. Each member of the group was to pen a horror story and present it to the group. Several members of the group wrote a story, but only Mary Shelley's remains extant today.

What began as a short story told to this illustrious group by Mary Shelley later emerged as the full-length work of fiction, *Frankenstein*. It was born out of a nightmare Shelley remembered. That nightmare, translated into the finest of Romantic fiction, is a frequently anthologized work in many of our secondary literature texts. What I hope to do in this chapter is to present ten young adult (YA) novels that may lead readers to a fuller understanding of Shelley's classic tale of the duality of humankind.

I already hear some grumbling from the audience. Before we proceed further, please erase the dreadful late-night images of Boris Karloff, Bela Lugosi, and Lon Chaney. They bear little resemblance to the work Shelley produced at the tender age of nineteen. Her novel deserves close scrutiny as a prime example of Romantic literature. This retelling of the Prometheus myth resonates with the monstrous and the macabre as well as startling reality.

Follow me into a twisted labyrinth as we examine the horror within in *Frankenstein* and ten related YA novels. In order to accomplish the goals and objectives of so varied and extensive a reading list as that which follows, a "novel" approach is necessary. So, before we proceed into the twists and turns we will take with Shelley's work, let us examine one way of incorporating at least some of the YA titles discussed along with a study of Romantic literature and *Frankenstein*.

The Intensive and Extensive Approaches to Reading

A common practice in schools is to take the intensive approach to the study of literature. In an intensive approach, students spend a great deal of time in a detailed analysis of a few selected works. They dissect the literature one piece at a time. On the other hand, an extensive approach to literature allows students to read a wider variety of literature, much of which is self-selected. It is an approach which utilizes a rapid reading of a larger amount of literature within the same time period as the intensive approach. How does extensive reading work?

In 1927, an erstwhile doctoral student added an important element to the growing body of research about the teaching of literature. Nancy Coryell's evaluation of extensive and intensive approaches to reading with 11th graders challenged the prevailing tradition of intensive analysis of a few selected works in English classes. Coryell examined the test results of two groups of 11th grade students: Group One, the Intensive Group, spent 10 days reading *Julius Caesar*. Group Two, the Extensive Group, in the same span of time read *Julius Caesar* as well as another self-selected Shakespearean play and an Elizabethan play not written by the Bard. Both groups were administered the same test at the end of this 10-day period. Students in the extensive group scored as well as the students in the intensive group on this examination. They also fared as well as their intensive group counterparts on state and other standardized tests of English and literature.

Nor were these results a one–time phenomenon. Later in the semester, while studying contemporary poetry, the extensive group read 345 poems; during that same period of time, the intensive group read 60 poems. Despite the fact that the extensive group had read nearly six times the number of poems, their scores on the core poetry examination were no lower than the intensive group. A major benefit of the extensive approach was seen in the attitude toward reading on the part of the extensive participants. They generally had more positive and more enthusiastic reactions to their method of instruction.

What Coryell confirmed nearly 70 years ago still holds true for today's English classrooms. Research has born out similar results. The extensive study of literature is an approach that allows us to utilize the fine array of YA literature available for today's adolescents while not ignoring the enormous contributions of the classics of literature. The extensive approach, as Vera Thomas suggested in a 1935 article in *The English Journal*, develops in students a liking for reading and a love of literature; Dora Smith (1930) concurred. If we broaden students' knowledge of language by lots of reading in its natural context, we can create more lifetime readers. Therefore, what I propose is that *Frankenstein* become a centerpiece for a thematic study in an extensive approach to YA literature that features the theme of duality of character.

Frankenstein

For those of you who have only the midnight "creature-feature" image of this story, a summary of the work may serve to allay your skepticism. Shelley, concerned with what science and industry were doing to the world, was fascinated with the science of the time and obsessed with the technological knowledge being conveyed by the men and women of science of the 19th century. This Faustian quest for knowledge became one of the central themes of Shelley's remarkable work.

The novel opens with a series of letters to a Mrs. Saville in England from her brother, Robert Walton, who is lonely and longing for a companion in his journey. He has been exploring the Arctic for several years without a friend to whom he can confide; he is on a Romantic quest of sorts. His wish for a companion appears to be granted when he rescues a man from an ice floe. The man is near death, but recovers and begins to tell the saga of how he came to be tragically isolated in this frigid region of the world. What follows is a classic tale of invention gone haywire.

The rescued man is Victor Frankenstein. His story is, at first, one of a warm and close family. It is when Victor leaves his family to attend the university that the story begins to take a sinister turn. Victor, too, had engaged in a quest—a search for the very meaning of life. It is here that the Prometheus theme of the story is first evident. Victor wishes to create life and conquer death. He is not the mad scientist of the movies but a dedicated scholar who wishes to contribute to society. He sets about creating life, but once he has finished, he is horrified at what he has done.

His monster is ugly to behold, and Victor cannot bear looking at it. Thus, Victor abandons the monster and longs to be able to destroy his creation. Victor's creation makes an attempt to reconcile, as it were, but Victor cannot bring himself even to gaze upon this monster much less connect with it. This sets in motion events that are to lead, ultimately, to several tragedies in Victor's life. His brother is murdered, and Victor knows it is the monster who has done the deed, but he is at a loss as to how to convince others of this without seeming mad. A young woman, a friend of the Frankenstein family, is hanged for the murder. Finally, Victor's one true love, Elizabeth, is murdered, as is his childhood friend, Cherval. Now Victor is as abandoned as his creation.

He knows he must find a way to redeem himself for all the harm he has caused through his creation. Accordingly, he lures his monster to the Arctic area, hoping to cause its death. The novel closes as it opened, with letters from Robert to his sister in which he relates his encounter with the monster, who now has murdered Victor Frankenstein. The final scene is the disappearance of Victor's creation; the monster is intent upon self-immolation. It is, the monster feels, the only means of escape from the inhumanity it has suffered.

An Extensive Approach to *Frankenstein*

The duality of humanity is one of the central themes explored by Shelley in her novel. It is also a recurrent theme in many fine YA novels. Therefore, one approach to the utilization of *Frankenstein* in the secondary classroom might be to tie *Frankenstein* as the core novel to other thematically related YA works. What follows are brief summaries of ten YA novels that tackle the theme of duality. Following the plot synopses are some suggestions for follow-up activities for this unit of study.

These related books are presented in five categories. Within each category, a separate genre could become part of the thematic unit. With *Frankenstein* as the core novel, the teacher could utilize one or several of the related novels in an extensive approach in the classroom.

Historical Fiction

The True Confessions of Charlotte Doyle by Avi (232 pp.). This Newbery Honor Book recounts the adventures of an adolescent girl who finds herself the lone passenger on board a sailing ship bound for the United States in the early 19th century. Charlotte Doyle, the young heroine, becomes unwittingly involved in mutinous plans while aboard the *Seahawk*. Later, as she witnesses firsthand the cruelty of the captain, her participation in the mutiny is purposeful. She is ultimately sentenced to be hanged for her activity. She manages to escape this fate and returns home safely. The novel ends with Charlotte running away from the safety of her home to rejoin the crew on the open seas. Charlotte, brought up to be a refined young woman, discovers her dual nature when she is caught up in the events of the *Seahawk* mutiny. Her newfound skills and emotions compel her to seek further adventure.

Like Robert Walton, the unseen narrator of *Frankenstein*, Charlotte also experiences a voyage that tests the mettle of an individual. Charlotte becomes embroiled in a tumultuous situation not of her making, as does Walton. Like Walton, Charlotte feels compelled to participate in the adventure. In doing so, both become caught up in a dilemma.

Response should always begin with the personal or emotive reaction to the text. It is this level of response which then serves as the foundation upon which to build a more critical or evaluative response. Therefore, teachers might direct students' attention to the first letter of *Frankenstein* and the prologue of *The True Confessions of Charlotte Doyle*, and ask them for their initial responses before proceeding with further reading. Students might also transact with the text by placing themselves in one of the roles as the main character. How they would feel if they were either Charlotte or Robert Walton acts as a bridge between the purely personal response and a more critical stance.

Students should note the first-person narrative style employed by both authors. Avi utilizes Charlotte's diary whereas Shelley provides

Walton's letters home to his sister. Urge students to compare the impact this point of view has in these and other related novels. How might these works be different if the narrator were different or the point of view altered to third person?

Mary Reilly by Valerie Martin (263 pp.). Mary Reilly escapes a childhood of terror only to find herself as a maid in the home of the brilliant Dr. Jekyll. Through her young eyes, the reader sees her terror return when confronted with the specter of Mr. Hyde, Jekyll's alter ego. This riveting novel presents the classic tale of Jekyll and Hyde as told by an adolescent in the household.

The dual nature of man is evident from the start of the story as Mary experiences abuse at the hands of her stepfather, a man given to horrid rages when he has had too much to drink. At first, she is relieved to have found employment with the kindly Dr. Jekyll. Mary initially takes umbrage at the brutal disregard for civility shown by the mysterious Mr. Hyde, whom she naively assumes to be a visitor to the household. As the awful truth is revealed, she is repelled by Jekyll, a man for whom she once held the utmost respect.

Victor Frankenstein, too, appalled at what he feels is lacking in his creation, runs from the truth. He feels powerless, unable to destroy what he now deems evil. Mary Reilly, on the other hand, is made of sterner stuff. Encourage students to discuss the similarities and differences between Victor and Mary. Another intriguing piece of writing might result if students are asked to rewrite one of the chapters in *Frankenstein* as if Walton (or another character) were an adolescent. How might a younger narrator or character view and report the action differently?

This novel, like *Frankenstein*, presents an excellent opportunity for a read-aloud for the teacher. The opening scene, in which Mary Reilly finds herself locked in a dank closet with a rat, is sure to grab readers' attentions and perhaps provide incentive to read on. Similarly, since the core novel is told primarily in first person, read-aloud is an appropriate approach to begin the study of the work.

Wolf by the Ears by Ann Rinaldi (252 pp.). Harriet, the daughter of Sally Hemings, has always been happy at Monticello; it is the only home she has ever known. Rumors are running rampant that she is the daughter of her master, Thomas Jefferson. Harriet is forced to make a choice—to attempt to pass in the white world or to stay with her mother and family.

Jefferson is an interesting study in duality. Here is the man who penned the Declaration of Independence. Yet, he owned slaves himself and apparently fathered children by one of his slaves. Thomas Jefferson, like Victor Frankenstein, is a study in contrasts. Frankenstein wishes to create life from death. His meddling leads, ultimately, to disaster. When he is confronted by his failure, he is unable to cope. Likewise, Jefferson, in Rinaldi's novel, is torn between what is right and what society deems appropriate. Both men waver and hesitate and, by their inaction, cause irreparable damage to those whom they love.   *Hamlet* explores similar territory and would make an interesting comparison along with these works.

One possible topic of discussion for students might be why these characters are unable to deal with their failures.   Why is it impossible for Walton and Jefferson to admit that each has made an error in judgment? How might each story be different if the main character were able to deal swiftly with his mistake?   Would either novel make for interesting reading if this were the case?

Futurism—Science Fiction

Eva by Peter Dickinson (219 pp.).   Thirteen-year-old Eva awakens in a hospital room, aware that something is seriously wrong.   She can remember nothing but a pleasant picnic on a beach with her parents.   Haltingly, her mother explains that there was a horrific accident.   Eva's parents gave the doctors permission to do anything to save her life.   The doctors have indeed wrought a miracle, but their amazing medical techniques carry a high price for Eva and her family.   Eva is forced to live a wholly new kind of life, as a chimpanzee.   The human and animal nature of Eva battle against one another in this spell-binding novel of the future.

Dickinson, like Shelley, explores what happens when man meddles with nature and the natural course of events.   Unlike *Frankenstein*, Dickinson sets his novel in the future and in a society which he creates; Shelley utilizes the England of her time.   Have students explore how these two distinct settings account for some of the differences between Frankenstein's monster and Eva.   In addition, students should be aware of the "open endings" of each work.   Readers are not told exactly what happens to each of the creations.   Even though we know that Eva dies, her children, the result of her mating with the monkeys, may have some effect on the evolution of future generations.   Readers are never sure whether the monster really dies. Why Shelley and Dickinson opted for such open endings is a great topic of discussion.

The Giver by Lois Lowry (179 pp.).   One of the most frightening visions of the future is found in this novel.   Jonas, a 12-year-old boy, is assigned his role in this society.   He is to be the new "Receiver of Memory." Jonas does not know what this job will entail, and he is scarcely prepared for what occurs during his meetings with "The Giver of Memories."   Lowry tackles many of the ills of contemporary society in this riveting book.

There are several characters who exemplify the duality of humankind. Perhaps most disturbing is Jonas' father, a man who is caring and nurturing, and yet in charge of "releasing" infants, a euphemism for killing them if they fail to "thrive."   Perhaps one of the most horrific scenes in *The Giver* occurs when Jonas discovers the true meaning of the release.   Lowry has chosen to show, rather graphically, the deliberate murder of a baby at the hand of Jonas' father.   Shelley, on the other hand, in the true tradition of the Gothic novelist, reveals none of the blood and gore usually associated with cinematic adaptations of *Frankenstein*. The grisly details of graveyard robberies were an invention of the film industry's versions of the novel.

Does the omission of the lurid details of the monster's creation lessen the impact of its murderous rampages? Why has Lowry chosen to include some of the more bloody scenes? Students should be asked to discuss how each novelist handles these scenes. An interesting comparative paper might result from this focus. Persuasive writing might also be a possibility as students attempt to decide which author is more effective in conveying horror and why.

House of Stairs by William Sleator (166 pp.). Five 16-year-old orphans who are living in state institutions are suddenly brought to a place that is not a hospital or prison—a place composed of nothing but stairs, white stairs running in all directions. The only break in all the startling whiteness is the red machine, a machine which can provide them the food they need to survive. But the machine demands certain behavior before food will be released. The behavior becomes increasingly violent until Lola and Peter refuse to participate in the violence. Sleator explores how easily people can be forced to change their behavior in this novel that explores ground similar to that in Orwell's classic *1984*.

In *Frankenstein*, the monster's actions are, at first, not deliberately evil or murderous. Like the orphans who find themselves in the House of Stairs, the monster harms only accidentally. Once the monster is rebuffed by its creator, however, its killing is deliberate and meant to hurt Frankenstein deeply. The orphans are initially violent only as a result of their frustration at their inability to make the machine release food to them. However, once they sense that the violent behavior is expected for food, they are willing to be deliberately physical with one another. When Lola and Peter separate from the others, they place themselves in jeopardy. Students might chart the changes in the monster and the orphans as each plot progresses.

Fantasy Fiction

Strange Objects by Gary Crew (216 pp.). This winner of the Children's Book Council of Australia Book of the Year Award is similar in format to Avi's *Nothing but the Truth*. That is, the story is told entirely through diary entries, newspaper stories, letters, and other artifacts which an anthropologist might utilize to piece together a report of a lost civilization.

Steven Messenger stumbles across an unusual discovery on a school field trip when he uncovers an iron pot containing a journal and a severed hand; a ring adorns the mummified hand. The ring accidentally finds its way home with Steven, who mysteriously disappears. Steven's character undergoes abrupt changes as he has visions of the past, peopled by the characters in the journal, which is being translated in the local papers.

Steven, like Robert Walton, is an unwitting participant at first. Steven and Walton both find themselves drawn inextricably toward participation, though how they become involved is dissimilar. The use of journals and letters is also a similarity between these two works. Once again, readers might examine how the use of first person affects their reading. They might also study the contrast between the two works. While Crew opts to use only documents to tell the story of Steven Messenger, Shelley moves from the letters of Robert Walton to the first-person narrative of Victor Frankenstein.

Shoebag by Mary James (135 pp.). M.E. Kerr, writing under a pseudonym, creates a Kafkaesque fantasy in which a young cockroach discovers himself transformed into a human. Shoebag can no longer live with his family. Instead, he becomes part of the Biddle household as Stuart Bagg. He is soon enrolled in school where he uncovers others like himself. Shoebag still longs for his roachdom, his home sweet home. Kerr probes the split personalities of several of the characters in this witty and wicked fantasy where things are not always what they appear to be.

Appearances may be deceiving; certainly Stuart Bagg, or Shoebag, comes to this conclusion. Frankenstein, too, is confronted with this problem. Ask students to identify instances where characters are not exactly what they seem to be on the surface in these and other thematically related works.

Modern Realism

We All Fall Down by Robert Cormier (193 pp.). At 9:02 P.M., three adolescents enter a house. When they leave at 9:46 P.M., they leave behind broken mirrors, slashed furniture, urine- and vomit-splattered walls and rugs, and an unconscious Karen Jerome, who made the mistake of arriving home early and unexpected. Karen's family tries to cope with this invasion into their lives. Karen's older sister, Jane, unknowingly begins dating one of the intruders, a young boy who is attempting to atone for his participation. Jane herself faces suspicion: Could she have been an accessory?

Cormier, as always, explores how seemingly nice kids can become destructive. Shelley, too, shows how easily the best intentions can go awry. Frankenstein initially is searching for a means to bring life from that which is dead. His experiments lead to a grisly end for many of the innocent people who are a part of his life. The same can be said for Karen and for the young man who wishes to obtain absolution for his actions in the home invasion.

Cormier, like Shelley, uses a third person, an outside party as it were, to play the role of the narrator. At first, readers believe that this narrator is simply a neutral observer. It becomes rapidly apparent, however, that each narrator has some sort of stake in the story. Ask students to identify the reasons why Walton and The Avenger, the narrator of Cormier's work, become personally involved in the action of the stories.

A Lighter Touch: Humor

Frank and Stein and Me by Kin Platt (108 pp.). Jack Hook wins an all-paid trip to Paris, not exactly his dream prize, but he decides to go. Jack gets into trouble almost immediately on his journey when he agrees to deliver a package for a strange man who approaches him in the Paris airport. Jack soon discovers that the police are after the package and, of course, after him as well. He escapes, only to land in the clutches of Dr. Stein, who introduces him to Frank, his monster. Jack is off on a wild and rollicking adventure in this spoof of *Frankenstein*.

Readers should note how the original version of Shelley's work serves as the core for this wacky variation. What qualities exist in both novels? What are the qualities which serve to separate the two?

Other YA Literature Worth Considering

Here are a handful of other fine YA short stories and novels which explore the theme of duality.

"Ethan Unbound" by Gary Blackwood

This story, in Gallo's collection entitled *Short Circuits*, tells of a young man trapped after hours in the public library with a librarian out to zap him into oblivion.

Tunes for Bears To Dance To by Robert Cormier (101 pp.)

Henry, grief-stricken by the sudden death of his beloved older brother, discovers that he is capable of doing anything to purchase a fitting monument for his brother's grave—even if it means destroying the life of an innocent old man.

Kim/Kimi by Hadley Irwin (200 pp.)

Kim, the daughter of a Japanese-American who died before she was born, searches for her identity. Is she Kim Andrews or Kimi Yogushi?

Interstellar Pig by William Sleator (196 pp.)

Barney, a high school student, is thrilled to be allowed to hang around with a group of college students, until he discovers that each is an alien bent on destroying Earth.

Strange Attractors by William Sleator (169 pp.)

Max discovers a device that allows him to travel through time, a tempting situation which draws him inexorably toward a meeting which may change his life: a meeting with himself!

The Devil's Arithmetic by Jane Yolen (170 pp.)

Hannah learns the true meaning of the Passover symbolism when she finds herself suddenly transported back in time to Poland of the 1940s and destined for a Nazi death camp.

A Final Note

Any one or all or a combination of these works for adolescents would make for an interesting unit of study. Works of nonfiction such as psychological studies of the duality of humanity would also be appropriate. Essays, poems (I would suggest "The Rime of the Ancient Mariner" as one startling pairing), and short stories should also find a place in such an extensive approach. Karen Kutiper (1983) provides an outstanding example of the construct of such a unit in her *English Journal* article entitled "Extensive Reading: A Means of Reconciliation." Film and video are also natural tie-ins to this unit of study.

According to Livaudais (1985), secondary students prefer post-reading activities that require peer interaction. Students prefer oral activities and short writing activities that have audiences other than the teacher. What types of follow-up ideas would then be appropriate?

Debates and panel discussions seem almost ideally suited to the theme of duality. Students could defend or argue against, for example, Eva's parents' decision to have her brain neurons implanted into the brain of a chimp. Beyond this, students might generalize the debate or discussion to one which concerns medical ethics in contemporary society. What of fetal tissue research? DNA testing? Assisted suicide?

Writing assignments that require students to assume the role of one of the characters caught up in his or her duality would also be useful. What if the narrator in *We All Fall Down* were Jane instead of "The Avenger"? How might the story change? Students might be instructed to rewrite a chapter or a scene from another point of view.

Finally, activities that ask students to compare and contrast the various novels and other works included within the unit would be most valuable. Having students make comparisons among works emphasizes critical thinking skills and, more importantly, is one of the behaviors associated with good readers. Whether students trace the theme of duality from novel to novel or compare and contrast a series of characters or events or even authors' styles, they are forging new connections among various literary works, seeing how themes emerge, realizing that one theme may be explored in a variety of ways. Surely, these are important insights for secondary English students.

List of References

Avi. (1990). *The true confessions of Charlotte Doyle*. New York: Avon.

Blackwood, G. (1992). Ethan unbound. In D.R. Gallo (Ed.), *Short circuits*. New York: Dell.

Coleridge, S.T. (1986). *The rime of the ancient mariner*. New York: Chelsea House.

Cormier, R. (1992). *Tunes for bears to dance to*. New York: Delacorte Press.

Cormier, R. (1991). *We all fall down*. New York: Delacorte Press.

Coryell, N.G. (1927). *An evaluation of extensive and intensive teaching of literature*. Unpublished doctoral dissertation, Columbia University, New York.

Crew, G. (1993). *Strange objects*. New York: Simon & Schuster.

Dickinson, P. (1988). *Eva*. New York: Delacorte Press.

Irwin, Hadley. (1988). *Kim/Kimi*. New York: Viking/Penguin.

James, M. (1990). *Shoebag*. New York: Scholastic.

Kutiper, K. (1983, November). Extensive reading: A means of reconciliation. *English Journal*, **72** (7), pp. 58–61.

Livaudais, M.F. (1985). *A survey of secondary (grades 7–12) students' attitudes toward reading motivational activities*. Unpublished doctoral dissertation, University of Houston, Texas.

Lowry, L. (1993). *The giver*. Boston: Houghton Mifflin.

Martin, V. (1990). *Mary Reilly*. New York: Bantam Doubleday Dell.

Orwell, G. (1949). *1984*. New York: Harcourt, Brace, & Jovanovich.

Platt, K. (1982). *Frank and Stein and me*. New York: Scholastic.

Rinaldi, A. (1991). *Wolf by the ears*. New York: Scholastic.

Shakespeare, W. (1959). *Hamlet*. New York: Pocket Books.

Shelley, M. (1965). *Frankenstein*. New York: Signet Classics.

Sleator, W. (1990). *Strange attractors*. New York: Dutton.

Sleator, W. (1984). *Interstellar pig*. New York: Bantam.

Sleator, W. (1974). *House of stairs*. New York: E.P. Dutton.

Smith, D.V. (1930, June). Extensive reading in junior high. *English Journal*, **19** (6), pp. 449–462.

Thomas, V.N. (1938, September). Extensive reading in practice. *English Journal*, **27** (7), pp. 574–579.

Yolen, J. (1988). *The devil's arithmetic*. New York: Viking.

CHAPTER 11

JANET S. ALLEN

Exploring the Individual's
Responsibility in Society in
The Giver and
Brave New World

It is good to have an end to journey toward; but it is the journey that matters, in the end.
                                                                        —*Ursula K Le Guin*

Introduction

It has become an impossibility to get through a day without reading about, listening to, or discussing what's wrong with our society. The social ills of poverty, homelessness, disease, aging, abuse, lack of medical care, violence, and political corruption do not begin to scratch the surface of the problems we experience, either personally or vicariously, every day. Although most would not want to believe that life in the United States in the 1990s could be characterized as a dystopia, many would agree that we have come dangerously close to the imaginative warnings of 20th-century fiction writers. Books such as Orwell's *1984* and *Animal Farm*; Rand's *Anthem*; Bradbury's *Fahrenheit 451*; and Huxley's *Brave New World* have been staples in the English curriculum for many years, yet for many of our students, their warnings have been seen as distant messages unrelated to their lives. Lois Lowry's Newbery Medal winner *The Giver* brings those societal issues into focus for today's young adults by examining a "perfect" society as seen through the eyes of an adolescent. When this young adult (YA) novel is used in connection with Aldous Huxley's *Brave New World*, students gain both a personal and a world view of the individual's responsibility in society.

Although there are many themes which could be explored in these two novels, the theme I have chosen to examine is that of one person's responsibility in changing and rebuilding a society where the people have lost their freedom, choice, and power. Jonas in *The Giver* and Bernard and John in *Brave New World* are strong characters who take action to survive in a society that has gone very wrong. Additionally, both Jonas and John learn that society's problems are not someone else's responsibility. They discover that change comes from within each individual or it does not occur at all. Exploring the characteristics and the logistics of individuals making a societal difference can be a powerful model for all readers, especially for young adults.

The Utopia/Dystopia Context

Donelson and Nilsen (1989) state that utopian literature has not typically been popular with most readers because it "lacks excitement and fast-moving plots needed for fast reading and easy appeal" (p. 209). I have found that for many readers the message is too heavy, the thought processes of the characters too complex, and the settings too unfamiliar for adolescents to feel comfortable and conversant with the literature. But, writers of utopias do not want readers to feel comfortable.

Utopian literature developed because there were writers who were concerned and dissatisfied with society as it existed for them. Those individuals created, either in the mind or in reality, what they considered to be the perfect society. Perhaps the fascination with dreaming of that perfect place comes in part from the Greek origin of the word *utopia* which has two, seemingly contradictory, meanings: "good place" and "no place." The irony occurs when writers, by describing the good place, the perfect place, create a society that, in reality, is terribly flawed.

These "utopias" are the dystopias of literature, and Orwell, Huxley, Rand, and Bradbury have created such places. Now Lois Lowry in *The Giver* has written about a seemingly perfect world that is all the more horrific when seen through the eyes of a young boy. Like all dystopias, this novel warns readers by presenting the possibilities that exist if a society becomes too perfect, stable, and disease-free. Readers experience the sentiments of Bob Seger's lyrics, "Every point of refuge has its price."

The "Perfect" Society in the Two Core Novels

Brave New World

Aldous Huxley's *Brave New World*, first published in 1932, is as startling today as it was when it was first published. For decades, other writers have used this text as an example of a society suffering the ill effects of "perfection." The World State Motto in this new world is *Community, Identity, Stability* which makes the D. H. C., Director of Hatcheries and Conditioning, an extremely powerful person.

Readers immediately gain a relationship with the main character, Bernard Marx. Although Bernard is somewhat of a social outcast because of his physical characteristics, he remains part of the upper class because he is an Alpha Plus. Bernard's strangeness has been attributed, at least in terms of rumor, to alcohol contamination while he was still in the Embryo Store. Whatever the source of his difference, Bernard's choice to spend much of his time alone further alienates his peers. In Utopian-like terms, this picture of a disease-free civilization is built around the stability which comes from conformity. Unfortunately for Bernard, he cannot or will not conform.

John comes into the picture when Bernard and Lenina discover him on their trip to a Savage Reservation. Savage Reservations, unlike the civilized Brave New World, continue in the backward ways. There are competition, hunger, disease, aging, and death. But there are also love, marriage, books, and parents. When Bernard finds out that John is the son of the Director, he takes him back to the new world—and civilization.

The conflicts in terms of personal responsibility occur after Bernard and John return to civilization. Although John finds many of the comforts initially appealing, he is appalled at the lack of personal connections within the society. When Bernard finds that his status has risen because of his discovery of John, he finds himself to be more of a conformist than he wants to believe. As these two men grapple with their individual choices and the subsequent responsibilities that go along with those choices, readers are led to examine their own ideas about what they might or might not be willing to give up in order to have community, identity, and stability.

The Giver

Lois Lowry's *The Giver* appears to paint a picture of an ideal world, because it is a world devoid of conflicts, poverty, divorce, unemployment, and injustice. Or so it seems, if only readers could let go of the first line of the novel: "It was almost December, and Jonas was beginning to be frightened." Readers experience this fear through the eyes of Jonas, an almost 12-year-old. As Jonas waits for the Ceremony of the Twelves and the "Assignment" he will receive at that ceremony, readers come to understand that this society has amazing similarities to the society in Huxley's *Brave New World*.

As Jonas' anticipation of the mysterious assignment heightens, one realizes that Jonas is different than the other children. Thus, it is no surprise to the reader that Jonas receives the most unusual assignment; he is the Receiver of Memories. As Jonas receives memories, he also develops an awareness of the "perfect" society he and his "family" inhabit. Only as we live through Jonas' new understandings, his pain, and his ultimate decision to take a stand against his community, do we come to realize the magnitude of this assignment.

Assessing and Building Background Knowledge

Before beginning any major unit of study, it is helpful to assess students' background knowledge of the topic or theme of study. One excellent way to have students do this is through an anticipation guide (Readence, Bean & Baldwin, 1985). An anticipation guide can support students' reflections on and expressions of opinions related to statements that challenge or confirm their beliefs (see Figure 11–1). Students respond to the belief statements in the guide before reading any of the texts. The guide helps to generate a great deal of student discussion, which serves as a transition to reading and exploring the two core novels.

Students first respond individually, and then discuss their responses in a think-pair-share strategy. This strategy allows students time for individual reflection and response (think); time to discuss responses with a self-selected other (pair); and opportunity to discuss or debate responses within the context of the larger group (share). At the end of the unit, students use the guide to see if their beliefs have been challenged or have changed. This is accomplished by asking students to respond from their post-reading views, as well as the projected views of the authors in the two core novels.

When students finish their initial discussions of the statements within the guide, there are three short stories that can be read aloud which help students refine their beliefs about these complex issues. All three stories explore aspects of the core novels and are short enough to fit into one class period. In addition, interest and readability will make these stories accessible to most readers.

"Harrison Bergeron" by Kurt Vonnegut, Jr. is an excellent story to read aloud. Found in many literature anthologies, this short story has enough action for the most reluctant reader and enough complexity for the most thoughtful reader. The story begins, "The year was 2081, and everybody was finally equal." By Constitutional Amendments, members of this society are made to wear masks if beautiful, mental handicappers if intelligent, and weights if graceful in order to make everyone equal. The society functions at the whim of the Handicapper General, Diana Moon Glampers, until tall, beautiful, and intelligent Harrison expresses his individuality.

"Do You Want My Opinion" by M.E. Kerr seems more superficial than Vonnegut's story if taken at the surface level. The first-person story is told through the eyes of the young protagonist, John, as he grapples with the societal belief that exchanging ideas is the most intimate behavior. Although more light-hearted, this story is like *Brave New World* in its attitude that sexuality is something normal which should not only be allowed, but expected. When John says, "It isn't fair to ask a girl out when all you really want is only one thing" (1984, p. 98), he is not talking about sex.

"The Children's Story" by James Clavell is childlike in presentation but frightening in the intensity of its message. Clavell states in the afterword that he wrote the story in response to his daughter's rote memorization and complete lack of understanding of the Pledge of Allegiance. The story recounts the 25 minutes, from 8:58 A.M. to 9:23 A.M., in which a new teacher enters an elementary classroom and completely brainwashes the children by questioning them about saying words they don't understand. Connections to *Brave New World* are numerous because of the brainwashing and chants. *The Giver* has a very similar scenario, in that all children are involved each morning in the chanting of the morning anthem. The message to all readers is frightening in its clarity.

Figure 11–1
Anticipation Guide: Individual Responsibility in Society

Directions: Before we begin reading *Brave New World* and *The Giver*, I would like you to read the following statements and decide whether you Agree (A) or Disagree (D) with each one. After we finish reading the two novels, I will ask you to look at the guide again and decide if the authors would have agreed or disagreed with each statement and if you have changed your opinions related to the statements now that you have read two related books. Room is left after each statement for comments.

Before   **After**   **Huxley**   **Lowry**

_____   1.   It is the responsibility of our parents to help us develop our image of what it means to be responsible.

_____   _____   _____

Comments:

_____   2.   The government has the right to make laws which keep people from knowing things that will cause them pain.

_____   _____   _____

Comments:

_____   3.   When one discovers injustice it is the individual's responsibility to make the injustice right.

_____   _____   _____

Comments:

_____   4.   When people are more similar than different, it makes it easier for people to be less competitive.

_____   _____   _____

Comments:

_____   5.   Everything in life is a trade-off. In order to get something, we must give up something.

_____   _____   _____

Comments:

Exploring the Core Novels

The Giver

Since *The Giver* is more engaging in terms of language, point-of-view, and complexity of plot, I recommend beginning by reading this novel aloud. Because the language in the text is relatively easy, the novel could also be read in small cooperative groups or as independent, silent reading. The predictive and suspenseful nature of the text, however, does make this an effective read-aloud.

Students should lead the discussions each day by generating and discussing their own responses to the text, but there are certain passages and questions that ought to be included (See Figure 11–2). Most of these are likely to be generated by the students but, if not, I encourage teachers to try and work them into the discussion since they are connections that lend themselves to the reading of *Brave New World*.

Students' discussions of related topics of their own choosing will be intense. Keeping a list of unresolved issues from *The Giver* as students move into reading *Brave New World* will give students support as they move to a related, but more complex, work of literature.

Brave New World

If all students in a heterogeneous class are going to read *Brave New World*, the book will require more teacher support than *The Giver*. Although parts of this book provide excellent passages that could be read aloud, the text does not lend itself to that format. For those students who need the voice support, making the text available in a recorded book format provides students with the help they need with unfamiliar words and concepts. If neither reading aloud, nor recorded books, meets the needs of a particular class, then group reading and response in a read-and-retell format (Brown & Cambourne, 1987) will help students to clarify words or situations that might be confusing.

Another way to help students understand this complex novel is to have them make a group re-creation of the "brave new world" presented in the text. Building a prototypical community with buildings labeled by name and function will help all readers, especially those who are visual and/or tactile kinesthetic, to visualize the setting and the way the society functions within that setting. Concrete visuals such as the Neo-Pavlovian Conditioning Rooms, the Social Predestination Room, and the Fordson Community Singery give students a base for imagining a society very different from theirs.

Figure 11–2
Key Passages and Questions

- In what ways does the first line, "It was almost December, and Jonas was beginning to be frightened," lead readers to expect that this society might have some imperfections?
- Defend the humanity or inhumanity of the RELEASE.
- Why do you think the teachers and other adults were so adamant about the precision of language?
- What was the role of the nurturer in society? Is there an equivalent role in our society?
- What is the function and form of the comfort objects?
- Jonas' society believes that drawing attention to individual differences is rude. Why would a society foster such a belief? What impact does this belief have on their society? How does this compare with "Harrison Bergeron"?
- Why do you think the society has no need for mirrors? "Mirrors were rare in the community; they weren't forbidden, but there was no real need of them." (p. 21)
- What rules are in place in the society to teach children to be interdependent? What rules are in place to allow them gradual independence? Do we have any similar rites of passage?
- Although being a birth mother is considered an important job, it lacks prestige. Why do you think birth mothers are held in such low esteem?
- What is the role (or non-role) of books in society? What did the leaders hope to gain, or lose, through this attitude toward books?
- Jonas says, "I thought there was only us. I thought there was only now." (p. 78) What had the society done to make Jonas believe this? Why would the elders have seen this as preferable to studying and building upon historical events?
- Jonas learns as he begins to receive memories that everything in life is a tradeoff. See pages 83–84 in order to generate a beginning list of things that had to be given up in order to get the "perfect" society.
- Why do you think the Giver makes the point that "great honor is not the same as great power"? (p. 84) Is that true in our society?
- "...a something—he could not grasp what—that lay beyond the place where the thickness of snow brought the sled to a stop." (p. 88) What predictions could individual students make about the "something"?
- Looking specifically at page 89. What comparisons and contrasts can be made between the school curriculum as it exists for Jonas and as it exists for students today?
- How are the young and old treated similarly in this society? How does that compare with our society's treatment of the young and old?
- What is the society's rationale for taking away individual choice? See pages 98–103 for support as you defend or denounce this position.
- How does Jonas' concept of the term "family" expand as the book progresses?

Wanderings & Wonderings: Dialogue Journals

One way for students to support each other during the reading of the core novels is through the use of dialogue journals. Whether students are reading independently, in small groups, or with a read-aloud, students will benefit by choosing a reading partner for dialogue throughout their reading of the texts. Using one of the short stories or a reading of the first chapter in a novel as a model, I recommend that the teacher discuss with students the purpose for and logistics of having a dialogue journal partner.

After choosing a partner, students vertically fold pages in a notebook and respond on the left-hand side of the paper to each reading of the text. Each day, when students come to class, they should have a response ready for their dialogue journal partners. Students take the first 10–15 minutes to respond to their partners' writing, on the right-hand side, and then together choose a quotation, an issue, or a point of debate for whole class discussion. This method provides an arena for everyone's voice as well as a forum for asking questions and exploring misconceptions. Students may choose to put illustrations, questions, comparisons, related poetry, connected news articles, as well as their written responses to the assigned readings in their dialogue journals.

Language Archeology

Although there are many avenues that can be explored in these novels, one of the most interesting features of each book is the rich language. As I reread these two core texts together, I felt as if I were a member of an archeological dig. An interesting word in *Brave New World* would remind me of an analogous term in *The Giver*. Students can also enjoy the same kind of language excavation after they have read both texts (See Figure 11–3). Figure 11–3 is a comparison/contrast graphic organizer in which students can record relatively equivalent words, phrases, and customs among *The Giver*, *Brave New World*, and our society.

Writing to Extend Thinking

The writing possibilities for these two novel are endless. There are many rich opportunities presented for extended writing, not only within the context of social issues, but also in terms of related personal responsibility. I have listed a few writing prompts that ask students to look critically at the text, examine their own views, and extend that thinking to other texts and content areas.

Figure 11–3
Language Archeology

Directions: The two novels we have read are rich in language that depicts a society very different from the one we are experiencing today. Or, do they? Perhaps our society is more like *Brave New World* than we might want to admit. Working cooperatively in your reader-response groups, gather data that support or reject the notion that the more things change, the more they stay the same. I have completed two of the cells as a model for your data collection. As in all good excavations, you should be creating categories from language artifacts you find that have not been listed on this organizer. Please add those to your list.

	The Contemporary Giver	Brave New World	Society
Words or phrases that have been coined for a particular process in society.	Release	Death conditioning	?
Leisure activities available.			
Phrases that tell us of the culture's values.			
Words for social class standing.			

---

1. When Lois Lowry wrote *The Giver*, her 85-year-old mother was dying. Shortly before publication of the novel, her mother died. Discuss your thoughts related to the impact you think that event might have had on the author's writing. Support your discussion of this possibility with "evidence" from the novel.

2. We have examined societies in two novels and two short stories at this point. Write an imaginative piece in which you explore something in our society that could take us to a "brave new world."

3. Memories and the past are bad things in both *The Giver* and *Brave New World.* If you had a limited amount of time to transmit a significant memory to someone, what would that memory be? Why have you chosen this memory? Is this a memory which you believe would sustain and regenerate this person after you are gone, or is it one you wish to last only for the moment?

4. We have seen several examples of unusual families in our reading—at least in terms of our definition of family. Redefine "family" in a new time and a new place. What would "family" units be like and why would they be different from our current understanding of family?

5. We all, in some sense, have experienced givers in our lives. In *Brave New World*, Linda might not be as warm and caring as the Giver in Lowry's novel; nevertheless, she does give memories to John. Write a letter to the person, either living or dead, who has been a giver for you.

6. All three main characters in *Brave New World*, *The Giver*, and "Harrison Bergeron" can be seen as individuals who take responsibility for speaking and acting out against social ills. They also can be seen as individuals who are basically self-destructive. Choose and defend one of these points of view.

7. How far are we from our version of the *Brave New World*? Using our society as a springboard, imagine what our current values, trends, and culture might be like in the future.

8. Choice is an element that has been summarily taken from the citizens in all the societies about which we have read. In what ways is our current society at risk because of the individual choices our citizens enjoy?

9. If everything in life is a tradeoff, what would you trade and for what?

Interdisciplinary Possibilities

Although all of the activities at this point have been related to reading and writing, the content area connections are endless. Whether teachers are part of an integrated curriculum or must work alone to help students make those connections, these two novels provide many opportunities for that extended research and thinking (see Figure 11–4). Teachers may wish to allow students to choose from this beginning list of possibilities, build other content options, or ask students to find the content connections in which they have an interest.

Figure 11–4
Content Connections

Science	**Art**
genetic engineering	absence of color
genocide	visual "elsewheres"
euthanasia	visual memories
	comfort objects

History	**Music**
Oneida	Bergeron's dance
the Shakers	Feelies' music
Zoar, Ohio	sound spigots
Icarian community, Corning, Ohio	
censorship	

Sociology

homelessness
aging
death and dying
families
nurture vs. nature
traditions
poverty
prejudice
the senses—a sixth sense

Conclusion

There are many works of young adult and traditionally classic literature that can build on and extend the ideas students have explored in the core texts. Some classic connections with related topics have been mentioned in the introduction. Many YA titles can also help readers continue to think about the issue of the individual's role in society. Further reading can be completed as independent reading, or students can work in small groups and read a common text. In either scenario, students can continue exploring the ways in which individuals have stood alone, or with others of like mind, against an issue or a society that has taken the wrong path.

If we want students to see themselves as participants in our society who are capable of thinking critically, then it is our responsibility to help them challenge their thinking with many readings that portray adolescents taking an active role in society. A beginning list of those literary connections is offered (see Figure 11–5) in the hope that readers of all ages can share in the gift which Jonas, The Giver, experiences: "Behind him, across vast distances of space and time, from the place he had left, he thought he heard music too. But perhaps it was only an echo" (p. 180).

Figure 11–5
Young Adult Connections

The Butterfly Revolution by William Butler (221 pp.)

    What initially appears to be a typical summer camp experience winds up becoming a riveting story of suspense. When one of the members of the camp society takes over the leadership, the other boys begin to realize the powerless feeling of being controlled by a sick leader. As a microcosmic study of revolution in society, this novel has all of the aspects of the attractive, yet dangerous, web of power.

The White Mountains by John Christopher (214 pp.)

    The characterizations are so believable in this science fiction novel that once the reader believes in the ruling Tripods, it reads as if it were realistic fiction. Will Parker, the main character, lives in a world that has abandoned memories. Each young boy is Capped by the Tripods and this settles his fate. Will Parker and two newly-found friends embark on an adventure that will help them escape the Capping if they can make it to the White Mountains—a place not ruled by Tripods.

Lord of the Flies by William Golding (208 pp.)

    This novel first appeared in 1954 and has been standard fare in the English curriculum since the 1960s. Although widely read, it has been the object of much criticism because of the harsh picture of the way society is created when children are left to their own devices. Given the social implications of the shipwrecked society, this novel provides close connections to the core novels.

The War between the Classes by Gloria Miklowitz (158 pp.)

    Students engage in a class experiment that helps them come to deeper understandings of both class and racial prejudice. When Amy realizes that the game is no longer a game to many of her friends, she has to decide whether to play or stand against the crowd.

Figure 11–5 Continued
Young Adult Connections

Z for Zachariah by Robert C. O'Brien (249 pp.)

Ann is young, alone, and surviving in a post-nuclear radiation society. While alone, she is able to establish her own patterns and goals. Once another member is added to her society, the rules all change. As readers experience Ann's survival instincts, they also learn about the dynamics of interpersonal relationships.

The Wave by Todd Strasser (143 pp.)

This novel exposes how easily brainwashed and thus easily led people can be and is based on a true incident that occurred in Palo Alto, California, in 1969. Like students in *The War Between the Classes*, students in this novel participate in a game that has them locked in a Nazi-like regime. Also like *The War Between the Classes*, two of the students must decide whether or not to expose the inherent evil in the game.

Bless the Beasts and Children by Glendon Swarthout (127 pp.)

A group of young boys, who name themselves the Bedwetters, have "triumphant" coming-of-age stories. As these boys form their own society out of necessity, this becomes a study of roles and leadership within such a society. It is also a touching example of young people finally taking a stand.

The Taking of Mariasburg by Julian Thompson (258 pp.)

Although the premise of Maria's newly acquired millions from a wealthy father she never met requires a near suspension of disbelief, the issues that Maria and her friends experience seem all–too–real. Maria uses her money to buy a town in order for her and her friends to establish a society that has none of the problems they have while living at home. Together they experience the pain of learning to lead, to follow, to survive, and to compromise.

List of References

Bradbury, R. (1953). *Fahrenheit 451.* New York: Ballantine.

Brown, H. & Cambourne, B. (1987). *Read and retell.* Portsmouth, NH: Heinemann.

Butler, W. (1979). *The butterfly revolution.* New York: Ballantine.

Christopher, J. (1988). *The white mountains.* New York: Collier.

Clavell, J. (1981). *The children's story.* New York: Bantam.

Donelson, K.L. & Nilsen, A.P. (1989). *Literature for today's young adults.* Glenview, IL: Scott, Foresman, & Company.

Golding, W. (1954). *Lord of the flies.* New York: Putnam.

Huxley, A. (1946). *Brave new world.* New York: Harper & Row.

Kerr, M.E.   (1984).   Do you want my opinion?   In *Sixteen: Short stories by outstanding writers for young adults*. New York: Dell.

Lowry, L. (1993). *The giver*. New York: Houghton Mifflin.

Miklowitz, G. (1986). *The war between the classes*. New York: Dell Laurel-Leaf.

O'Brien, R.C. (1987). *Z for Zachariah*. New York: Collier.

Orwell, G. (1949). *1984*. New York: Harcourt, Brace, & Jovanovich.

Orwell, G. (1946). *Animal farm*. New York: Harcourt, Brace, & Jovanovich.

Rand, A. (1946). *Anthem*. New York: Penguin.

Readence, J.E., Bean, T.W., & Baldwin, R.S. (1985). *Content area reading: An integrated approach*. Dubuque, IA: Kendall/Hunt.

Strasser, T. (1981). *The wave*. New York: Dell.

Swarthout, G. (1984). *Bless the beasts and children*. New York: Pocket Books.

Thompson, J.F. (1988). *The taking of Mariasburg*. New York: Scholastic.

Vonnegut, K. (1968). Harrison Bergeron. In *Welcome to the monkey house: A collection of short works*. New York: Delacorte Press.

CHAPTER 12

Beyond Camelot: Poetry, Song, and Young Adult Fantasy

TERI S. LESESNE

Introduction

She sits alone on a distant island high above the world. No one has seen her; no human waits on her. Her small world provides all that she needs, and she is happy in it. From time to time she sings a cheerful song as she watches the world below her through a glass in one wall of her station above the world; and she records its pictures regularly. Making these records is what she has been chosen for; at times, though, she wishes she could know more of the lives of that world than the images that the glass reveals of its people.

A character from volume two of a new fantasy trilogy? The next episode in the "Star Wars" series? No, as you have no doubt guessed, she is Tennyson's Lady of Shalott:

> There she weaves by night and day
> A magic web with colors gay.
> She has heard a whisper say,
> A curse is on her if she stay
>   To look down to Camelot.
> She knows not what the curse may be,
> And so she weaveth steadily,
> And little other care hath she,
>   The Lady of Shalott. (p. 179)

And she does—as any good fantasy heroine must—encounter disasters:

> She left the web, she left the loom,
> She made three paces through the room,
> She saw the water lily bloom,
> She saw the helmet and the plume,

> She looked down to Camelot.
> Out flew the web and floated wide;
> The mirror cracked from side to side;
> "The curse is come upon me," cried
> The Lady of Shalott. (p. 181)

Tennyson's poem is one that is frequently taught in the upper middle school and high school grades, and it is often preceded or followed by an examination of the mythology of King Arthur. And it is, unfortunately, just as often rejected by students as irrelevant and pointless. Tennyson's use of a slightly archaic English also often annoys students—the type of student who says of all poetry, "Why didn't he just say what he had to say and get it over with!" And then too, we, with our biographical information about Tennyson ("POET LAUREATE"), our history of England ("And then when the Roman Empire began to withdraw..."), and our literary analysis ("And that is called *incremental repetition*"), have sometimes tended to drown the impact.

One Fictional Young Reader's Reaction

In Chapter XXVIII, titled "The Unfortunate Lily Maid," in *Anne of Green Gables*, L.M. Montgomery describes the reactions of Anne and her friends to another of Lord Tennyson's Arthurian poems, "Lancelot and Elaine" from the *Idylls of the King* that has many similarities to "The Lady of Shalott":

> It was Anne's idea that they dramatize Elaine. They had studied Tennyson's poem in school the preceding winter, the Superintendent of Education having prescribed it in the English course for the Prince Edward Island schools. They had analyzed and parsed it and torn it to pieces in general until it was a wonder there was any meaning at all left in it for them, but at least the fair lily maid and Lancelot and Guinevere and King Arthur had become very real people to them, and Anne was devoured by secret regret that she had not been born in Camelot. Those days, she said, were so much more romantic than the present. (p. 221)

And so begins a funny but potentially dangerous adventure in which Anne attempts to re-enact the poem: "'Well, I'll be Elaine,' said Anne, yielding reluctantly, for, although she would have been delighted to play the principal character, yet her artistic sense demanded fitness for it and this, she felt, her limitations made impossible" (p. 222). The parts having been doled out and the barge having been covered with black and gold,

> For a few minutes Anne, drifting slowly down,
> enjoyed the romance of her situation to the full.   Then

something happened not at all romantic. The flat began to leak. In a very few moments it was necessary for Elaine to scramble to her feet, pick up her cloth of gold coverlet and pall of blackest samite and gaze blankly at a big crack in the bottom of her barge through which the water was literally pouring. (p. 223)

Anne is, of course, saved, or there would not have been the many popular sequels. And, being Anne, she eventually sees a positive side to her near disaster:

"And today's mistake is going to cure me of being too romantic. I have come to the conclusion that it is no use trying to be romantic in Avonlea. It was probably easy enough in towered Camelot hundreds of years ago, but romance is not appreciated now. I feel quite sure that you will soon see a great improvement in me in this respect, Marilla."

"I'm sure I hope so," said Marilla skeptically.

But Matthew, who had been sitting mutely in his corner, laid a hand on Anne's shoulder when Marilla had gone out.

"Don't give up all your romance, Anne," he whispered shyly, "a little of it is a good thing—not too much, of course—but keep a little of it, Anne, keep a little of it." (p. 227)

Fantasy and "The Lady of Shalott"

And, of course, Matthew is right: Romance is clearly possible in our age as it was in Anne's and King Arthur's. Other than biographies chronicling the scandals of the famous and near or want-to-be famous, few types of books are published in greater numbers than fantasies. Nearly all of them are inspired by medievalism, many by aspects of the King Arthur legends. And important to notice is that poetry plays a large role in most of the fantasies as songs, chants, inscriptions, and the like. For example, in the very popular *Mossflower* by Brian Jacques there are several poems and songs, including the following:

> To the mountain offire where badgers go,
> The path is fraught with danger.
> The way is long and hard and slow,
> Through foe and hostile stranger.
> The warrior's heart must never fail,
> Or falter on his quest.
> Those who live to tell the tale,
> Must first turn the quest. (p. 111)

Though not popular with every student, these contemporary "romances" and their technological adventure counterparts, *Star Wars*, *Star Trek*, and "Dungeons and Dragons," have the potential to draw them into the legend-heavy world of "The Lady of Shalott." Many students will recognize the names of Steven Spielberg, Monica Hughes, Jane Yolen, Stephen Roddenberry, and Brian Jacques. As Teri Lesesne points out in a recent article in *The ALAN Review*,

> In a recent survey (Lesesne, 1992), middle school students selected fantasy as one of their favorite topics or genres for books. Nearly one-third of the boys and one-fourth of the girls in the survey chose fantasy. Nearly one-half of the boys surveyed also selected science fiction as one of their favorite topics or genres. (p. 25)

What is fantasy? Isaac Asimov wrote, in an introduction to a book for young adult readers, the following about fantasy:

> Ordinary fiction is a story that isn't true, but might be. Fantasy is a story that isn't true, and *can't* be.
> In ancient time, when people didn't know much about the world, fantasy wasn't really fantasy. It was just fiction. Most people were quite ready to believe that dragons did exist, as well as giants and ogres, or witches and wizards, or ghosts and demons, or unicorns and fairies, and so on.
> With time, though, people discovered that all these things—and many others—simply didn't exist, and fantasies grew less popular. People went about saying, "Oh, that's just a fairy story" and would dismiss it. This was a shame because fantasies are very exciting, and when you're shivering over the villainy of a wicked witch, it's annoying to be told, "Witches don't exist, you know."
> Nowadays, therefore, fantasies are often written for young people because the world is new to them, and their imaginations are still so active. They are ready to believe in dragons and fairies and all the rest, and they can still enjoy fantasies. (p. viii)

Clearly, then, medievalism, the Arthurian legends, and fantasy in general are alive and well in the lives of many teenagers and have the potential to help them see the wonder of the story of the Lady in her tower watching the world through a mirror and weaving the images that she sees. Indeed, as Suzy McKee Charnas maintains, "I believe that fantasy literature is the strongest literature for children and young people right up through adolescence because it deals with the crucial question of childhood and you: *power.*" She goes on to suggest that children feel powerless and that "The only place you have real power is in your own imagination" (p. 22).

And I think I should point out that the division between fantasy and science fiction that is sometimes drawn by lovers of one and not of the other really does not apply to this look at the Lady in her tower or perhaps to any fantasy. Pamela F. Service has commented, "First, though, I should say that although the questions referred only to fantasy, I would lump science fiction in there as well. I know the purists will object, but both in reading and in writing, many of the same considerations apply to each genre. They are both speculative fiction dealing with realities that do not quite exist" (p. 17). The very fact that Asimov edited a book of fantasy stories suggests that, although there is fantasy that is not science fiction and science fiction that is not fantasy, there is much literature that is clearly both, as *Star Wars*, with its Emperor, Obi Wan Kenobi, Princess Leia, and the embodiment of evil, Darth Vader, illustrates.

Tennyson was, of course, much taken with the legends of King Arthur, and his fascination with the subject later culminated in the long and complex set of poems titled *The Idylls of the King*, of which "Lancelot and Elaine" is one. "The Lady of Shalott," though not the earliest of his efforts to turn the Arthurian milieu into verse, was written relatively early. It was included in the 1832 collection entitled *Poems*, in which also appeared the equally well known poem, "The Lotos-Eaters."

> Ricks, in his biographical/critical study of Tennyson, indicates that Impatience with "The Lady of Shalott" for being a 'tale of magic symbolism' and not that more conclusive thing, an allegory, manifested itself immediately on publication... (p. 79)

However, Ricks quotes R. H. Hutton as having provided the best "allegorical pointer":

> [The poem] has for its real subject the emptiness of the life of fancy, however rich and brilliant, the utter satiety which compels any true imaginative nature to break through the spell which entrances it in an unreal world or visionary joys...The curse, of course, is that she shall be involved in mortal passions, and suffer the fate of mortals, if she looks away from the shadow to the reality. Nevertheless, the time comes when she braves the curse. (p. 79)

And so the Lady, protected so long by her second-hand viewing of life, is drawn out of fantasy and into life and is destroyed by it. In that sense, the curse that "She has heard a whisper say" is "on her" (p. 179) is, perhaps, the curse that comes from engaging with life, a curse that we all suffer from and are eventually destroyed by. It is important to note that Tennyson does not say that she has been cursed, that is, that someone has *placed* a curse on her; rather, he uses the expression "a curse is on her" and "'The curse is come upon me'" (p. 181), suggesting that the curse is a part of her, not something set upon her from the outside, perhaps by a wizard.

She seems happy in her state. In Part I of the poem, Tennyson creates a lovely setting for her tower:

> On either side the river lie
> Long fields of barley and of rye,
> That clothe the world and meet the sky;
> And through the field the road runs by
>   To many-towered Camelot... (p. 178)

Her tower "Overlook[s] a space of flowers" and a "shallop flitteth silken-sailed" past her island (p. 178). She sings "a song that echoes cheerly," although she is a mysterious figure to the workers who hear that song (pp. 178–179).

In Part II, we learn that "she weaves by night and day" and "has heard a whisper say,/ A curse is on her if she stay/ To look down to Camelot" (p. 179). But we also learn that she does not know the nature of the curse, and it does not seem to bother her, for Tennyson says, "little other care hath she" (p. 179)—not an expression one would expect to be used to describe someone who was unhappy. She has heard of the curse, then; but she is happy in her weaving and largely care-less.

Indeed, Tennyson describes for us what she sees in her mirror, and it is a lively and colorful array: "surly village churls," "red cloaks of market girls," "damsels glad," "an abbot," "a curly shepherd lad," a "long-haired page in crimson clad," and "knights...riding two and two" (p. 179). We are told that "She hath no loyal knight and true" (p. 179), perhaps a sad state. Nevertheless, we are also told that "...in her web she still delights" (p. 179).

Then with the sudden shifts that mark key parts of the poem, Tennyson introduces a note of sadness and frustration: "'I am half sick of shadows,' said/ The Lady of Shalott" (p. 180), thus setting up the conflict for the crucial next section.

When, in Part III, she sees Lancelot, his brilliance is overwhelming: "From the bank and from the river/ He flashed into the crystal mirror" (p. 181). Tennyson pours into his depiction of Lancelot language that repeats in line after line the flash of the knight: "dazzling," "flamed," "sparkled," "yellow field," "glittered," "stars," "golden," "blazoned," "silver," "thick-jeweled shone," "burned like one burning flame," "starry clusters bright," "bearded meteor, trailing light," and so on until he flashes in that "crystal mirror" (pp. 180–181).

Ricks suggests that Tennyson intended a special interaction between the river and the mirror:

> The "crystal" mirror suggests the river; for the only time in the poem, a word rhymes with itself—a perfect reflection: *river/ river*. Nor is there another reference to the river's reflecting in the poem—notably, given that there is so much about the river and about dazzling light. Her mirror constituted a protection against life for the Lady; it cracks after she sees somebody doubly mirrored—"From the bank and from the river"—within the mirror. It is as if the protection is canceled out: re-re-flection = flection, the impact itself. (p. 81)

The effect of the dazzling Lancelot is in strong contrast to the images Tennyson describes her seeing and weaving at the end of Part II just before Lancelot, "A bowshot from her bower eaves" (p. 180), appears:

> For often through the silent nights
> A funeral, with plumes and lights
>   And music, went to Camelot;
> Or when the moon was overhead,
> Came two young lovers lately wed:
> "I am half sick of shadows," said
>   The Lady of Shalott. (p. 180)

The Lancelot that Tennyson describes is certainly no shadow.

And so the Lady leaves her secluded life, crosses the room and

> She saw the water lily bloom,
> She saw the helmet and the plume,
>   She looked down to Camelot. (p. 181)

She sees not fantasy but the reality of life in the form of the blooming of the flower of a water lily, the regalia of a young and vigorous knight, and the brilliance of a grand towered city. With that involvement in the vibrancy of life, her artificial tapestry of life flew out and floated away; and the mirror that reflected but was not life, "cracked from side to side" (p. 181).

In another sudden shift, in Part IV of the poem, the images Tennyson uses become somber:

> In the stormy east wind straining,
> The pale yellow woods were waning,
> The broad stream in his banks complaining,
> Heavily the low sky raining
> > Over toward Camelot... (p. 181)

The weather has turned stormy; the day has turned to evening; and the season has turned into autumn:

> Lying, robed in snowy white
> That loosely flew to left and right—
> The leaves upon her falling light—
> Through the noises of the night
> > She floated down to Camelot... (p. 182)

The poem in its final version ends with dread among "All the knights at Camelot" except Lancelot:

> But Lancelot mused a little space;
> He said, "She has a lovely face;
> God in his mercy lend her grace,
> > The Lady of Shalott." (p. 183)

A masterpiece of rhythm and rhyme and image, the poem maintains to these very last lines a mystery and pathos, a dream-like quality. It is a fantasy, a song sung in a fantasy. Indeed, "The Lady of Shalott" is a song, sung in its entirety by Loreena McKennitt on her recent album *The Visit*. It is a song, but it also shows us the conflict between fantasy and reality. As Ricks puts it,

> But it creates an intensely memorable myth in which the wish
> not to face reality and the wish to face it, the impulse toward
> life and the impulse toward death, an inexplicable guilt and a
> timorous innocence, shine as from a cracked mirror. (p. 82)

Teaching "The Lady of Shalott"

An approach to the poem might begin by asking the students to imagine the world described at the start of this chapter, that is, the world of the Lady, but in terms of the fantasy and fantasy-science-fiction that they are familiar with:

> She sits alone on a distant island high above the
> world. No one has seen her; no human waits on her. Her
> small world provides all that she needs, and she is happy in

it. From time to time she sings a cheerful song as she watches the world below her through a glass in one wall of her station above the world; and she records its pictures regularly. Making these records is what she has been chosen for; at times, though, she wishes she could know more of the lives of that world than the images that the glass reveals of its people.

They might be asked whether it could be a world created by Stephen Spielberg? One encountered by the crew of the Enterprise? A novel by Susan Cooper or J. R. R. Tolkein? Monica Hughes or Anne McCaffrey? They might then be asked to write in their readers' notebooks brief answers to the following questions:

1. Where does she live?

2. Who is she?

3. What has happened to her?

4. What would she think and feel in her separate world?

5. What might happen to her?

They should understand that there are no answers to these questions, only each of their ideas, each interesting to consider. They will be imagining, therefore, limited only by a context, as Tennyson did with the world of King Arthur, not a story already written or a received legend.

After they have shared those speculations, they might be asked to remember a world that they have read about or seen in a movie or on television that, in Asimov's words, "doesn't exist" (p. viii) and share these worlds with each other. The purpose of this reflection is to bring their thoughts to bear on the pervasive role of fantasy in our world. Books they have read by Monica Hughes, Anne McCaffrey, Madeleine L'Engle are likely to be mentioned; movies and television programs they have seen—*Star Trek*, *Star Wars*, *Aladdin*—and computer games and video games are all appropriate for this listing of worlds. And a list should be made for future reference.

Because fantasy literature depends so heavily on medievalism, it is likely that many will describe worlds with unicorns, sorcerers, dragons, and the like. At this point, the teacher might say something like, "Well, I have a favorite fantasy world and here's a song about it" and read "The Lady of Shalott" aloud as a bard might have done in the time of Arthur. Once the reading is complete, students would be ready to think about the Lady and her world, now with the insights that Tennyson has given his readers.

In their readers' notebooks, they might consider the same questions they did earlier, always remembering that the songwriter's vision is one among many.

1. Where does she live?

2. Who is she?

3. What has happened to her?
4. What would she think and feel in her separate world?

5. What might happen to her?

After the students have shared their second set of reactions to the questions—and some will surely like their own first answers as well as or better than Tennyson's—the teacher could ask the students to point to parts of each other's answers that they think would make good elements of a story about the Lady. Acting for Tennyson, then, the teacher might read the song again, pointing to a few parts that make it a good look at the basic story, being careful not to say it is the best look, or even a better look than those the students have come up with. This might also be a good place to play the McKennitt version from the album *The Visit*.

Following Up on the Theme of the Poem

Since "The Lady of Shalott" may be read in a unit dealing with fantasy and reality, students might be asked to consider the question, "What is the difference between fantasy worlds and the real world?" After they have had a chance to consider this question in their readers' notebooks and perhaps in small group discussions, the class might make two lists, one headed "The Real World" and the other, "Fantasy Worlds."

After the listing has created a variety of items under each heading, the students might be ask to consider another question: "Is one better than the other?" Again, lists might be created for each under the following headings: "Fantasy World: Pro," "Fantasy World: Con," "Real World: Pro," and "Real World: Con."

As a final question for individual thought, students might be asked to consider one of the following:

1. Should the Lady of Shalott have left her fantasy world for the real world?

2. What happens if one lives only in a fantasy world?

3. What happens if one lives only in the real world?

Following Up on the Idea of Fantasy

This may, of course, be enough. "The Lady of Shalott" is a lovely poem, as generations of readers have recognized. But to have today's students see it as a part of their world, as a song from a fantasy like those they read and watch, may be the best experience for them; though, as teachers and readers, we would probably want more.

However, if an additional spark seems to have been lit, if the discussion of fantasy has brought to the surface wide-spread interest in it, more might be done.

Follow-up Activities

So, assuming that interest in fantasy is extensive enough—and not to propose that "The Lady of Shalott" should be lost in a fantasy unit—let me suggest that students might pursue the following follow-up activities:

1. Obviously, there are many poems, stories, novels, and works of nonfiction that students can read that deal with the King Arthur legends. Tennyson's own "Idylls of the King" might interest some, as might Cooper's "The Dark Is Rising" and J.R.R. Tolkien's "Lord of the Rings" trilogy (See Additional Reading and Other Popular Fantasies). Students might decide to write about the ways in which the authors of the books they have read have dealt with King Arthur in their fantasy worlds. Corbet, in writing about "The Dark Is Rising" series, suggests, "The appeal of these books goes beyond the invitation to study further about Arthur and the Matter of Britain, but any student who reads these books should be encouraged to search through the literature, fiction and nonfiction, so that they may come to their own conclusions about Arthur and his importance in their lives" (p. 47).

2. Some students might like to concentrate on the ways in which Tennyson uses the legends of King Arthur in his other poems. A comparison of "The Lady of Shalott" with "Lancelot and Elaine" from *The Idylls of the King* would be interesting from the perspective of a teenage reader of "The Dark Is Rising" or "The Lord of the Rings" series, although *The Idylls* present major reading problems because of Tennyson's extensive use of archaic language. They might find thought-provoking Anne's efforts in *Anne of the Green Gables* to act out one of them. Would they be tempted to act out "The Lady of Shalott"?

3. Students might wish to pursue their own story of the Lady from their original and later thoughts after hearing and reading

Tennyson's "The Lady of Shalott." These stories could lead in many directions different from those of Tennyson, each as interesting as his.

4. There are many songs in recent fantasies. Students who are interested in music may want to work with the music teacher in the school to set these songs to music. The musical settings of Donald Swan (see Additional Reading) can serve as guides for such activities. The students might also consider the musical setting sung by McKennitt on *The Visit*.

5. The story of the Lady that Tennyson created may inspire some students to create their own stories or poems, expanding on the stories that Tennyson tells in "The Idylls of the King." Or they may want to go back to the original King Arthur legends and retell them. Or, perhaps, they might wish to tell an Arthur-like legend from their own perspective, as Susan Cooper and J. R. R. Tolkein did.

6. Students might wish to go back to the list of other creators of worlds that do not exist and explore one or more other works of fantasy, perhaps with a medieval setting, perhaps not. They might choose to look at fantasies with cats or mice or unicorns as major characters. Others might want to pursue the works of a single author, such as Madeleine L'Engle.

7. The world at the time that King Arthur is thought to have lived may have been very different from that shown in the legends and described in Tennyson's poems. Some students may wish to look at the reality of the life and time of Arthur and the other characters in the myths, and compare the romanticized version to what life was really like then.

8. Every land has its own mythology, and students may wish to explore the myths of another country, either as myths or in works of literature that use elements of that mythology. Laurence Yep's "Dragon" series is an excellent example of the latter. The author has commented about the writing of the series in an article in *The ALAN Review*, in which he states, "It [the experiences of the dragon, Shimmer, that is the main character] not only fit what I knew of her character but let me root my fantasy firmly in history—for the best fantasy is nurtured by the past" (p. 8).

9. A few irreverent students may see humor in fantasy and wish to parody its conventions, as Mark Twain did in *A Connecticut Yankee in King Arthur's Court*.

Additional Reading

Any number of stories of fantasy exist from which students will have drawn their responses to the activities described above. If the interest is there, the teacher can take a cue from those mentioned by the students. A couple that are likely to be mentioned are those discussed in the following.

The Dark Is Rising by Susan Cooper (244 pp.)

Susan Cooper's critical and commercial success, "The Dark Is Rising" series, has won many awards and many readers. Corbett says of it,

> Cooper's five books deal with the mythological Arthur. There is no story here of holding back the Saxons. This is a tale that the old bards might have told—of monsters and magic, of kings, queens, gods, and goddesses, and above all, of the on-going battle between good and evil, the Light and the Dark, not necessarily interpreted as Christianity and Paganism. (p. 47)

The novel with the series title, *The Dark Is Rising*, was a Newbery Honor book in 1974 and begins the story of the renewal of the fight between Good and Evil, into which characters from the King Arthur legends are drawn, along with the guardians of the Light called the Old Ones:

> When the Dark comes rising, six shall turn it back,
> Three from the circle, three from the track;
> Wood, bronze, iron; water, fire, stone;
> Five will return and one go alone. (p. 37)

Will Stanton, the principal character of the novel and the last of the Old Ones, lives in two worlds that shift for him as he tries to help in the battle against evil, the Dark:

> It ["delicate music"] had gone again. And when he looked back through the window, he saw that his own world had gone with it. In that flash, everything had changed. The snow was there as it had been a moment before, but not piled now on roofs or stretching flat over lawns and fields. There were no roofs, there were no fields. There were only trees. Will was looking over a great white forest: a forest of massive trees, sturdy as towers and ancient as rock. (p. 17)

And his world continues to shift, as on Christmas Eve,

There before him rose the great doors, the great carved doors that he had first seen on a snow-mounded Chiltern hillside, and Merriman raised his left arm and pointed at them with his five fingers spread wide and straight. Slowly the doors opened, and the elusive silvery music of the Old Ones came swelling up briefly to join the accompaniment of the carol, and then was lost again. And he walked forward with Merriman into the light, into a different time and a different Christmas...(p. 78)

The battle against the renewed power of evil continues, with Will at its center. The fourth in the series, *The Grey King*, won the Newbery Award in 1976; and poetry and song continued to play a part by both explaining and obscuring, as they do in all fantasy:

> By the pleasant lake the Sleepers lie,
> On Cadfan's Way where the kestrels call;
> Though grim from the Grey King shadows fall,
> Yet singing the golden harp shall guide
> To break their sleep and bid them ride. (p. 37)

Near the close of the novel, the golden harp does awake the Sleepers:

They were horsemen, riding. They came out of the mountain, out of the lowest slopes of Cader Idris that reached up from the lake into the fortress of the Grey King. They were silvery-grey, glinting figures riding horses of the same strange half-colour, and they rode over the lake without touching the water, without making any sound... . They wore tunics and cloaks. Each one had a sword hanging at his side. Two were hooded. One wore a circlet about his head, a gleaming circlet of nobility, though not the crown of a king... .

... Then the riders wheeled back suddenly towards the slope of the mountain, and before Will could wonder at it, he saw that Bran stood there on the slope, halfway up the loose scree, near the ledge that had broken his fall earlier that day... . It was not for ordinary men to see that the Sleepers, woken out of their long centuries of rest, were riding now to the rescue of the world from the rising Dark... .

... The six riders, glinting silver-grey on their silver-grey mounts, curved round after their leader and paused for a moment in line before the place on the hillside where Bran stood. Each drew his sword and held it up right before his face in a salute, and kissed the flat of its blade in homage as to a king. And Bran stood there slim and erect as a young tree, his white hair gleaming in a silver crest, and bent his head gravely to them with the quiet arrogance of a king granting a boon. (pp. 200–201)

The Lord of the Rings by J. R. R. Tolkien (1,193 pp.)

No fantasy has captured the enthusiasm of both young and old readers more than J. R. R. Tolkien's *The Lord of the Rings*. A trilogy made up of *The Fellowship of the Ring, The Two Towers*, and *The Return of the King*, but using characters introduced in the earlier novel, *The Hobbit*, these books, partly of the medieval world, have, for many readers, produced their own world nearly as real as the modern one in which they live.

Characters created by Tolkien have become as much a part of our culture as those created by Shakespeare or Dickens: Bilbo Baggins, the Goloub, Ents, Sauron, Gandalf, Galadriel, Strider, Gondor, and, of course, Frodo ("FRODO LIVES!").

The novels, written in the 1940s, tell the story of the battle between good and evil, of the innocent who is chosen to combat evil, and the temporary success of good over evil, leaving evil weakened but ready to return. In that way, they cover ground that has been part of the literature of humankind since its first recorded words. And they cover the ground that "The Dark Is Rising" series later looked at in the Seventies. But they are more, much more. They are a world into which many young readers (and this older one) fall happily. In fact, there is even an "atlas" of the journey of Frodo to confront evil, *Journeys of Frodo: An Atlas of J. R. R. Tolkien's "The Lord of the Rings"* (109 pp.) by Barbara Strachey.

Not every student will want to read all three plus one of the series. Many will not want to read any of them, though *The Hobbit* has been known to seduce many a not-very-interested-in-fantasy reader into the series. But they are filled with episodes that can be read for their own sake, and the books contain songs and poems that both ornament them and echo their stories. The most famous is one that changes as the novels progress from start to finish of a journey. Here is how it begins its transformation:

> The Road goes ever on and on
> Down from the door where it began.
> Now far ahead the Road has gone,
> And I must follow, if I can,
> Pursuing it with eager feet,
> Until it joins some larger way
> Where many paths and errands meet.
> And whither then? I cannot say. (*Fellowship*, p. 62)

Indeed, when Donald Swan created a song cycle of eight of Tolkien's lyrics, he gave it the title of "The Road Goes Ever On." There are many other songs that might have been but do not seem to have been set to music, especially one that begins "Where now the horse and the rider? Where is the horn that was blowing?   Where is the helm and the hauberk, and the bright hair flowing?"

Other Popular Fantasies

To list all the popular books and authors of novels of fantasy, even those with a medieval flavor, would fill this book; and I know that whatever list I provide will cause some readers to say, "Why didn't he include ———?" But with that risk, in addition to "The Dark Is Rising" and "The Lord of the Rings," I offer the following as a limited bibliography of modern fantasy that teachers might read if they have not and that they might suggest to their students who are drawn into this magical world by that wonderful Lady of Shalott.

Visions of Fantasy edited by Isaac Asimov & Martin H. Greenberg (192 pp.).

The Silver Glove by Suzy McKee Charnas (162 pp.).

The Bronze King by Suzy McKee Charnas (189 pp.).

The Golden Thread by Suzy McKee Charnas (209 pp.).

The Ghatti's Tale: Book One, Finders-Seekers by Gayle Greeno (506 pp.).

The Ghatti's Tale: Book Two, Mindspeakers' Call by Gayle Greeno (527 pp.).

The Keeper of the Isis Light by Monica Hughes (136 pp.).

The Promise by Monica Hughes (156 pp.).

Sandwriter by Monica Hughes (158 pp.).

Many Waters by Madeleine L'Engle (310 pp.).

A Ring of Endless Light by Madeleine L'Engle (332 pp.).

A Swiftly Tilting Planet by Madeleine L'Engle (334 pp.).

A Wind in the Door by Madeleine L'Engle (262 pp.).

A Wrinkle in Time by Madeleine L'Engle (190 pp.).

Dragon Cauldron by Laurence Yep (312 pp.).

Dragon of the Lost Sea by Laurence Yep (213 pp.).

Dragon Steel by Laurence Yep (276 pp.).

Dragon War by Laurence Yep (313 pp.).

Conclusion

Well, she still sits in her tower; she is still weaving; she is still drawn from her glass to look directly at Lancelot and Camelot; and Lancelot still comments on her lovely face. Her story—poem, song, fantasy, and parable of the conflict between fantasy and reality, between dwelling in one's own world and venturing into the world of the rest of humankind—can be for our students more than a dead monument of Victorian poetry. It can be more than a "major work" by a "poet laureate." Fantasy—Princess Leia in *Star Wars* or Olwen in *The Keeper of the Isis Light*—may be the hook to draw students into Tennyson's song of the Lady who has seen the world only through the "screen" of her mirror, who has recorded in the "log" of her web, and who is drawn by the flash of intense reality to join that world—and who is destroyed by her new vision. Many questions are raised by the poem, as many questions are raised by all fantasies. And, like the poem, fantasies are not about answers, at least not single correct answers. "The Lady of Shalott" can entrance not only through its song but also through the puzzles it opens for its readers, puzzles that can tease our students into reading, listening to it, wondering about the Lady. It is then a good choice if come at through the angle of fantasy.

List of References

Asimov, I. & Greenberg, M.H. (Eds.). (1989). *Visions of fantasy*. New York: Doubleday.

Charnas, S.M. (1992, spring). A case for fantasy. *The ALAN Review*, **19** (3), 20–22.

Charnas, S.M. (1989). *The golden thread*. New York: Bantam.

Charnas, S.M. (1989). *The silver glove*. New York: Bantam.

Charnas, S.M. (1985). *The bronze king*. Boston: Houghton Mifflin.

Cooper, S. (1980). *Silver on the tree*. New York: Macmillan.

Cooper, S. (1976). *The grey king*. New York: Atheneum.

Cooper, S. (1973). *The dark is rising*. New York: Atheneum.

Cooper, S. (1973). *Greenwitch*. New York: Macmillan.

Cooper, S. (1966). *Over sea, under stone*. New York: Harcourt Brace.

Corbett, L. (1993, fall). 'Not wise the thought—A grave for Arthur.' *The ALAN Review*, **21** (1), 45–48.

Elledge, S. (Ed.). (1990). *Wider than the sky: Poems to grow up with*. New York: HarperCollins, 178–183.

Greeno, G. (1994). *The Ghatti's tale: Book two, Mindspeakers' call*. New York: DAW Books.

Greeno, G. (1993). *The Ghatti's tale: Book one, Finders-seekers*. New York: DAW Books.

Hughes, M. (1989). *The promise*. New York: Simon & Schuster.

Hughes, M. (1988). *Sandwriter*. New York: Henry Holt & Company.

Hughes, M. (1985). *The keeper of the isis light*. New York: Atheneum.

Jacques, B. (1988). *Mossflower*. New York: Avon.

Jacques, B. (1986). *Redwall*. New York: Philomel.

L'Engle, M. (1993). *A wind in the door*. New York: Dell.

L'Engle, M. (1993). *A swiftly tilting planet*. New York: Dell.

L'Engle, M. (1992). *Many waters*. New York: Dell.

L'Engle, M. (1980). *A ring of endless light*. New York: Dell.

L'Engle, M. (1976). *A wrinkle in time*. New York: Dell.

Lesesne, T. (1994, spring). Forming *connections* and awakening *visions*: Using short story collections in the classroom. *The ALAN Review*, **21** (3), 24–26.

McKennitt, L. (1992, April). The lady of Shalott. *The visit*. Burbank, CA: Warner Brothers.

Montgomery, L.M. (1987). *Anne of green gables.* New York: Bantam Books (originally published in 1908).

Ricks, C. (1972). *Tennyson.* New York: Macmillan.

Service, P.F. (1992, spring). On writing sci fi and fantasy for kids. *The ALAN Review*, **19** (3), 16–18.

Strachey, B. (1981). *Journeys of Frodo: An atlas of J. R. R. Tolkien's The lord of the rings.* New York: Ballantine.

Swan, D. & Tolkien, J.R.R. (1978). *The road goes ever on: A song cycle.* Boston: Houghton Mifflin.

Tolkien, J.R.R. (1988). *The return of the king.* New York: Ballantine.

Tolkien, J.R.R. (1986). *The two towers.* New York: Ballantine.

Tolkien, J.R.R. (1986). *The fellowship of the ring.* New York: Ballantine.

Tolkien, J.R.R. (1986). *The hobbit.* New York: Ballantine.

Yep, L. (1992, spring). A garden of dragons. *The ALAN Review*, **19** (3), 6–8.

Yep, L. (1992). *Dragon war.* New York: Harper & Row.

Yep, L. (1991). *Dragon cauldron.* New York: HarperCollins.

Yep, L. (1985). *Dragon steel.* New York: Harper & Row.

Yep, L. (1982). *Dragon of the lost sea.* New York: Harper & Row.

Adolescent
Literature
as a

Complement
to the
CLASSICS

REFERENCES

Alexander, R.P. & Lester, J. (Eds.). (1970). *Young and black in America*. Westminster, MD: Random House.

Andrews, W.L. (1991). *Critical essays on Frederick Douglass*. New York: Macmillan.

Applebee, A.N. (1993). *Literature in the secondary school: Studies of curriculum and instruction in the United States*. Urbana, IL: National Council of Teachers of English.

Asimov, I. & Greenberg, M.H. (Eds.). (1989). *Visions of fantasy*. New York: Doubleday.

Beach, R. (1993). *A teacher's introduction to reader response theories*. Urbana, IL: National Council of Teachers of English.

Blair, L. (1991, December). Developing student voices with multicultural literature. *English Journal*, **80** (8), 24–28.

Blockson, C.L. (1987). *The Underground Railroad: First person narratives of escapes to freedom in the North*. New York: Prentice Hall.

Bodart, J. (1980). *Booktalk! Booktalking and school visiting for young adult audiences*. New York: H.W. Wilson.

Bontemps, A. (1969). *Great slave narrative*. Boston: Beacon Press.

Bushman, J.H. & Bushman, K.P. (1993). *Using young adult literature in the English classroom*. New York: Merrill/Macmillan.

Cable, M. (1971). *Black odyssey: The case of the slave ship Amistad*. New York: Viking.

Campbell, J. & Moyers, B. (1988). *The power of myth*. New York: Doubleday.

Carey, M. (1993). Hero. *Music box* (Columbia compact disc 53205), Carey (lyrics) and Carey and Afanasieff (music). Nashville: Sony Songs, Inc.

Carey-Webb, A. (1991, April). Auto/Biography of the oppressed: The power of testimonial. *English Journal*, **80** (4), 44–47.

Carlsen, R.G. & Sherrill, A. (1988). *Voices of readers: How we come to love books*. Urbana, IL: National Council of Teachers of English.

Carrier, W. (Ed.). (1980). *Guide to world literature*. Urbana, IL: National Council of Teachers of English.

Charnas, S.M. (1992, spring). A case for fantasy. *The ALAN Review*, **19** (3), 20–22.

Corbett, L. (1993, fall). 'Not wise the thought—A grave for Arthur.' *The ALAN Review*, **21** (1), 45–48.

Coryell, N.G. (1927). *An evaluation of extensive and intensive teaching of literature*. Unpublished doctoral dissertation, Columbia University, New York.

Cross, B.E. (1993, May). How do we prepare teachers to improve race relations? *Educational Leadership,* 50 (8), 64–65.

Davis, C.T. & Gates, H.L., Jr. (Eds.). (1991). *The slave's narrative.* Cary, NC: Oxford University Press.

Dionisio, M. (1991, January). Responding to literary elements through mini-lessons and dialogue journals. *English Journal,* 80 (1), 40–44.

Donelson, K.L. & Nilsen, A.P. (1989). *Literature for today's young adults.* Glenview, IL: Scott, Foresman, & Company.

Elkind, D. (1967). Egocentrism in adolescence. In J. Gardner (Ed.), *Readings in developmental psychology.* 2nd. ed. Boston: Little, Brown & Company, 383–390.

Farrell, E. (1966, January). Listen my children and you shall read. *English Journal,* 55 (1), 39–45.

Freedman, R. (1987). *Lincoln: A photobiography.* New York: Clarion.

Gardner, H. (1983). *Frames of mind: The theory of multiple intelligences.* New York: Basic Books.

Gates, H.L., Jr. (Ed.). (1987). *The classic slave narratives.* New York: The New American Library.

Gates, H.L., Jr. & Appiah, K.A. (Eds.). (1994). *Frederick Douglass: Critical perspectives past and present.* New York: Amistad Press.

Gibson, W. (1956). *The miracle worker.* New York: Tamarack Productions, Ltd.

Glasser, J.E. (1994, February). Finding Ithaca: *The Odyssey* personalized. *English Journal,* 83 (2), 66–69.

Hamilton, V. (1993). *Anthony Burns: The defeat and triumph of a fugitive slave.* New York: Alfred A. Knopf.

Haskins, J. (1976). *Witchcraft, mysticism and magic in the black world.* New York: Dell.

Haskins, J. (1987). *Black music in America: A history through its people.* Scranton, PA: Thomas Y. Crowell.

Haskins, J. (1990). *Black dance in America: A history through its people.* Scranton, PA: Thomas Y. Crowell.

Heath, S.B. & Mangiola, L. (1991). *Children of promise: Literate activity in linguistically and culturally diverse classrooms.* Washington, D.C.: National Education Association.

Higuchi, C. (1993, May). Understanding must begin with us. *Educational Leadership,* 50 (8), 69–71.

Hodgkinson, H. (1993, April). American education: The good, the bad, and the task. *Phi Delta Kappan,* 74 (8), 619–623.

Huggins, N.I. (1987). *Slave & citizen: The life of Frederick Douglass.* New York: HarperCollins.

Hughes, L., Meltzer, M., & Lincoln, E. (1973). *A pictorial history of black Americans.* Westminster, MD: Crown.

Jordan, J. (1972). *Dry victories.* New York: Holt, Rinehart & Winston.

Kane, S. (1991, February). Turning teenagers into reader response researchers. *Journal of Reading,* 34 (5), 400–401.

Karolides, N.J. (1992). The transactional theory of literature. In N.J. Karolides (Ed.), *Reader response in the classroom: Evoking and interpreting meaning in literature.* White Plains, NY: Longman, 21-32.

Katz, W. (1977). *Black people who made the old West.* Scranton, PA: HarperCollins.

Katz, W.L. (Ed.). (1968). *Five slave narratives: A compendium*. Arno Press and *The New York Times*.

Kaywell, J.F. (1993). *Adolescents at risk: A guide to fiction and nonfiction for young adults, parents, and professionals*. Westport, CT: Greenwood Press.

Kirby, D., Liner, T., & Vinz, R. (1988). *Inside out: Developmental strategies for teaching writing*. 2nd ed. Portsmouth, NH: Heinemann.

Kuklin, S. (1993). *Speaking out: Teenagers take on race, sex, and identity*. New York: Putnam.

Kutiper, K. (1983, November). Extensive reading: A means of reconciliation. *English Journal, 72* (7), pp. 58–61.

Langer, J.A. (1989). *Literature instruction: A focus on student response*. Urbana, IL: National Council of Teachers of English.

Lesesne, T. (1994, spring). Forming *connections* and awakening *visions*: Using short story collections in the classroom. *The ALAN Review, 21* (3), 24–26.

Lester, J. (1986). *To be a slave*. New York: Scholastic.

Lindgren, M.V. (Ed.). (1991). *The multicolored mirror: Cultural substance literature for children and young adults*. Fort Atkinson, WI: Highsmith Press.

Livaudais, M.F. (1985). *A survey of secondary (grades 7–12) students' attitudes toward reading motivational activities*. Unpublished doctoral dissertation, University of Houston, Texas.

McFreeley, W.S. (1992). *Frederick Douglass*. New York: Simon & Schuster.

Mee, S. (1986, September 8). I am. *Scholastic Voice*.

Meltzer, M. (1987). *The Black Americans: A history in their own words 1619–1983*. New York: Harper Trophy.

Miller-Lachmann, L. (Ed.). (1992). *Our family, our friends, our world: An annotated guide to significant multicultural books for children and teenagers*. New Providence, NJ: Bowker.

Milner, J.O. & Milner, L.F.M. (1993). *Bridging English*. New York: Merrill.

Murphy, J. (1990). *The boys' war: Civil War letters to their loved ones from the blue and gray*. New York: Clarion.

Neeld, E.C. (1986). *Writing*. Glenview, IL: Scott, Foresman.

O'Neil, J. (1993, May). A new generation confronts racism. *Educational Leadership, 50* (8), 60–63.

Pace, B.G. (1992, September). The textbook canon: Genre, gender, and race in U.S. literature anthologies. *English Journal, 81* (5), 33–38.

Penn, A. (1962). *The miracle worker*. Playfilm Productions, Inc. (VHS video by United Artists, 1987), 105 mins.

Petry, A. (1991). *Harriet Tubman: Conductor on the Underground Railroad*. North Bellmore, NY: Marshall Cavendish Corporation.

Phillips, L. (1989, March). First impressions: Introducing Monet to Megadeth. *English Journal, 78* (3), 31–33.

Pine, G.J. & Hilliard, A.G. (1990, April). Rx for racism: Imperatives for America's schools. *Phi Delta Kappan, 71* (8), 593–600.

Polakow-Suranski, S. & Ulaby, N. (1990, November). Students take action to combat racism. *Phi Delta Kappan, 71* (8), 601–606.

Probst, R.E. (1984). *Adolescent literature: Response and analysis*. New York: Merrill.

Purves, A.C., Rogers, T., & Soter, A.O. (1990). *How porcupines make love II: Teaching a response centered literature curriculum*. New York: Longman.

Quarles, B. (1991). *Black abolitionists*. New York: Da Capo Press.

Rappaport, D. (1988). Escape from slavery: Five journeys to freedom. In Dorothy Sterling (Ed.). *Black foremothers*. New York: Feminist Press.

Ray, D. (1991). *Behind blue and gray: The soldier's life in the Civil War*. New York: Lodestar Books.

Reed, A.J.S. (1993). *A teacher's guide to the signet edition of the Narrative of Frederick Douglass: An American slave, written by himself*. New York: Penguin.

Reed, A.J.S. (1994). *Reaching adolescents: The young adult book and the school*. New York: Merrill.

Rhodes, R.H. (1992). *All for the Union: The Civil War diary and letters of Elisha Hunt Rhodes*. New York: Vintage Books.

Ricks, C. (1972). *Tennyson*. New York: Macmillan.

Rico, G. (1983). *Writing the natural way*. Los Angeles, CA: J.P. Tarcher.

Robertson, S.L. (1990, January). Text rendering: Beginning literary response. *English Journal*, 79 (1), 80–84.

Rochman, H. (1993). *Against borders: Promoting books for a multicultural world*. Chicago, IL: American Library Association.

Rosenblatt, L.M. (1938). *Literature as exploration*. New York: Modern Language Association.

Rosenblatt, L.M. (1978). *The reader, the text, the poem: The transactional theory of the literary work*. Carbondale, IL: Southern Illinois University Press.

Rosenblatt, L.M. (1989). Writing and reading: The transactional theory. In J.M. Mason (Ed.), *Reading and writing connections*. Needham Heights, MA: Allyn Bacon, 153–176.

Rosenblatt, L.M. (1991). The lost reader of democracy. In *The triumph of literature: The fate of literacy: English in the secondary school curriculum*. Teachers College Press, 114–144.

Sauve, P. (1993). Class handout. Campbell Hall School, North Hollywood, CA.

Service, P.F. (1992, spring). On writing sci fi and fantasy for kids. *The ALAN Review*, 19 (3), 16–18.

Siebert, W.H. (1968). *The Underground Railway from slavery to freedom*. Arno Press and the *New York Times*.

Slade, L.A., Jr. (1991, spring). Growing up as a minority in America: Four African-American writers' testimony. *The ALAN Review*, 18 (3), 9–11.

Smagorinsky, P. (1992, December). Towards a civic education in a multicultural society: Ethical problems in teaching literature. *English Education*, 24 (4), 212–228.

Small, R.C. (1977, October). The junior novel and the art of literature. *English Journal*, 66 (7), 55–59.

Small, R.C. (1979, October). The YA novel in the composition program: Part II. *English Journal*, 68 (7), 75–77.

Small, R., & Kenney, D.J. (1978). The slide-tape review and the reader support kit. In Gene Stanford (Ed.), *Activating the passive student*. Urbana, IL: NCTE, 7–11.

Smith, B.H. (1983). Contingencies of value. *Critical Inquiry*. 10 (1), 1–35.

Smith, D.V. (1930, June). Extensive reading in junior high. *English Journal*, 19 (6), pp. 449–462.

Still, W. (1968). *The Underground Railroad*. Arno Press and the *New York Times*.

Stover, L. (1991, spring). Exploring and celebrating cultural diversity and similarity through young adult novels. *The ALAN Review*, 18 (3), 12–15.

Stover, L. & Karr, R. (1990, December). Glasnost in the classroom: Likhanov's 'shadows across the sun.' *English Journal, 79* (8), 47–53.

Strachey, B. (1981). *Journeys of Frodo: An atlas of J.R.R. Tolkien's The lord of the rings.* New York: Ballantine.

Sundquist, E.J. (Ed.). (1990). *Frederick Douglass: New literary and historical essays.* Cambridge, NY: Cambridge University Press.

Tannen, D. (1990). *You just don't understand: Talk between the sexes.* New York: William Morrow.

Tchudi, S. & Mitchell, D. (1989). *Explorations in the teaching of English.* New York: Harper & Row.

Thomas, V.N. (1938, September). Extensive reading in practice. *English Journal, 27* (7), 574–579.

Tiedt, P.L. & Tiedt, I.M. (1986). *Multicultural teaching: A handbook of activities, information and resources.* 2nd ed. Boston: Allyn & Bacon.

Trimmer, J. & Warnock, T. (Eds.). (1992). *Understanding others: Cultural and cross-cultural studies and the teaching of literature.* Urbana, IL: National Council of Teachers of English.

Vann, K.R. & Kunjufu, J. (1993, February). The importance of an Afrocentric, multicultural curriculum. *Phi Delta Kappan, 74* (6), 490–491.

Weld, T. (1968). *American slavery as it is: Testimony of a thousand witnesses.* Arno Press and the *New York Times.*

Wigginton, E. (1992). Culture begins at home. *Education Leadership, 49* (4), 60–64.

Wood, K., McDonnell, H., Pfordresher, J., Fite, M.A., & Lankford, P. (Eds.). (1991). *Classics in world literature: America reads, teacher's annotated edition.* Glenview, IL: Scott, Foresman, & Company.

Yep, L. (1992, spring). A garden of dragons. *The ALAN Review, 19* (3), 6–8.

Zaharias, J. (1984, fall). Promoting response agility through literature for young adults. *The ALAN Review, 12* (1), 36–41.

Adolescent
Literature
as a
Complement
to the
CLASSICS

CONTEMPORARY AND
CLASSICS BIBLIOGRAPHY

Achebe, C. (1991). *Things fall apart*. New York: Fawcett Crest.

Alighieri, D. (1973). *Dante's vita nova*. Translated by Mark Musa. Bloomington: Indiana University Press.

Angelou, M. (1971). *I know why the caged bird sings*. New York: Bantam.

Aristophanes. (413 B.C.). *Lysistrata*. Translated by Charles T. Murphy. *The Norton anthology of world masterpieces*. New York: Norton.

Babin, M.T. & Steiner, S. (Eds.). (1974). *Borinquen: An anthology of Puerto Rican literature*. New York: Alfred A. Knopf.

Beckett, S. (1987). *Waiting for Godot*. New York: Chelsea House.

Bierce, A. (1992). A horseman in the sky. In B. Bernstein (Ed.), *Language and literature*. Evanston, IL: McDougal Littell, 304–309.

Bradbury, R. (1953). *Fahrenheit 451*. New York: Ballantine.

Brecht, B. (1963). *Mother Courage and her children: A chronicle of the Thirty Years' War*. Adapted by Eric Bentley. New York: Samuel French.

Bruchac, J. (1993). *Native American stories*. Colorado: Fulcrum Publishing.

Buck, P. (1992). The old demon. In R. Craig Goheen (Ed.), *Language and literature*. Evanston, IL: McDougal Littell, 35–43.

Camus, A. (1954). *The stranger*. New York: Random House.

Carrison, M.P. (1987). *Cambodian folk stories from the Gatiloke*. Translated by The Venerable Kong Chhean. Rutland, VT: Tuttle.

Chopin, K. (1976, originally published in 1899). *The awakening*. In B. Solomon (Ed.), *The awakening and selected stories of Kate Chopin*. New York: Signet/NAL.

Clarke, A. (1968). *2001: A space odyssey*. New York: Penguin.

Clavell, J. (1981). *The children's story*. New York: Bantam.

Coleridge, S.T. (1986). *The rime of the ancient mariner*. New York: Chelsea House.

Crane, S. (1981). *The red badge of courage*. Mahwah, NJ: Watermill Press.

The Epic of Gilgamesh. (1960). Translated by N.K. Sandars. New York: Penguin Classics.

Forbes, E. (1971). *Johnny Tremain*. New York: Dell.

Golding, W. (1954). *Lord of the flies*. New York: Putnam.

Hansberry, L. (1988). *A raisin in the sun*. New York: Signet Classic/NAL.

Hemingway, E. (1989). In another country. In Scribner's literature series: *American literature*. Mission Hills, CA: Glencoe, 490–495.

Hersey, J. (1992). Survival. In B. Bernstein (Ed.), *Language and literature*. Evanston, IL: McDougal Littell, 795–805.

Homer. (1963). *The odyssey.* Translated by Robert Fitzgerald. New York: Anchor Books.

Homer. (1988). *The odyssey.* Translated by Samuel Butler. New York: Amsco School Publications.

Hugo, V. (1938). *Les Miserables.* Translated by Lascalles Wraxall. New York: The Heritage Press.

Hurston, Z.N. (1994). How it feels to be colored me. In A. Applebee, A. Bermudez, J. Langer, & J. Marshall (Sr. Consultants), *Literature and language: American literature.* Evanston, IL: McDougal Littell, 786–788.

Huxley, A. (1946). *Brave new world.* New York: Harper & Row.

Ibsen, H. (1951). *An enemy of the people.* Adapted by Arthur Miller. New York: Viking.

Ibsen, H. (1992). *A doll house.* In *Four Major Plays, Volume I.* New York: Signet Classics, 43–114.

Keller, H. (1954). *The story of my life.* New York: Doubleday & Company.

Knowles, J. (1959). *A separate peace.* New York: Macmillan.

Knowles, J. (1982). *Peace breaks out.* New York: Bantam.

Kuan-Chung, L. (1976, 1320). *Three kingdoms.* Translated by Moss Roberts. New York: Pantheon.

Kurtz, J. (1991). *Ethiopia: The roof of Africa.* New York: Dillon Press.

The Lay of Thrym. From the *Elder Edda.* (1969). Translated by Paul B. Taylor & W.H. Auden. New York: Random House.

Lee, H. (1988). *To kill a mockingbird.* New York: Warner Books.

Lee, P.H. (Ed.). (1990). *Modern Korean literature: An anthology.* Honolulu: University of Hawaii Press.

Marcelin, P. (1986). *The beast of the Haitian hills.* San Francisco, CA: City Lights Books.

McCullough, C. (1977). *The thorn birds.* New York: Harper & Row.

McKennitt, L. (1992, April). The lady of Shalott. *The visit.* Burbank, CA: Warner Brothers.

Meridiam, E. (1992). Metaphor. In J. Beatty (Ed.), *Literature and language.* Evanston, IL: McDougal Littell, 576.

Montgomery, L.M. (1987). *Anne of green gables.* New York: Bantam Books (originally published in 1908).

Morrison, T. (1992). *Beloved.* New York: Alfred A. Knopf.

O'Brien, T. (1992). Ambush. In B. Bernstein (Ed.), *Language and literature.* Evanston, IL: McDougal Littell, 331–332.

O'Flaherty, L. (1992). The sniper. In Richard Craig Goheen (Ed.), *Language and literature.* Evanston, IL: McDougal Littell, 649–651.

Orwell, G. (1946). *Animal farm.* New York: Harcourt, Brace, & Jovanovich.

Orwell, G. (1949). *1984.* New York: Harcourt, Brace, & Jovanovich.

Paz, O. (1990). *The monkey grammarian.* New York: Arcade Publishing.

Peare, C.O. (1959). *The Helen Keller story.* New York: Thomas Y. Crowell.

Plath, S. (1960). Metaphor. In X.J. Kennedy (3rd Ed.), (1983). *Literature: An introduction to fiction, poetry, and drama.* Boston: Little, Brown & Company, 1461.

Rand, A. (1946). *Anthem.* New York: Penguin.

Remarque, E.M. (1929). *All quiet on the western front.* Translated by A.W. Wheen. Boston: Little, Brown & Company.

Rilke, R.M. (1934). *Letters to a young poet.* Translated by M.D. Herter Norton. New York: W.W. Norton.

Rosenberg, D. (Ed.). (1991). *World literature.* Lincolnwood, IL: National Textbook Company.

Shakespeare, W. (1959). *Hamlet.* New York: Signet Classics.

Shakespeare, W. (1969). *Julius Caesar.* London: Cornmarket.

Shelley, M. (1965). *Frankenstein.* New York: New American Library.

Siddiqi, S. (1991). *God's own land: A novel of Pakistan.* Translated by David J. Matthews. Kent, England: Paul Norbury/UNESCO.

Sienkiewicz, H. (1906). *On the field of glory.* Cambridge: The University Press.

Singh, K. (1956). *Mano majra.* New York: Grove Press.

Solzhenitsyn, A. (1963). *One day in the life of Ivan Denisovich.* Translated by Max Haywood & Ronald Hingley. New York: Praeger.

Stowe, H.B. (1852). *Uncle Tom's cabin.* New York: Signet Classic/NAL.

Swan, D. & Tolkien, J.R.R. (1978). *The road goes ever on: A song cycle.* Boston: Houghton Mifflin.

Swift, J. (1960). *Gulliver's travels.* New York: Penguin.

Terada, A.M. (Ed.). (1989). *Under the starfruit tree: Folktales from Vietnam.* Honolulu: University of Hawaii Press.

Thurber, J. (1939). *The last flower, A parable in pictures.* New York: Harper & Brothers.

Tolkien, J.R.R. (1986). *The hobbit.* New York: Ballantine.

Tolkien, J.R.R. (1986). *The fellowship of the ring.* New York: Ballantine.

Tolkien, J.R.R. (1986). *The two towers.* New York: Ballantine.

Tolkien, J.R.R. (1988). *The return of the king.* New York: Ballantine.

Twain, M. (1940). *The adventures of Tom Sawyer.* New York: Heritage Press.

Twain, M. (1981). *The adventures of Huckleberry Finn.* New York: Bantam.

Vonnegut, K. (1968). Harrison Bergeron. In *Welcome to the monkey house: A collection of short works.* New York: Delacorte Press.

Walker, A. (1992). *The color purple.* New York: Harcourt, Brace, & Jovanovich.

Walker, A. (1994). In search of our mothers' gardens. In L. King (Ed.), *Hear my voice: A multicultural anthology of literature from the United States.* Menlo Park, CA: Addison-Wesley, 127–134.

Wallace, S.J. (1992). *Back home.* Essex, England: Longman Carribean.

Wray, E., Rosenfield, C. & Bailey, D. (1972). *Ten lives of the Buddha.* New York: Weatherhill.

Wright, R. (1940). *Native son.* New York: Harper & Brothers.

Yoshimoto, B. (1988). *Kitchen.* New York: Grove Press.

Adolescent
Literature
as a

Complement
to the
CLASSICS

YOUNG ADULT
BIBLIOGRAPHY

Aikath-Gyaltsen, I. (1991). *Daughters of the house.* New York: Ballantine.

Anaya, R. (1992). *Bless me, Ultima.* New York: Warner Books.

Appleman-Jurman, A. (1990). *Alicia: My story.* New York: Bantam.

Armstrong, W. (1969). *Sounder.* New York: Harrow Books.

Avery, G. (1964). *Maria's Italian springtime.* New York: Simon & Schuster.

Avi. (1984). *The fighting ground.* Philadelphia: J.B. Lippincott Company.

Avi. (1990). *The true confessions of Charlotte Doyle.* New York: Avon.

Baker, K. (1993). *The dove's letter.* New York: Harcourt, Brace, & Jovanovich.

Beake L. (1993). *Song of Be.* New York: Henry Holt & Company.

Beatty, P. (1991). *Jayhawker.* New York: William Morrow.

Beatty, P. & Robbins, P. (1990). *Eben Tyne, Powdermonkey.* New York: William Morrow.

Bender, A. (1992). The story of my life. In A. Herschfelder (Ed.), *Rising voices: Writings of young Native Americans.* New York: Charles Scribner's Sons.

Bennett, J. (1985). *The voyage of the Lucky Dragon.* New York: Prentice Hall.

Berry, J. (1987). *A thief in the village.* New York: Orchard Books.

Betancourt, J. (1990). *More than meets the eye.* New York: Bantam.

Blackwood, G. (1992). Ethan unbound. In D.R. Gallo (Ed.), *Short circuits.* New York: Dell.

Blos, J. (1990). *A gathering of days: A New England girl's journal.* New York: Macmillan.

Blume, J. (1973). *Deenie.* New York: Dell Laurel-Leaf.

Blume, J. (1982). *Tiger eyes.* New York: Dell.

Bode, J. (1989). *New kids on the block: Oral histories of immigrant teens.* New York: Franklin Watts.

Bodker, C. (1975). *The leopard.* Translated by Gunnar Poulsen. New York: Atheneum.

Bontemps, A. (1992). *Black thunder.* Boston: Beacon Press.

Bontemps, A. (1993). A summer tragedy. In D. Worley & J. Perry (Eds.), *African American literature: An anthology of nonfiction, fiction, poetry, and drama.* New York: National Textbook Company.

Brady, E.W. (1976). *Toliver's secret.* New York: Bullseye.

Brancato, R. (1988). *Winning.* New York: Alfred A. Knopf.

Bridgers, S.E. (1981). *Notes for another life.* New York: Alfred A. Knopf.

Bridgers, S.E. (1987). *Permanent connections.* New York: Harper & Row.

Bridgers, S.E. (1990). *All together now.* New York: Bantam.

Brooks, B. (1984). *The moves make the man.* New York: Harper & Row.

Brooks, B. (1986). *Midnight hour encores.* New York: Harper Keypoint.

Brooks, B. (1989). *No kidding.* New York: Harper & Row.

Brown, F. (1986). *Our love.* New York: Ballantine/Fawcett-Juniper.

Bunting, E. (1990). *The wall.* New York: Clarion.

Buss, F.L. & Cubias, D. (1991). *Journey of the sparrows.* New York: Lodestar.

Butler, W. (1979). *The butterfly revolution.* New York: Ballantine.

Caraker, M. (1991). *The faces of Ceti.* Boston: Houghton Mifflin.

Carey, L. (1991). *Black ice.* New York: Alfred A. Knopf.

Carter, F. (1986). *The education of Little Tree.* New Mexico: University of New Mexico Press.

Charnas, S.M. (1985). *The bronze king.* Boston: Houghton Mifflin.

Charnas, S.M. (1989). *The golden thread.* New York: Bantam.

Charnas, S.M. (1989). *The silver glove.* New York: Bantam.

Childress, A. (1973). *A hero ain't nothin' but a sandwich.* New York: Avon.

Choi, S.N. (1991). *Year of impossible goodbyes.* New York: Dell.

Christopher, J. (1988). *The white mountains.* New York: Collier.

Cisneros, S. (1988). *The house on mango street.* Houston, TX: Arte.

Clapp, P. (1977). *I'm Deborah Sampson: A soldier in the war of the revolution.* New York: Lothrop, Lee, & Shepard.

Clapp, P. (1986). *The tamarack tree.* New York: Penguin USA.

Cleary, B. (1989). *A girl from Yamhill.* New York: Dell.

Cliff, M. (1991). *Abeng.* New York: Penguin.

Coerr, E. (1977). *Sadako and the thousand paper cranes.* New York: Yearling.

Cole, B. (1987). *The goats.* New York: Farrar, Straus & Giroux.

Cole, B. (1989). *Celine.* New York: Farrar, Straus & Giroux.

Collier, J., & Collier, C. (1974). *My brother Sam is dead.* New York: Scholastic.

Collier, J. & Collier, C. (1978). *The winter hero.* New York: Four Winds Press.

Collier, J. & Collier, C. (1985). *The bloody country.* New York: Scholastic.

Collier, J.L. & Collier, C. (1987). *Jump ship to freedom.* New York: Dell.

Collier, J.L. & Collier, C. (1987). *War comes to Willy Freeman.* New York: Dell.

Collier, J.L. & Collier, C. (1987). *Who is Carrie?* New York: Dell.

Conover, T. (1987). *Coyotes.* New York: Vintage Books.

Cooper, S. (1966). *Over sea, under stone.* New York: Harcourt Brace.

Cooper, S. (1973). *The dark is rising.* New York: Atheneum.

Cooper, S. (1973). *Greenwitch.* New York: Macmillan.

Cooper, S. (1976). *The grey king.* New York: Atheneum.

Cooper, S. (1980). *Silver on the tree.* New York: Macmillan.

Cormier, R. (1974). *The chocolate war.* New York: Pantheon.

Cormier, R. (1977). *I am the cheese.* New York: Dell.

Cormier, R. (1979). *After the first death.* New York: Avon.

Cormier, R. (1991). *We all fall down.* New York: Delacorte Press.

Cormier, R. (1992). *Tunes for bears to dance to.* New York: Delacorte Press.

Covington, D. (1991). *Lizard.* New York: Delacorte Press.

Cox, C. (1991). *Undying glory: The story of the Massachusetts 54th Regiment.* New York: Scholastic.

Cox, C. (1993). *The forgotten heroes: The story of the buffalo soldiers.* New York: Scholastic.

Crew, G. (1993). *Strange objects*. New York: Simon & Schuster.

Crew, L. (1990). *Children of the river*. New York: Delacorte Press.

Criddle, J.D. & Mam, T.B. (1989). *To destroy you is no loss: The odyssey of a Cambodian family*. New York: Anchor/Doubleday Books.

Crutcher, C. (1987). *The crazy horse electric game*. New York: Greenwillow.

Crutcher, C. (1991). *Athletic shorts: Six short stories*. New York: Greenwillow.

Crutcher, C. (1993). *Staying fat for Sarah Byrnes*. New York: Greenwillow.

Dangarembwa, T. (1989). *Nervous conditions*. Seattle, WA: Seal Press.

Danziger, P. (1986). *It's an aardvark eat turtle world*. New York: Dell Laurel-Leaf.

David, J. (Ed.). (1969). *Growing up black*. New York: Pocket Books.

Davis, J. (1993). *Checking on the moon*. New York: Dell.

Davis, O. (1990). *Escape to freedom: A play about young Frederick Douglass*. New York: Puffin.

de Trevino, E. (1965). *I, Juan de Pareja*. New York: Farrar, Straus & Giroux.

Dickinson, P. (1988). *Eva*. New York: Delacorte Press.

Dorris, M. (1988). *A yellow raft in blue water*. New York: Warner Books.

Duncan, L. (1973). *I know what you did last summer*. New York: Archway Paperbacks.

Duncan, L. (1978). *Killing Mr. Griffin*. Boston: Little, Brown & Company.

Elledge, S. (Ed.). (1990). *Wider than the sky: Poems to grow up with*. New York: HarperCollins, 178–183.

Emberley, B. (adaptor). (1967). *Drummer Hoff*. Englewood Cliffs, NJ: Prentice-Hall.

Fast, H. (1961). *April morning*. New York: Crown.

Fast, H. (1974). *Freedom road*. New York: Bantam.

Flanigan, S. (1988). *Alice*. New York: St. Martin's Press.

Fox, P. (1991) *The slave dancer*. New York: Dell.

Fox, P. (1993). *Monkey island*. New York: Dell.

Fritz, J. (1967). *Early thunder*. New York: Coward, McCann, & Geoghegan.

Fritz, J. (1982). *Homesick: My own story*. New York: Dell.

Gaines, E.J. (1987). *The autobiography of Miss Jane Pittman*. New York: Doubleday.

Garland, S. (1992). *Song of the buffalo boy*. San Diego: Harcourt, Brace, & Jovanovich.

Garland, S. (1993). *The lotus seed*. New York: Harcourt, Brace, & Jovanovich.

Garland, S. (1993). *Shadow of the dragon*. New York: Harcourt, Brace, & Company.

Garza, D. (1990). Everybody knows Tobie. In C. Tatum (Ed.), *Mexican American literature*. Orlando: Harcourt, Brace, & Jovanovich.

Geisel, T.S. (Dr. Seuss). (1984). *The butter battle book*. New York: Random House.

George, J. (1983). *The talking earth*. New York: Harper Trophy.

Gilson, J. (1985). *Hello, my name is Scrambled Eggs*. New York: Lothrop, Lee, & Shepard Books.

Gleitzman, M. (1990). *Two weeks with the queen*. London: Macmillan.

Gonzalez, G. (1977). *Gaucho*. New York: Alfred A. Knopf.

Gordon, S. (1989). *Waiting for the rain*. New York: Bantam.

Gordon, S. (1990). *The middle of somewhere: A story of South Africa*. New York: Orchard Books.

Graham, R.L. (1972). *Dove*. New York: Harper & Row.

Graham, R.M. (1970). *The happy sound*. Chicago: Follett.

Greenberg, J. (1989). *Of such small differences*. New York: Signet Books.

Greene, B. (1973). *The summer of my German soldier*. New York: Dial Press.

Greene, B. (1991). *The drowning of Stephan Jones*. New York: Bantam.

Greeno, G. (1993). *The Ghatti's tale: Book one, Finders-seekers*. New York: DAW Books.

Greeno, G. (1994). *The Ghatti's tale: Book two, Mindspeakers' call*. New York: DAW Books.

Guy, R. (1983). *The friends*. New York: Bantam.

Guy, R. (1985). *The disappearance*. New York: Puffin.

Guy, R. (1989). *Ruby*. New York: Puffin.

Guy, R. (1990). *And I heard a bird sing*. New York: Puffin.

Guy, R. (1990). *My love, my love or the peasant girl*. New York: Henry Holt & Company.

Guy, R. (1992). *Edith Jackson*. New York: Dell.

Hale, J.C. (1991). *The owl's song*. New York: Bantam.

Hamilton, V. (1979). *Arilla sun down*. New York: Dell.

Hamilton, V. (1979). *Paul Robeson: The life and times of a free black man*. New York: Dell.

Hamilton, V. (1983). *Sweet whispers, brother Rush*. New York: Avon.

Hamilton, V. (1984). *The house of Dies Drear*. New York: Collier.

Hamilton, V. (1985). *A little love*. New York: Berkley Books.

Hamilton, V. (1985). *Junius over far*. New York: HarperCollins.

Hamilton, V. (1986). *The magical adventures of pretty Pearl*. New York: Harper & Row.

Hamilton, V. (1986). *The planet of Junior Brown*. New York: Collier.

Hamilton, V. (1986). *Zeely*. New York: Aladdin.

Hamilton, V. (1987). *The mystery of Drear house*. New York: Greenwillow.

Hamilton, V. (1987). *A white romance*. New York: Philomel.

Hamilton, V. (1989). *Justice and her brothers*. San Diego: Harcourt, Brace, & Jovanovich.

Hamilton, V. (1993). *M.C. Higgins, the great*. New York: Aladdin.

Hansen, J. (1992). *Which way freedom?* New York: Avon.

Haskins, J. (1979). *The story of Stevie Wonder*. New York: Dell.

Haskins, J. (1988). *Winnie Mandela: Life of struggle*. New York: Putnam.

Haskins, J. (1992). *One more river to cross*. New York: Scholastic.

Hayslip, L.L. (1990). *When heaven and earth changed places*. New York: Plume.

Head, A. (1968). *Mr. and Mrs. Bo Jo Jones*. New York: Signet Books.

Hentoff, N. (1982). *The day they came to arrest the book*. New York: Delacorte Press.

Hickok, L.A. (1961). *The touch of magic*. New York: Dodd, Mead & Company.

Hinton, S.E. (1971). *That was then, this is now*. New York: Dell.

Hinton, S.E. (1979). *Tex*. New York: Delacorte Press.

Hinton, S.E. (1989). *The outsiders*. New York: Dell.

Hirschfelder, A.B. & Singer, B.R. (Eds.). (1992). *Rising voices: Writings of young native Americans*. New York: Charles Scribner's Sons.

Ho, M. (1990). *Rice without rain*. New York: Lothrop, Lee, & Shepard.

Hobbs, W. (1989). *Bearstone*. New York: Avon Camelot.

Hobbs, W. (1991). *Downriver*. New York: Bantam.

Hobbs, W. (1992). *The big wander*. New York: Atheneum.

Hodge, M. (1993). *For the life of Laetitia*. New York: Farrar, Straus, & Giroux.

Holland, I. (1990). *The unfrightened dark*. New York: Fawcett Juniper.

Holme, A. (1980). *The hostage*. Translated by Patricia Crampton. London: Methuen.

Houston, J.W. & Houston, J.D. (1990). *Farewell to Manzanar*. New York: Bantam.

Hughes, M. (1985). *The keeper of the isis light*. New York: Atheneum.

Hughes, M. (1988). *Sandwriter*. New York: Henry Holt & Company.

Hughes, M. (1989). *The promise*. New York: Simon & Schuster.

Hunt, I. (1986). *Across five Aprils*. New York: Berkley Books.

Hurmence, B. (1982). *A girl called boy*. New York: Clarion.

Hurmence, B. (1984). *Tancy*. New York: Clarion.

Irwin, Hadley. (1984). *I be somebody*. New York: Atheneum.

Irwin, Hadley. (1988). *Kim/Kimi*. New York: Viking/Penguin.

Jacques, B. (1986). *Redwall*. New York: Philomel.

Jacques, B. (1988). *Mossflower*. New York: Avon.

James, M. (1990). *Shoebag*. New York: Scholastic.

Jen, G. (1994). In the American society. In Laurie King (Ed.), *Hear my voice: A multicultural anthology of literature from the United States*. Menlo Park, CA: Addison-Wesley, 174–187.

Johnson, C. (1991). *Middle passage*. New York: Plume.

Jones, T. (1980). *Go well, stay well*. New York: Harper & Row.

Keith, H. (1957). *Rifles for Watie*. New York: Troll.

Kent, D. (1978). *Belonging*. New York: Ace Books.

Kent, D. (1989). *One step at a time*. New York: Scholastic.

Kerr, M.E. (1984). Do you want my opinion? In *Sixteen: Short stories by outstanding writers for young adults*. New York: Dell.

Kincaid, J. (1985). *Annie John*. New York: Farrar, Straus & Giroux.

Kingman, L. (1985). *Head over wheels*. New York: Dell Laurel-Leaf.

Kingsolver, B. (1988). *The bean trees*. New York: HarperCollins.

Klass, D. (1987). *Breakaway run*. New York: E.P. Dutton.

Lasky, K. (1981). *Night journey*. London: Puffin.

Lasky, K. (1983). *Beyond the divide*. New York: Macmillan.

Lawrence, M. (1975). *Touchmark*. New York: Harcourt, Brace, & Jovanovich.

Leaf, M. (1984). *The story of Ferdinand*. New York: Scholastic.

Lee, M.G. (1992). *Finding my voice*. Boston: Houghton Mifflin.

Le Guin, U.K. (1968). *A wizard of Earthsea*. New York: Bantam.

Le Guin, U.K. (1990). *Tehanu*. New York: Atheneum.

L'Engle, M. (1976). *A wrinkle in time*. New York: Dell.

L'Engle, M. (1980). *A ring of endless light*. New York: Dell.

L'Engle, M. (1989). *The young unicorns*. New York: Dell.

L'Engle, M. (1992). *Many waters*. New York: Dell.

L'Engle, M. (1993). *A wind in the door*. New York: Dell.

L'Engle, M. (1993). *A swiftly tilting planet*. New York: Dell.

Lester, J. (1985). *This strange new feeling*. New York: Scholastic.

Levinson, N.S. (1990). *Annie's world*. Washington, D.C.: Kendall Green.

Levitin, S. (1987). *The return*. New York: Ballantine.

Levy, M. (1982). *The girl in the plastic cage*. New York: Ballantine.

Levy, M. (1989). *Love is not enough*. New York: Ballantine/Fawcett Juniper.

Likhanov, A. (1983). *Shadows across the sun*. New York: Harper & Row.

Lindbergh, A. (1975). *Gift from the sea*. New York: Pantheon.

Lipsyte, R. (1987). *The contender*. New York: Harper & Row.

Lipsyte, R. (1991). *The brave*. New York: HarperCollins.

Lobel, A. (1967). *Potatoes, potatoes*. New York: Harper & Row.

Lord, B.B. (1986). *In the year of the Boar and Jackie Robinson*. New York: Harper & Row.

Lowry, L. (1989). *Number the stars*. New York: Bantam.

Lowry, L. (1993). *The giver*. Boston: Houghton Mifflin.

Mahy, M. (1989). *Memory*. New York: Dell Laurel-Leaf.

Martin, V. (1990). *Mary Reilly*. New York: Bantam Doubleday Dell.

Matas, C. (1993). *Sworn enemies*. New York: Bantam.

Mathabane, M. (1986). *Kaffir boy: The true story of a black youth's coming of age in apartheid South Africa*. New York: Plume.

Mathis, S.B. (1990). *Listen for the fig tree*. New York: Puffin.

Mazer, N.F. (1987). *After the rain*. New York: William Morrow.

Mazer, N.F. & Mazer, H. (1992). *Bright days, stupid nights*. New York: Bantam.

Meyer, C. (Ed.). (1986). *Voices of South Africa: Growing up in a troubled land*. San Diego: Harcourt, Brace, & Jovanovich.

Meyer, C. (1990). *Killing the kudu*. New York: Margaret K. McElderry.

Miklowitz, G.D. (1986). *The war between the classes*. New York: Dell Laurel-Leaf.

Mohr, N. (1973). *Nilda*. New York: Harper & Row.

Mongoshi, C. (1972). *Coming of the dry season*. Nairobi: Oxford University Press.

Mongoshi, C. (1975). *Waiting for the rain*. London: Heinemann Educational.

Moore, M. (1993). "In the dark." Young Playwrights Program. Washington, D.C.: John F. Kennedy Center for the Performing Arts.

Mori, K. (1993). *Shizuko's daughter*. New York: Fawcett Juniper.

Mukherjee, B. (1989). *Jasmine*. New York: Fawcett Crest.

Myers, W.D. (1977). *Mojo and the Russians*. New York: Viking.

Myers, W.D. (1978). *It ain't all for nothin'*. New York: Viking.

Myers, W.D. (1983). *Hoops*. New York: Dell.

Myers, W.D. (1987). *Crystal*. New York: Viking.

Myers, W.D. (1987). *Motown and Didi: A love story*. New York: Dell.

Myers, W.D. (1988). *Fallen angels*. New York: Scholastic.

Myers, W.D. (1988). *Fast Sam, cool Clyde, and stuff*. New York: Puffin.

Myers, W.D. (1988). *Me, Mop and the moondance kid*. New York: Delacorte Press.

Myers, W.D. (1989). *The young landlords*. New York: Puffin.

Myers, W.D. (1990). *Scorpions*. New York: Harper.

Myers, W.D. (1991). *Now is your time! The African-American struggle for freedom*. Scranton, PA: HarperCollins.

Myers, W.D. (1992). *Mop, Moondance, and the Nagasaki knights*. New York: Delacorte Press.

Myers, W.D. (1992). *The mouse rap*. New York: Harper Trophy.

Myers, W.D. (1992). *Somewhere in the darkness.* New York: Scholastic.

Naidoo, B. (1990). *Chain of fire.* Philadelphia: J.B. Lippincott.

Naqvi, T. (1994). Paths upon water. In L. King (Ed.), *Hear my voice: A multicultural anthology of literature from the United States.* Menlo Park, CA: Addison-Wesley, 12–23.

Naughton, J. (1989). *My brother stealing second.* New York: Harper & Row.

Neufeld, J. (1971). *Twink.* New York: Signet Books.

Ngugi. (1967). *A grain of wheat.* Portsmouth, NH: Heinemann.

Oates, J. (1993). Where are you going, where have you been? In H. Rochman & D. McCampbell (Eds.), *Who do you think you are? Stories of friends and enemies.* Boston: Little, Brown/Joy Street, 14–35.

O'Brien, R.C. (1987). *Z for Zachariah.* New York: Collier.

O'Dell, S. (1977). *Carlota.* Boston: Houghton Mifflin.

O'Dell, S. (1978). *Kathleen, please come home.* Boston: Houghton Mifflin.

O'Dell, S. (1980). *Sarah Bishop.* Boston: Houghton Mifflin.

O'Dell, S. (1989). *My name is not Angelica.* Boston: Houghton Mifflin.

O'Dell, S. (1990). *Sing down the moon.* New York: Dell Laurel-Leaf.

O'Kimoto, J.D. (1990). *Jason's women.* New York: Dell.

Olsen, T. (1994). I stand here ironing. In A. Applebee, A. Bermudez, J. Langer, & J. Marshall (Sr. Consultants), *Literature and language: American literature.* Evanston, IL: McDougal Littell, 756–762.

Oneal, Z. (1986). *In summer light.* New York: Bantam.

Paterson, K. (1980). *Bridge to Terabithia.* New York: Avon.

Paterson, K. (1981). *Jacob have I loved.* New York: Avon Flare.

Paterson, K. (1986). *Come sing, Jimmy Jo.* New York: E.P. Dutton.

Paterson, K. (1988). *Park's quest.* New York: E.P. Dutton.

Paulsen, G. (1978). *The night the white deer died.* New York: Dell.

Paulsen, G. (1990). *Canyons.* New York: Delacorte Press.

Paulsen, G. (1990). *The crossing.* New York: Dell Laurel-Leaf.

Paulson, G. (1987). *Hatchet.* New York: Bradbury Press.

Peck, R.N. (1972). *A day no pigs would die.* New York: Dell.

Peck, R. (1986). *Remembering the good times.* New York: Dell.

Peck, R. (1987). *Princess Ashley.* New York: Delacorte Press.

Perez, N.A. (1990). *The slopes of war.* Boston: Houghton Mifflin.

Pettepiece, T. & Aleksin, A. (Eds.). (1990). *Face to face: A collection of stories by celebrated Soviet and American writers.* New York: Philomel.

Pettit, J. (1992). *My name is San Ho.* New York: Scholastic.

Platt, K. (1982). *Frank and Stein and me.* New York: Scholastic.

Pullman, P. (1992). *The broken bridge.* New York: Alfred A. Knopf.

Reeder, C. (1989). *Shades of gray.* New York: Avon.

Reit, S. (1988). *Behind rebel lines: The incredible story of Emma Edmonds, Civil War spy.* New York: Gulliver Books.

Richmond, S. (1988). *Wheels for walking.* New York: Signet Books.

Rinaldi, A. (1986). *Time enough for drums.* Mahwah, NJ: Troll.

Rinaldi, A. (1991). *A ride into morning: The story of Tempe Wick.* New York: Gulliver Books.

Rinaldi, A. (1991). *Wolf by the ears.* New York: Scholastic.

Robinet, H. (1991). *Children of the fire.* New York: Macmillan.

Robinson, M.A. (1990). *A woman of her tribe*. New York: Ballantine.

Rochman, H. (Ed.). (1988). *Somehow tenderness survives: Stories of Southern Africa*. New York: HarperCollins.

Rodriquez, R. (1983). *Hunger of memory: The education of Richard Rodriquez*. New York: Bantam.

Rylant, C. (1989). *But I'll be back again*. New York: Orchard Books.

Rylant, C. (1992). *Missing May*. New York: Orchard Books.

Rylant, C. (1993). *I had seen castles*. New York: Harcourt, Brace, & Jovanovich.

Sacks, M. (1989). *Beyond safe boundaries*. New York: Penguin.

Santiago, D. (1983). *Famous all over town*. New York: American Library.

Schami, R. (1990). *A handful of stars*. Translated by R. Lesser. New York: E.P. Dutton.

Scott, V.M. (1986). *Belonging*. Washington, D.C.: Gallaudet College Press.

Sebestyen, O. (1983). *Words by heart*. New York: Bantam.

Sebestyen, O. (1989). *The girl in the box*. New York: Bantam.

Sender, R.M. (1990). *The cage*. New York: Bantam.

Service, P. (1989). *Vision quest*. New York: Fawcett Juniper.

Sevela, E. (1989). *We were not like other people*. Translated by Antonin Bouis. New York: Harper & Row.

Shaara, M. (1974). *The killer angels*. New York: Ballantine.

Shura, M.F. (1991). *Gentle Annie: The true story of a Civil War nurse*. New York: Scholastic.

Sleator, W. (1974). *House of stairs*. New York: Dutton.

Sleator, W. (1984). *Interstellar pig*. New York: Bantam.

Sleator, W. (1990). *Strange attractors*. New York: E.P. Dutton.

Smith, R.K. (1984). *The war with grandpa*. New York: Delacorte Press.

Smucker, B. (1977). *Runaway to freedom: A story of the Underground Railroad*. New York: Harper & Row.

Snyder, A. (1987). *The truth about Alex*. New York: Signet Books.

Sommer, K. (1987). *New kid on the block*. Elgin, IL: Chariot Books/David C. Cook Publishing Company.

Soto, G. (1985). *Living up the street*. San Francisco: Strawberry Hill Press.

Soto, G. (1986). *Small faces*. Houston: University of Houston.

Soto, G. (1990). *Baseball in April and other stories*. New York: Harcourt, Brace, & Jovanovich.

Soto, G. (1990). The jacket. In C. Tatum (Ed.), *Mexican American literature*. Orlando: Harcourt, Brace, & Jovanovich, 392–395.

Soto, G. (1992). *Pacific crossing*. San Diego: Harcourt, Brace, & Jovanovich.

Southall, I. (1988). *Josh*. New York: Macmillan.

Specht, R. (1990). *Tisha*. New York: Bantam.

Spinelli, J. (1991). *There's a girl in my hammerlock*. New York: Simon & Schuster.

Staples, S.F. (1989). *Shabanu: Daughter of the wind*. New York: Alfred A. Knopf.

Strasser, T. (1981). *The wave*. New York: Dell.

Sutcliff, R. (1980). *Frontier wolf*. New York: E.P. Dutton.

Swarthout, G. (1984). *Bless the beasts and children*. New York: Pocket Books.

Taylor, M. (1978). *Song of the trees*. New York: Bantam.

Taylor, M. (1991). *Let the circle be unbroken*. New York: Puffin.

Taylor, M. (1991). *Roll of thunder, hear my cry*. New York: Puffin.

Taylor, M. (1992). *The road to Memphis.* New York: Penguin.

Taylor, T. (1990). *The cay.* New York: Doubleday.

Telemaque, E.W. (1978). *It's crazy to stay Chinese in Minnesota.* Nashville: Thomas Nelson.

Thesman, J. (1991). *The rain catchers.* Boston: Houghton Mifflin.

Thomas, J.C. (Ed.). (1990). *A gathering of flowers: Stories about being young in America.* New York: Harper & Row.

Thomas, P. (1978). The konk. In Piri Thomas *Stories from El Barrio.* New York: Alfred A. Knopf.

Thompson, J.F. (1988). *The taking of Mariasburg.* New York: Scholastic.

Townsend, P. (1983). *The girl in the white ship.* New York: Holt, Rinehart, & Winston.

Tsuchiya, Y. (1988). *Faithful elephants: A true story of animals, people, and war.* Translated by Tomoko Tsuchiya Dykes. New York: Harcourt, Brace, & Jovanovich.

Uchida, Y. (1994). Tears of autumn. In A. Applebee, A. Bermudez, J. Langer, & J. Marshall (Sr. Consultants), *Literature and language: American literature.* Orlando: McDougal Littell, 647–652.

Van Allsburg, C. (1988). *Two bad ants.* New York: Houghton Mifflin.

Voigt, C. (1981). *Homecoming.* New York: Fawcett Juniper.

Voigt, C. (1982). *Dicey's song.* New York: Fawcett Juniper.

Voigt, C. (1985). *The runner.* New York: Atheneum.

Voigt, C. (1987). *Izzy, willy-nilly.* New York: Fawcett Juniper.

Wartski, M.C. (1982). *A long way from home.* New York: Signet Books.

Wartski, M.C. (1988). *A boat to nowhere.* New York: Signet Books.

Watkins, Y.K. (1986). *So far from the bamboo grove.* London: Puffin.

Webb, S. & Nelson, R.W. (1980). *Selma, Lord, Selma: Girlhood memories of the Civil Rights days.* New York: William Morrow.

Wells, R. (1993). *Waiting for the evening star.* Bergenfield, NJ: Penguin USA.

Williams-Garcia, R. (1988). *Blue tights.* New York: E.P. Dutton.

Yanagisawa, R. (1993). "The invisible room." Young Playwrights Program. Washington, D.C.: John F. Kennedy Center for the Performing Arts.

Yates, E. (1989). *Amos Fortune, free man.* New York: Puffin.

Yep, L. (1975). *Dragonwings.* New York: Harper & Row.

Yep, L. (1982). *Dragon of the lost sea.* New York: Harper & Row.

Yep, L. (1985). *Dragon steel.* New York: Harper & Row.

Yep, L. (1990). *Child of the owl.* New York: Harper & Row.

Yep, L. (1991). *Dragon cauldron.* New York: HarperCollins.

Yep, L. (1991). *The lost garden.* Englewood Cliffs, NJ: Julian Messner.

Yep, L. (1991). *The star fisher.* New York: William Morrow.

Yep, L. (1992). *Dragon war.* New York: Harper & Row.

Yolen, J. (1988). *The devil's arithmetic.* New York: Viking.

Yoshimoto, B. (1988). *Kitchen.* New York: Grove Press.

Young, A. (1988). *Never look back.* Worthington, OH: Willowisp Press.

Zee, A. (1979). *The sound of dragon's feet.* Translated by Edward Fenton. New York: E.P. Dutton.

Zieman, J. (1975). *The cigarette sellers of Three Crosses Square.* Translated by
    Janina Davide. New York: Lerner.
Zindel, P. (1983). *The pigman.* New York: Bantam.

Adolescent
Literature
as a

Complement
to the
CLASSICS

AUTHOR AND
TITLE INDEX

Adolescent
Literature
as a
Complement
to the
CLASSICS

SUBJECT INDEX

Chapter 3

Chapter 4

Adolescent
Literature
as a
Complement
to the
CLASSICS

CONTRIBUTORS

JOAN F. KAYWELL is Associate Professor of English Education at the University of South Florida where she won Undergraduate Teaching Awards in 1991 and 1994. She is passionate about assisting preservice and practicing teachers in discovering ways to improve literacy. She donates her time extensively to the NCTE and its affiliate, FCTE, and holds these offices: She is on the Advisory Board for the NCATE/NCTE Folio Review Committee, is the Second Vice President for FCTE, and serves on NCTE's CEE's commission on English Education and English Studies. She is published in *English Journal*, *Florida English Journal*, *The ALAN Review*, *Notes Plus*, *Clearing House*, *Middle School Journal*, *High School Journal* and has two textbooks: *Adolescent Literature as a Complement to the Classics* with Christopher-Gordon Publishers and *Adolescents At Risk: A Guide to Fiction and Nonfiction for Young Adults, Parents, and Professionals* with Greenwood Press.

JANET ALLEN currently teaches English Education at the University of Central Florida in Orlando. Prior to this, she taught English at a high school in northern Maine for 20 years. In 1991, she received the Milken Foundation's National Educator Award for her literacy work with at-risk students. Her book, *It's Never Too Late: The Power of Literacy in the Secondary School*, will be published by Heinemann in early 1995.

LYNNE ALVINE, a former high school English teacher, is Associate Professor of English Education at Indiana University of Pennsylvania. She teaches courses in adolescent literature, reading theory, and English teaching methods, and serves as co-director of the Southcentral Pennsylvania Writing Project. An active member of ALAN and NCTE, she currently chairs the NCTE Women in Literature and Life Assembly (WILLA).

PAMELA SISSI CARROLL is an Assistant Professor of English Education at Florida State University in Tallahassee, Florida. A former teacher of middle and high school English, she is particularly interested in helping practicing and prospective teachers find ways to integrate the language arts in second English language arts classrooms and across the disciplines. She is particularly interested in the promotion of multicultural literature for today's students and teachers, and is constantly seeking books that have both literary merit and thematic appeal for today's diverse population of adolescents. She is an active member of ALAN, NCTE, and chairs the Florida Council of Teachers of English Commission on Multicultural Education. She is also involved with the National Writing Project as Director of the North Florida Writing Project.

PAM B. COLE is a former secondary English teacher at Whitewood High School in Whitewood, Virginia. She is currently pursuing a Ph.D. in Curriculum and Instruction at Virginia Polytechnic Institute and State University. Her primary areas of interest are young adult literature, writing assessment, and multicultural issues.

PATRICIA L. DANIEL taught middle schoolers for 12 years in Oklahoma. She is an Assistant Professor of Language Arts Education at the University of Kentucky where she teaches adolescent literature, elementary and secondary English language arts methods, content area reading, and approaches to teaching writing courses.

DEVON DUFFY taught tenth grade English at Derry area Senior High in Pennsylvania in the fall of 1993. She holds a B.A. in English and an M.A. in teaching English from Indiana University of Pennsylvania. She looks forward to increasing her involvement in the activities of ALAN and NCTE.

BONNIE O. ERICSON is a Professor of Secondary Education at California State University, Northridge, where she supervises English student teachers and teachers English methods and literacy across the curriculum classes. She reviews young adult books for *The ALAN Review* and currently edits the "Resources and Reviews" column for *English Journal*. Her two daughters and their friends help keep her current in the field of adolescent literature.

PATRICIA P. KELLY, a Professor of English Education at Virginia Tech in Blacksburg, Virginia, is co-editor of *The ALAN Review*. A past president of ALAN, she is also co-editor of *Virginia English Bulletin* and co-director of he Southwest Virginia Writing Project.

TERI S. LESESNE is an Assistant Professor in the Department of Library Sciences at Sam Houston State University in Texas where she teaches courses in children's and young adult literature. A past Board Member of ALAN, she write the "Books for Adolescents" column in *The Journal of Reading*. Teri also reviews books for other publications including *The ALAN Review*.

J. S. ARTHEA "Charlie" REED is currently Professor of Education and Chair of the Education Department at the University of North Carolina at Asheville. She is author of *Reaching Adolescents: The Young Adult Book and the School. In the Classroom: An Introduction to Education,* and *Comics to Classics: A Guide to Books for Teens and Preteens.*

ROBERT SMALL is currently Dean of the College of Education and Human Development at Radford University in Radford, Virginia. He is a past president of ALAN and current co-editor of *The ALAN Review*. He is also the immediate past-chair of SIGNAL, former chair of the IRA Intellectual Freedom Committee, and he also chaired the Intellectual Freedom Committee of YALSA, the ALA young adult librarian division of ALA. He is the current chair of NCTE's Standing Committee on Teacher Preparation and Certification.

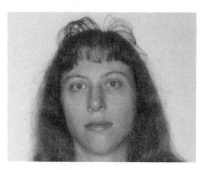

LOIS T. STOVER is Associate Professor of Education at Towson State University where she teaches introductory methods courses, courses in the Masters of Professional writing Program, and young adult literature. She is currently serving as co-editor of the 13th edition of *Books for You*, editor for the "Young Adult Literature" column for *English Journal*, and is on the Board of Directors for ALAN. She has published articles in *English Journal, Language Arts, The Journal of Teaching Writing, Action in Teacher Education*, and several book chapters on young adult literature.

CONNIE S. ZITLOW, a former English and music teacher, is Associate Professor of Education at Ohio Wesleyan University where she directs Secondary Education and teaches reading, young adult literature, and secondary method courses. She has published in *English Journal, Language Arts, Teacher Education Quarterly*, state journals, and a book on literacy. She reviews books for *The ALAN Review* and *Books for You*, serves on the editorial board for *English Journal* and *Reading Teacher*, and is President-Elect of the Ohio Council Teachers of English Language Arts.